Foundation Mathematics 2

David Rayner
Head of Mathematics, Richard Hale School, Hertford

Philip Cutts
Richard Hale School, Hertford

 **Ward Lock Educational**

WARD LOCK EDUCATIONAL CO. LTD.
1 CHRISTOPHER ROAD
EAST GRINSTEAD
SUSSEX RH19 3BT
UNITED KINGDOM

A MEMBER OF THE LING KEE GROUP
HONG KONG • SINGAPORE • LONDON • NEW YORK

© Ward Lock Educational Co. Ltd.
All rights reserved. No part of this publication may be reproduced, stored in a retrieval system, or transmitted in any form or by any means, electronic, mechanical, photocopying, recording or otherwise, without the prior written permission of the Publisher.

Text © David Rayner and Philip Cutts 1984

First published – 1984
Reprinted – 1992 (twice)

ISBN 0-7062-4273-4

Answers are published in a separate book

Printed in Hong Kong

Preface

Foundation Mathematics is a five-book series for pupils in the first three to four years of secondary school. The books contain a wealth of exercises and may either be used as a complete course, or to provide supplementary practice.

Each topic is introduced by brief notes and worked examples. The exercises that follow contain questions carefully graded to allow the majority of pupils to experience success. Sufficient questions are included to provide thorough practice and stretch able pupils. Wherever possible, questions involve objects and situations familiar to pupils, and emphasize practical aspects of mathematics.

The material covered is developed sequentially throughout the series, but no specific teaching order is presupposed, allowing teachers to choose a scheme of work appropriate to their pupils' needs.

Revision exercises are included on pages 21, 52 and 87, and Quick Tests which may be used for mental arithmetic practice are provided on pages 21, 33, 52 and 87.

Numerical answers to the questions in all five books are available in a separate book.

D.R.
P.C.

Contents

1 Whole numbers
    Mental arithmetic   1
    Adding and subtracting   1
    Multiplying and dividing   3
    Using brackets   6

2 Fractions
    Adding and subtracting   8
    Multiplying fractions   8
    Dividing fractions   10
    Multiplying and dividing mixed numbers   10
    Multiplying fractions by decimals   11

3 Nets
    Three-dimensional shapes: nets   14
    Constructing and using nets   15

4 Time
    24-hour clock   18
    Time intervals   19
    Timetables   19

Revisions exercises 1   21

5 Decimal numbers
    Adding and subtracting decimals   25
    Multiplying decimals by whole numbers   26
    Money   27
    Multiplying decimals together   28
    Dividing decimals by whole numbers   30
    Dividing decimals by decimals   31

6 Charts and graphs
    Bar charts   34
    Line graphs   38

7 Angles
    Angles and straight lines   45
    Angles at a point   46
    Angles and parallel lines   47
    Angles in triangles   49

Revision exercises 2   52

8 The metric system
    Length   55
    Perimeters   58
    Areas   59
    Weight   60
    Volume of a liquid   60

9 Algebra
    Simple equations   61
    Values of expressions   61
    Solving harder equations   63
    Values of harder expressions   63
    Powers and indices   64

10 Area
    Triangles   66
    Kites   69
    More complicated shapes   72

11 Symmetry
    Line symmetry   76
    Reflections   82

Revision exercises 3   87

1 Whole numbers

Mental arithmetic

There is sometimes a quick way of working out simple problems in your head.

Examples

(a) $65 + 99$
Work out $65 + 100$ and then subtract 1
i.e. $165 - 1$
$= 164$

(b) $57 - 19$
Work out $57 - 20$ and then add 1
i.e. $37 + 1$
$= 38$

(c) 9×15
Work out 10×15 and then subtract 15
i.e. $150 - 15$
$= 135$

Try some of these ideas in the following tests.

Exercise 1.1

Do the following calculations.

Test 1
1. $25 + 9$
2. $37 + 9$
3. $85 + 9$
4. $25 + 99$
5. $33 + 99$
6. $47 + 99$
7. $45 + 98$
8. $65 + 98$
9. $27 + 99$
10. $45 + 97$
11. $56 + 98$
12. $112 + 9$
13. $132 + 9$
14. $58 - 19$
15. $63 - 19$
16. $46 - 19$
17. $27 - 19$
18. $73 - 18$
19. $84 - 18$
20. $63 - 17$

Test 2
1. $60 - 15$
2. $70 - 25$
3. $100 - 86$
4. $78 - 19$
5. $65 - 19$
6. $57 - 18$
7. 9×14
8. 9×16
9. 9×18
10. 9×19
11. 9×23
12. 9×26
13. 99×7
14. 99×5
15. 99×8
16. 9×15
17. 9×17
18. 99×6
19. 99×9
20. 99×99

Adding and subtracting

Exercise 1.2

Do the following calculations.

1. $1344 + 279$
2. $6324 + 817$
3. $7238 + 1425$
4. $6924 + 2378$
5. $1883 + 298$
6. $4276 + 6185$
7. $572 + 3248 + 907$
8. $3709 + 130 + 705$
9. $7342 + 273 + 1082$
10. $787 + 342 + 7007$
11. $219 + 34$
12. $627 + 74$
13. $762 + 513$
14. $847 + 355$
15. $2072 + 95$
16. $3162 + 473$
17. $6929 + 487$
18. $7243 + 1666$
19. $279 + 3162$
20. $4907 + 624$
21. $624 + 315 + 67$
22. $2603 + 482 + 37$
23. $4112 + 3168 + 159$
24. $431 + 2167 + 284$
25. $32 + 6007 + 4238$
26. $217 + 318 + 4027 + 24$
27. $35 + 762 + 404 + 9$
28. $314 + 2162 + 341 + 2612$
29. $728 + 14321 + 8273 + 86$
30. $359 + 8778 + 98 + 77205$
31. Three jars contain 371, 209 and 88 marbles. How many marbles are there altogether?
32. At an auction, Mr Lewis buys the three articles below. How much does he spend?

2 Whole numbers

33. There are four schools in a town. They have 1242, 880, 906 and 643 pupils respectively. Find how many pupils attend school in the town altogether.
34. In a city there were three football matches played on a Saturday afternoon. If the crowds numbered 17 624, 14 216 and 6244, how many spectators were there altogether?
35. In an election there were four candidates. They gained 10 214, 7058, 5726 and 72 votes. Calculate how many people voted in the election.
36. If you bought five articles of furniture costing £64, £46, £215, £410 and £350, how much would you have to pay?
37. A travelling sales representative works from Monday to Friday. During a certain week she drove distances as given below.
    Monday 214 miles
    Tuesday 182 miles
    Wednesday 57 miles
    Thursday 208 miles
    Friday 143 miles.
    Find how many miles she travelled during that week.
38. Three shoals of herring consist of 4264, 8748 and 12 461 herring. If the shoals all join up to form one large shoal, find how many herring are in the new shoal.
39. During the first six months of the year, a decorator earned £422, £389, £400, £430, £494 and £427. How much did he earn altogether over that six-month period?
40. On a summer's day, a bumble bee visits 727 flowers, while her three friends visit 831, 646 and 1029 flowers respectively. How many flowers were visited by the four bees altogether, assuming that no flower was visited twice?

When doing subtraction questions it is very important to take the bottom figure away from the top figure, and not the other way round.

Exercise 1.3

Do the following calculations.

1. 348 − 132
2. 2684 − 1302
3. 426 − 119
4. 462 − 75
5. 624 − 241
6. 763 − 167
7. 983 − 347
8. 1488 − 529
9. 420 − 33
10. 2003 − 247
11. 377 − 58
12. 624 − 416
13. 308 − 213
14. 728 − 410
15. 940 − 381
16. 1245 − 422
17. 2042 − 638
18. 3626 − 174
19. 4713 − 326
20. 2262 − 169
21. 426 + 137 − 247
22. 734 + 73 − 37
23. 618 + 49 − 146
24. 209 + 246 − 213
25. 346 + 38 − 97
26. 199 + 72 − 43
27. 278 + 55 − 308
28. 643 + 276 − 517
29. 928 + 401 − 876
30. 1327 + 623 − 1722

31. Mr Stewart wishes to buy the settee shown below. If he only has £241, how much more does he have to save?

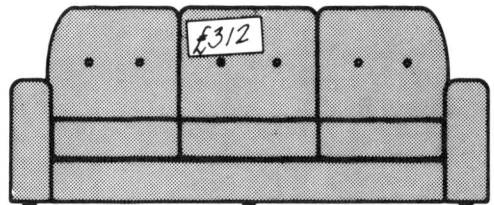

32. Mrs James has £424 in her bank account. If she takes out £147, how much is left in the account?
33. Devinder has to visit a relative who lives 257 miles away. If she stops for lunch after driving 173 miles, how much further does she still have to go?
34. In a wood there are just oak trees and hornbean trees. If there are 187 hornbeans, how many oaks are there, given that there are 374 trees altogether?
35. A library contains 4726 books of which 3819 are fiction, the rest are non-fiction. How many non-fiction books are there?
36. An article costing £147 is reduced in a sale to £129. Find how much you would save by buying it in the sale.
37. Mrs Payne earns £8130 per year. If £1855 is then deducted for tax, how much is she left with?
38. A factory ordered 7240 bolts. When they arrived, 128 of them were found to be faulty. How many good bolts were there?
39. If you wanted to buy a boat costing £2460, and you only had £554, how much more would you need to save?
40. An ants' nest contains 1475 ants. If a green woodpecker eats 258 ants how many are left?

Multiplying and dividing

Exercise 1.4

Do the following calculations.

1. 84 × 2
2. 37 × 4
3. 56 × 3
4. 45 × 5
5. 94 × 6
6. 142 × 8
7. 348 × 4
8. 132 × 7
9. 605 × 9
10. 1324 × 8
11. 473 × 5
12. 525 × 3
13. 617 × 2
14. 483 × 7
15. 513 × 4
16. 436 × 6
17. 627 × 8
18. 1259 × 9
19. 1447 × 7
20. 3248 × 6

21. On a supermarket shelf there are 57 boxes of eggs. If there are six eggs in each box, find the total number of eggs on the shelf.
22. If there are 36 matches in a box, how many matches are there altogether in 8 boxes?
23. A shop is selling Christmas trees for £5 each. On a certain day the shop sells 34 trees. How much money does the shop receive from the sale of those trees?

24. A boat is moving at a speed of 63 m every minute. Find how far it travels in 9 minutes.
25. A box-making machine costs £216. How much would a company have to pay if they wanted seven of these machines for their factory?
26. On a country estate there are 1748 rabbits at the beginning of the year. At the end of the year there are twice as many. Exactly how many rabbits are there at the end of the year?
27. In the spring each female blackbird in a forest lays 4 eggs. If there are 58 female blackbirds in the forest, how many blackbird eggs are laid altogether?
28. In a busy office, the telephone rings 47 times every hour. How many times does the telephone ring in a day, given that the working day lasts 8 hours?
29. At feeding time in the zoo, each penguin eats 6 fish. Find how many fish are required for the penguins, given that there are 64 penguins in the zoo.
30. There are 3 feet in a yard. How many feet are there in 185 yards?
31. 314 × 17
32. 273 × 15
33. 715 × 24
34. 508 × 36
35. 484 × 47
36. 625 × 58
37. A machine wraps 15 sweets every minute. How many sweets does it wrap in 35 minutes?
38. There are 16 ounces in a pound. Find how many ounces there are in 74 pounds.
39. A table costs £49. A restaurant owner wishes to order 18 of them. How much will she have to pay?
40. There are 36 inches in a yard. How many inches are there in 62 yards?

Exercise 1.5

Do the following calculations.

1. 2)86
2. 3)216
3. 2)74
4. 5)275
5. 4)528
6. 6)2556
7. 3)942
8. 7)2002
9. 8)3328
10. 4)2820
11. 3624 ÷ 6
12. 2241 ÷ 9
13. 6076 ÷ 7
14. 1428 ÷ 4
15. 1585 ÷ 5
16. 7230 ÷ 6
17. 10 218 ÷ 3
18. 10 532 ÷ 4
19. 3825 ÷ 9
20. 5000 ÷ 8

21. A sum of £436 is shared equally between 4 people. How much does each person receive?
22. A box of 105 daffodils is to be made up into 7 identical bunches. How many daffodils will there be in each bunch?
23. A machine takes 6 seconds to make a table-tennis ball. Find how many table-tennis balls it makes in 156 seconds.
24. A piece of wood is 184 cm long. How many pieces 8 cm long can be cut from it?
25. A sum of £243 is to be divided equally between you and eight other people. How much will you receive?

26. A shopkeeper has 245 aniseed balls left in a jar. He wishes to divide these equally between 5 bags. How many aniseed balls will there be in each bag?
27. There are 264 eggs in boxes on a supermarket shelf. If there are six eggs in each box, find how many boxes there are on the shelf.
28. If you decided to give away £777 equally to 3 different charities, how much would each charity receive?
29. Find how many pieces of string 7 cm long can be cut from a length of string 868 cm long.
30. There are 3 feet in a yard. How many yards are there in 5280 feet?
31. $315 \div 15$
32. $782 \div 17$
33. $848 \div 16$
34. $518 \div 14$
35. $2337 \div 19$
36. $13624 \div 26$
37. A sum of £645 is to be divided equally between 15 people. How much does each person receive?
38. A group of 414 boys is to be arranged in rows of 18. How many rows will there be?
39. An ordinary dozen is 12, but a baker's dozen is 13. How many baker's dozens are there in 442?
40. There are 14 pounds in a stone. A wrestler weighs 364 pounds. How many stones does he weigh?

Mixed calculations

Exercise 1.6

Do the following calculations.

1. $2435 + 1297$
2. 243×4
3. $248 - 74$
4. 317×7
5. $416 + 24 + 568$
6. $1032 \div 4$
7. 443×5
8. $627 + 659 + 649$
9. $4501 \div 7$
10. $612 - 254$
11. $92 + 794 + 2055$
12. 728×8
13. $2502 \div 3$
14. $670 - 274$
15. $27 + 270 + 7022$
16. 590×8
17. $15120 \div 5$
18. $4542 \div 6$
19. $918 - 742 + 94$
20. $413 + 679 + 205$
21. 1708×9
22. $246 + 554 - 197$
23. $4000 - 127 + 582$
24. $13536 \div 9$
25. $40240 \div 8$
26. $26 + 737 - 295$
27. 70989×2
28. $6923 \div 7$

29. There are 244 acorns in a sack. If we add 82 acorns and then remove 125, find how many acorns are left in the sack.
30. An athlete is training for a marathon. She runs 18 miles every day during January. How many miles does she run in January altogether?
31. How much would it cost a restaurant owner to buy 2 tables and 8 chairs, given that tables cost £155 each and chairs cost £24 each?
32. A chimney sweep works 6 days a week. During one week he earns £26 every day. At the end of the week he pays £47 in tax, gives £56 to his wife and puts £22 in the bank. How much does he have left?
33. In a florist's there are 58 tulips left at the end of a day. The next morning another 284 tulips are delivered. The manager of the shop wants all the tulips made up into bunches so that there are 9 tulips in each bunch. How many bunches will there be?
34. A man buys eight boxes of matches at the beginning of the year, each one containing 36 matches. He always uses exactly one match every day (to light his log fire). Assuming that it is *not* a leap year, how many more matches will he need so that he has enough for the whole year?
35. A forgetful grandfather buys one packet of sweets for each of his 6 grandchildren, each packet containing 24 sweets. He then remembers that he actually has 8 grandchildren, so he opens the packets, removes the sweets and divides them up into 8 equal shares. Find how many sweets each grandchild will get.
36. Shown below is the number of tennis balls delivered by the Acme 'Auto server' in one minute. The machine overheats after 1800 seconds. Find how many serves were completed before the machine broke down.

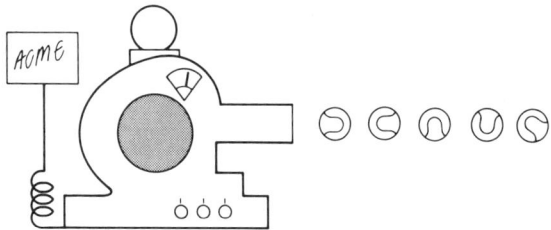

37. A man wishes to buy an article costing £392. He saves £8 a week for 48 weeks. During that time the price of the article increases by £45. How many pounds short is he at the end of the 48 weeks?
38. Five boys have 9 bags of humbugs between them, each bag containing 15 humbugs. The boys decide to share out the humbugs equally. Find how many each boy gets.
39. In a wood, there are 191 mice at the beginning of the summer. During the summer 522 new mice are born, 347 mice die or are killed, 132 move out of the wood and 76 move into the wood from elsewhere. How many mice are there in the wood at the end of the summer?

Order of calculations

When a calculation has a mixture of signs, we always do any × and ÷ parts *before* going from left to right.

Examples

(a) $\quad 5 + 2 \times 6$
$\quad = 5 + 12$
$\quad = 17$

(b) $\quad 4 \times 3 - 2$
$\quad = 12 - 2$
$\quad = 10$

(c) $\quad 16 - 12 \div 3$
$\quad = 16 - 4$
$\quad = 12$

(d) $\quad 5 \times 2 + 20 \div 2$
$\quad = 10 + 10$
$\quad = 20$

It is easier to follow your workings if you lay them out down the page.

Exercise 1.7

Do the following calculations.

1. $4 + 2 \times 3$
2. $7 + 5 \times 4$
3. $4 \times 4 + 3$
4. $3 \times 5 + 10$
5. $14 - 6 \times 2$
6. $4 \times 2 - 3$
7. $2 \times 7 + 1$
8. $11 + 3 \times 3$
9. $11 - 6 \times 1$
10. $4 \times 3 + 9$
11. $7 \times 4 - 8$
12. $31 - 10 \times 2$
13. $9 + 4 \times 0$
14. $10 + 6 \times 5$
15. $5 \times 2 - 10$
16. $4 \times 8 - 7$
17. $12 + 9 \times 2$
18. $5 + 5 \times 5$
19. $50 - 7 \times 6$
20. $8 \times 10 + 7$
21. $10 \div 2 + 3$
22. $7 - 12 \div 3$
23. $29 - 14 \div 2$
24. $11 \times 2 + 4$
25. $10 \times 3 + 12$
26. $20 \div 10 + 10$
27. $18 \div 3 + 7$
28. $12 \times 2 - 22$
29. $50 - 6 \times 6$
30. $7 \div 7 - 1$
31. $7 \times 3 + 13$
32. $12 - 22 \div 2$
33. $31 + 40 \div 5$
34. $7 \times 7 - 15$
35. $17 + 8 \times 7$
36. $47 - 5 \times 7$
37. $36 \div 12 + 11$
38. $8 \div 1 - 3$
39. $15 - 16 \div 4$
40. $18 + 9 \times 9$
41. $10 \times 7 + 18$
42. $21 \div 7 - 1$
43. $15 + 8 \times 9$
44. $4 \times 8 + 26$
45. $24 \div 3 - 2$
46. $21 + 10 \times 6$
47. $37 + 35 \div 5$
48. $5 \times 9 - 11$
49. $11 \times 5 + 9$
50. $29 - 27 \div 3$
51. $17 \times 7 + 246$
52. $78 + 15 \times 6$
53. $399 - 129 \div 3$
54. $140 \div 5 + 254$
55. $23 \times 5 - 76$
56. $52 + 46 \times 4$
57. $359 + 37 \times 6$
58. $300 \div 4 - 18$
59. $19 \times 8 + 231$
60. $34 + 564 \div 6$
61. $1000 - 4896 \div 8$
62. $316 + 28 \times 9$
63. $56 \times 3 + 217$
64. $93 \times 5 - 147$
65. $279 + 124 \times 7$
66. $132 + 581 \div 7$
67. $635 \times 9 - 2057$
68. $3765 \div 5 + 456$
69. $397 + 1116 \div 9$
70. $3000 - 277 \times 8$

Examples

(a) $\quad 5 \times 3 + 2 \times 10$
$\quad = 15 + 20$
$\quad = 35$

(b) $\quad 4 + 18 \div 3 - 7$
$\quad = 4 + 6 - 7$
$\quad = 3$

(c) $\quad 26 + 11 - 4 \times 4$
$\quad = 26 + 11 - 16$
$\quad = 21$

Exercise 1.8

Do the following calculations.

1. $5 \times 3 + 2 \times 4$
2. $10 \times 2 + 3 \times 5$
3. $6 \times 2 + 4 \times 3$
4. $7 \times 2 + 15 \div 3$
5. $10 \div 5 - 8 \div 4$
6. $9 \times 2 - 21 \div 3$
7. $12 \div 2 + 5 \times 5$
8. $16 \div 1 - 3 \times 4$
9. $7 \times 5 - 4 \times 8$
10. $6 \times 7 + 20 \div 4$
11. $30 \div 6 - 24 \div 6$
12. $7 \div 7 + 3 \times 6$
13. $5 \times 4 + 7 \times 8$
14. $18 \div 2 - 2 \times 2$
15. $7 \times 7 + 15 \div 5$
16. $9 \times 3 + 24 \div 3$
17. $5 \times 4 - 25 \div 5$
18. $11 \times 2 + 3 \times 10$
19. $12 \times 3 + 2 \times 2$
20. $10 \div 1 - 15 \div 5$
21. $7 \times 4 - 35 \div 7$
22. $8 \times 8 + 20 \div 5$
23. $3 \times 3 + 4 \times 4$
24. $10 \times 4 - 36 \div 6$
25. $7 \times 3 + 9 \times 2$
26. $27 \div 9 + 21 \div 7$
27. $50 \div 5 + 8 \times 2$
28. $6 \times 8 - 45 \div 5$
29. $11 \times 6 - 9 \div 9$
30. $3 \times 11 + 42 \div 6$
31. $9 \times 9 + 3 \times 5$
32. $40 \div 4 + 9 \times 6$
33. $1 \times 12 - 11 \times 0$
34. $10 \times 10 + 5 \times 11$
35. $20 \div 20 + 9 \times 10$
36. $8 \times 5 + 24 \div 2$
37. $8 \times 9 - 6 \times 11$
38. $100 \div 10 - 18 \div 6$
39. $4 \times 4 + 4 \div 4$
40. $9 \times 4 - 6 \times 5$
41. $5 + 3 \times 7 + 7$
42. $15 + 2 \times 8 - 10$
43. $6 + 6 \times 5 - 5$
44. $6 + 4 \times 7 + 9$
45. $20 - 30 \div 10 + 8$
46. $30 + 6 \times 11 - 11$
47. $15 - 24 \div 3 + 12$
48. $10 + 50 \div 5 + 22$
49. $20 + 8 \times 9 - 3$
50. $15 + 16 \div 2 + 13$
51. $2 + 17 + 3 \times 5$
52. $7 \times 3 + 5 - 16$
53. $14 + 9 - 4 \times 4$
54. $13 + 6 \times 2 - 3$
55. $16 + 23 + 20 \div 4$
56. $9 \times 4 + 3 + 21$
57. $70 + 2 \times 2 - 6$
58. $17 + 14 + 9 \div 3$
59. $42 + 37 - 7 \times 10$
60. $15 + 45 + 5 \times 7$
61. $74 \times 3 + 83 \times 4$
62. $67 \times 6 + 1458 \div 6$
63. $536 \div 4 - 18 \times 7$
64. $1638 \div 3 - 2736 \div 8$
65. $46 \times 9 + 2288 \div 8$
66. $73 \times 8 - 41 \times 5$
67. $128 \times 6 - 82 \times 7$
68. $64 \times 5 + 37 \times 9$
69. $279 \times 8 + 423 \times 5$
70. $4370 \div 5 + 5643 \div 9$

Using brackets

If a calculation contains brackets, the contents of these must be worked out first *before* going from left to right.

Examples

(a)   30 − (20 − 6)
    = 30 −   14
    = 16

(b)   2 × (11 − 3)
    = 2 ×   8
    = 16

(c)   (5 + 3) × (15 − 4)
   =   8   ×   11
   = 88

Exercise 1.9

Do the following calculations.

1. (11 − 5) − 3
2. 11 − (5 − 3)
3. (12 − 4) − 2
4. 12 − (4 − 2)
5. 9 − (6 − 1)
6. (9 − 6) − 1
7. 15 − (7 − 3)
8. (15 − 7) − 3
9. (20 − 11) − 2
10. 20 − (11 − 2)
11. 18 − (6 − 6)
12. (18 − 6) − 6
13. (12 ÷ 6) ÷ 2
14. 12 ÷ (6 ÷ 2)
15. 20 ÷ (10 ÷ 2)
16. (20 ÷ 10) ÷ 2
17. (50 ÷ 5) ÷ 5
18. 50 ÷ (5 ÷ 5)
19. (17 − 9) − 4
20. 17 − (9 − 4)
21. 3 × (4 + 3)
22. 5 × (6 − 2)
23. 6 × (7 + 3)
24. 2 × (15 − 6)
25. 10 × (3 − 3)
26. (8 + 3) × 3
27. (6 − 3) × 4
28. (18 − 13) × 6
29. (4 × 5) ÷ 2
30. 24 ÷ (15 − 7)
31. (7 + 2) − (7 − 2)
32. (12 + 7) − (12 − 3)
33. (17 + 12) − (16 − 5)
34. (23 + 11) − (25 − 4)
35. (18 + 17) − (15 + 7)
36. (17 − 2) − (7 + 3)
37. (7 + 2) × (5 − 3)
38. (6 + 2) × (12 − 2)
39. (11 + 1) × (5 − 4)
40. (12 + 7) × (17 − 17)
41. (15 − 6) × (8 − 6)
42. (4 + 3) × (11 − 4)
43. (8 + 2) × (15 − 5)
44. (6 + 5) × (6 − 1)
45. (17 + 3) ÷ (8 − 3)
46. (17 + 13) ÷ (5 + 5)
47. (6 + 2) ÷ (17 − 9)
48. (27 + 5) ÷ (8 ÷ 2)
49. (26 − 11) ÷ (10 ÷ 2)
50. (27 + 33) ÷ (25 − 19)
51. (247 − 138) − 84
52. 247 − (138 − 84)
53. 637 − (182 − 149)
54. (637 − 182) − 149
55. 3 × (432 + 82)
56. 7 × (625 − 48)
57. (248 + 375) × 8
58. (546 + 125) × (302 − 294)
59. (381 + 513) ÷ (53 − 47)
60. (627 + 466) × (528 − 519)

To summarize, when we do a calculation we do things in the following order.

(a) Work out any brackets.
(b) Do any × and ÷ parts.
(c) Go from left to right.

Remember, do not go from left to right until you have dealt with the first two operations.

Examples

(a)   6 + (5 − 2) × 7
   = 6 +   3   × 7
   = 6 +   21
   = 27

(b)   5 + (13 − 3) ÷ 2 − 7
   = 5 +   10   ÷ 2 − 7
   = 5 +   5 − 7
   = 3

Exercise 1.10

Do the following calculations.

1. 5 + (7 − 4) × 4
2. 10 + 7 × (9 − 6)
3. 4 × (2 + 2) + 6
4. (11 − 8) × 6 + 11
5. 26 − 10 × (9 − 7)
6. 5 × (5 + 6) − 15
7. 6 × (18 − 13) + 7
8. 3 + 3 × (5 + 3)
9. 22 − (5 + 4) × 2
10. 8 × (17 − 12) + 12
11. (17 − 10) × 4 − 25
12. 100 − 6 × (7 + 3)
13. 13 + (16 − 12) × 5
14. 5 + (7 + 4) × 3
15. 7 × (25 − 20) − 12
16. 6 × (4 + 2) − 14
17. 20 ÷ (12 − 8) + 26
18. 19 − (27 + 3) ÷ 3
19. 6 + 7 × (9 − 2)
20. 25 + (17 + 8) ÷ 5
21. 43 − 8 × (8 − 3)
22. (23 − 19) × 8 + 8
23. 55 ÷ (7 − 2) + 12
24. 12 × (10 − 7) + 4
25. 20 + 7 × (5 + 1)
26. 74 − (7 + 5) ÷ 12
27. 18 + (67 + 3) ÷ 7
28. 9 + 30 ÷ (11 − 1)
29. (4 + 4) × 7 − 5
30. 19 + 9 × (15 − 6)
31. 12 − (8 + 32) ÷ 5
32. 5 + 4 × (21 − 14)
33. (11 + 9) ÷ 5 + 13
34. 35 ÷ (17 − 12) − 2
35. 7 + (17 − 11) × 9
36. (30 − 20) × 10 + 27
37. 36 ÷ (30 − 26) + 19
38. 16 + 5 × (16 − 11)
39. 50 − (2 + 9) × 4
40. 15 + 9 × (40 − 35)

Exercise 1.11

Do the following calculations.

1. $4 + (8 - 5) \times 5$
2. $2 + 4 \times (6 - 4)$
3. $34 - (3 + 2) \times 6$
4. $7 + 2 \times (10 - 7)$
5. $16 \div (11 - 9) + 11$
6. $8 + (15 + 5) \div 4$
7. $9 - (11 + 7) \div 2$
8. $4 + 4 \times (9 - 5)$
9. $7 \times (12 - 10) + 9$
10. $12 + (19 + 2) \div 3$
11. $14 - 22 \div (23 - 21)$
12. $(7 + 3) \times 3 + 12$
13. $6 + (2 + 9) \times 4$
14. $29 - 8 \times (12 - 9)$
15. $(17 + 7) \div 6 + 13$
16. $25 \div (25 - 20) - 4$
17. $14 + 9 \times (21 - 18)$
18. $11 + (5 + 2) \times 5$
19. $(12 - 6) \times 6 - 5$
20. $5 + 8 \times (18 - 11)$
21. $1 - (7 + 2) \div 9$
22. $(17 - 8) \times 7 + 17$
23. $5 + (28 + 5) \div 3$
24. $37 - (31 - 23) \times 4$
25. $(23 - 11) \times 4 + 6$
26. $60 - 7 \times (20 - 13)$
27. $8 \times (8 + 1) - 5$
28. $41 + (47 + 8) \div 11$
29. $99 - 9 \times (100 - 91)$
30. $(41 + 39) \div 8 + 27$

Exercise 1.12

This exercise is only for those people who enjoy a challenge!

1. $7 + (9 - 4) \times 4 - (9 + 5) \div 7$
2. $4 \times (15 - 11) + (16 + 4) \div 4 + 11$
3. $(28 + 5) \div 3 + (5 + 3) \times 3 - 6$
4. $9 + 2 \times (3 + 7) - (20 - 13) \times 3$
5. $11 - (11 + 5) \div 2 + (18 - 11) \times 4$
6. $15 + 4 \times (20 - 11) - (54 + 12) \div 11$
7. $(15 - 5 \times 2) + (2 \times 2 + 3) \times (10 - 2 \times 4)$
8. $(3 + 5 \times 3) + (1 + 3 \times 3) \times (4 \times 5 - 16)$
9. $(3 + 4 \times 3) - (3 \times 2 - 4) \times (12 \div 2 - 1)$
10. $(5 \times 5 - 16) \times (14 - 6 \times 2) + (7 + 4 \times 5)$
11. $(39 - 6 \times 6) \times (8 \times 6 - 40) - (1 + 9 \times 1)$
12. $(7 + 2 \times 5) + (4 \times 4 + 6) \div (31 - 2 \times 10)$
13. $3 + 8 \times (15 - (10 - 3))$
14. $29 - ((3 + 9) \div 2) \times 4$
15. $(21 - (5 - 2)) - 3 \times ((7 - 4) \times 2)$
16. $10 + 2 \times ((7 - 2) \times (6 + 4))$
17. $5 \times (4 + (11 - 2 \times 4)) - 4$
18. $(40 - 7 \times 5) \times 3 + (40 \div (10 \div 2))$
19. $((10 - 7) \times 11) - (5 \times 3 - 2 \times 4)$
20. $((13 - (5 - 4)) \times 3) \div (19 - 2 \times 5)$

2 Fractions

Adding and subtracting

Examples

(a) $\quad \frac{7}{11} + \frac{2}{11}$
$= \frac{9}{11}$

(b) $\quad \frac{1}{2} + \frac{2}{5}$
$= \frac{5}{10} + \frac{4}{10}$
$= \frac{9}{10}$

(c) $\quad \frac{2}{3} - \frac{1}{6}$
$= \frac{4}{6} - \frac{1}{6}$
$= \frac{3}{6}$
$= \frac{1}{2}$

(d) $\quad 2\frac{1}{2} + 1\frac{1}{3}$
$= \frac{5}{2} + \frac{4}{3}$
$= \frac{15}{6} + \frac{8}{6}$
$= \frac{23}{6}$
$= 3\frac{5}{6}$

When we have the answer of a fraction question we always do two things.
 1. Look to see whether it is top-heavy. If it *is* top-heavy we change the answer to a mixed number.
 2. Look to see whether we can simplify (cancel).

Exercise 2.1

Do the following calculations.

1. $\frac{2}{11} + \frac{5}{11}$
2. $\frac{2}{5} + \frac{1}{5}$
3. $\frac{6}{7} - \frac{2}{7}$
4. $\frac{5}{9} - \frac{4}{9}$
5. $\frac{2}{13} + \frac{7}{13}$
6. $\frac{6}{7} + \frac{1}{7}$
7. $\frac{5}{8} - \frac{1}{8}$
8. $\frac{1}{6} + \frac{1}{6}$
9. $\frac{1}{10} + \frac{7}{10}$
10. $\frac{3}{4} - \frac{1}{4}$
11. $\frac{2}{3} - \frac{1}{2}$
12. $\frac{2}{5} + \frac{1}{3}$
13. $\frac{3}{5} + \frac{1}{10}$
14. $\frac{3}{4} - \frac{1}{6}$
15. $\frac{4}{5} + \frac{1}{2}$
16. $\frac{7}{10} + \frac{1}{4}$
17. $\frac{2}{3} - \frac{1}{8}$
18. $\frac{4}{5} - \frac{3}{4}$
19. $\frac{3}{10} + \frac{7}{20}$
20. $\frac{5}{6} + \frac{2}{3}$
21. $2\frac{1}{2} + 1\frac{1}{3}$
22. $3\frac{1}{5} - 1\frac{2}{3}$
23. $1\frac{1}{5} + 2\frac{1}{10}$
24. $2\frac{3}{4} - 1\frac{1}{6}$
25. $3\frac{1}{2} + \frac{3}{5}$
26. $4\frac{2}{3} + \frac{1}{12}$
27. $2\frac{1}{2} - \frac{7}{8}$
28. $2\frac{2}{5} - 1\frac{1}{4}$
29. $5\frac{1}{2} - 3\frac{3}{8}$
30. $2\frac{1}{10} + 1\frac{3}{20}$

31. If Leroy travels $\frac{4}{5}$ of a mile and then another $\frac{1}{2}$ mile, how far has he travelled altogether?
32. If Mary has to walk $\frac{7}{8}$ of a mile to school, find how much further she has to go after walking $\frac{1}{3}$ of a mile.
33. Mrs Williams has made a cake. At teatime she eats $\frac{3}{10}$ of it and Mr Williams eats $\frac{2}{5}$ of it. What fraction of the cake is left?
34. If Mr Patel works in the garden for $2\frac{1}{2}$ hours on a Saturday morning and then for $1\frac{3}{4}$ hours in the afternoon, how long has he spent working in the garden altogether?
35. Mr and Mrs Hughes are going to visit relatives who live $7\frac{1}{2}$ miles away. After travelling $4\frac{2}{3}$ miles the car breaks down. How much further do they still have to go?
36. A piece of string $1\frac{1}{4}$ metres long is cut from a piece $4\frac{5}{8}$ metres long. How much is left?
37. Ms Clarke wishes to walk to the shops which are $1\frac{1}{2}$ miles away. She walks for $\frac{7}{8}$ of a mile and then stops to talk to a friend. She then walks another $\frac{1}{3}$ of a mile and stops for a rest. How much further does she still have to go?
38. Three slugs are attacking a tomato in Mrs Dixon's garden. The first two slugs eat $\frac{2}{7}$ and $\frac{3}{5}$ of the tomato. What fraction is left for the third slug?
39. In a school, $\frac{3}{5}$ of the children have school lunch, $\frac{1}{8}$ of the children bring sandwiches and the rest go home for lunch. What fraction of the children go home for lunch?
40. In a container there are $4\frac{2}{3}$ litres of water. If we add $2\frac{3}{8}$ litres and then later on remove $1\frac{3}{4}$ litres, find how much water is in the container then.

Multiplying fractions

When multiplying fractions we use the following method:

(a) Multiply the numbers on top
(b) Multiply the numbers underneath
(c) Simplify the answer (if possible)

Examples

(a) $\quad \dfrac{2}{7} \times \dfrac{4}{5} = \dfrac{2 \times 4}{7 \times 5} = \dfrac{8}{35}$

(b) $\quad \dfrac{2}{3} \times \dfrac{1}{4} = \dfrac{2 \times 1}{3 \times 4} = \dfrac{\cancel{2}^{1}}{\cancel{12}_{6}} = \dfrac{1}{6}$

Exercise 2.2
Do the following calculations.

1. $\frac{1}{4} \times \frac{1}{3}$
2. $\frac{3}{4} \times \frac{1}{2}$
3. $\frac{2}{3} \times \frac{1}{5}$
4. $\frac{3}{4} \times \frac{3}{5}$
5. $\frac{2}{5} \times \frac{1}{6}$
6. $\frac{3}{4} \times \frac{3}{4}$
7. $\frac{1}{2} \times \frac{3}{5}$
8. $\frac{3}{5} \times \frac{1}{6}$
9. $\frac{2}{3} \times \frac{6}{7}$
10. $\frac{5}{6} \times \frac{2}{5}$
11. $\frac{4}{7} \times \frac{1}{4}$
12. $\frac{1}{12} \times \frac{3}{4}$
13. $\frac{4}{5} \times \frac{1}{8}$
14. $\frac{5}{9} \times \frac{3}{4}$
15. $\frac{3}{5} \times \frac{2}{3}$
16. $\frac{7}{4} \times \frac{3}{2}$
17. $\frac{6}{7} \times \frac{3}{2}$
18. $\frac{12}{5} \times \frac{3}{4}$
19. $\frac{2}{3}$ of $\frac{3}{7}$
20. $\frac{1}{5}$ of $\frac{3}{4}$
21. $\frac{2}{3}$ of $\frac{6}{7}$
22. $\frac{4}{5}$ of $\frac{5}{8}$
23. $\frac{7}{8}$ of $\frac{1}{2}$
24. $\frac{9}{10}$ of $\frac{5}{6}$
25. $\frac{3}{4} \times \frac{3}{1}$
26. $\frac{2}{5} \times \frac{4}{1}$
27. $\frac{5}{6} \times \frac{3}{1}$
28. $\frac{5}{9} \times 6$
29. $\frac{3}{5} \times 10$
30. $\frac{2}{9} \times 12$
31. $\frac{3}{5} \times 15$
32. $\frac{3}{4}$ of 8
33. $\frac{2}{9}$ of 12
34. $\frac{3}{5}$ of 20
35. $\frac{5}{6}$ of 30
36. $\frac{2}{15}$ of 60
37. $\frac{5}{18} \times \frac{9}{10}$
38. $\frac{7}{12} \times \frac{1}{7}$
39. $\frac{3}{7} \times \frac{9}{10}$
40. $\frac{1}{2} \times \frac{2}{3} \times \frac{3}{4}$
41. $\frac{1}{5} \times \frac{2}{3} \times \frac{1}{2}$
42. $\frac{3}{4} \times \frac{2}{5} \times \frac{1}{3}$
43. $\frac{5}{7} \times \frac{3}{4} \times \frac{1}{2}$
44. $\frac{3}{5} \times \frac{1}{4} \times \frac{1}{2}$
45. $\frac{4}{5} \times \frac{1}{4} \times 10$
46. $\frac{3}{4} \times \frac{1}{6} \times 9$
47. $\frac{1}{10} \times \frac{5}{6} \times \frac{2}{3}$
48. $\frac{8}{9} \times \frac{1}{3} \times \frac{3}{10}$

Example

$\frac{3}{5}$ of 20 kg $= \frac{3}{5} \times \frac{20}{1}$ kg

$= \frac{60}{5}$ kg

$= 12$ kg

Here the word 'of' means $\times$.

Exercise 2.3
Calculate the following

1. $\frac{3}{4}$ of 8
2. $\frac{5}{6}$ of 24
3. $\frac{2}{3}$ of 9
4. $\frac{2}{5}$ of 15
5. $\frac{1}{4}$ of 28
6. $\frac{2}{7}$ of 35
7. $\frac{3}{5}$ of 500
8. $\frac{2}{3}$ of 30 kg
9. $\frac{3}{4}$ of 32 km
10. $\frac{4}{5}$ of 100 tonnes
11. $\frac{1}{6}$ of 54 cm
12. $\frac{5}{8}$ of £40
13. $\frac{4}{7}$ of 3500 kg
14. $\frac{3}{11}$ of 132 km
15. $\frac{5}{6}$ of £15
16. $\frac{3}{8}$ of 12 hours
17. $\frac{5}{16}$ of $64
18. $\frac{2}{5}$ of 35 pence
19. $\frac{7}{12}$ of 66 cm
20. $\frac{17}{20}$ of £4000
21. $\frac{7}{10}$ of 55 minutes
22. $\frac{2}{3}$ of $\frac{1}{2}$ kg
23. $\frac{3}{4}$ of $\frac{1}{2}$ kg
24. $\frac{2}{5}$ of $\frac{3}{4}$ km
25. $\frac{1}{3}$ of $\frac{1}{3}$ tonne
26. $\frac{2}{5}$ of $\frac{1}{5}$ gram
27. $\frac{3}{8}$ of $\frac{1}{2}$ hour
28. $\frac{3}{7}$ of 1 m
29. $\frac{7}{12}$ of $\frac{1}{3}$ mile
30. $\frac{9}{10}$ of $\frac{1}{5}$ mile
31. $\frac{3}{4}$ of $\frac{3}{4}$ pint
32. $\frac{2}{5}$ of $\frac{1}{2}$ litre
33. $\frac{5}{6}$ of $\frac{4}{5}$ litre
34. $\frac{7}{8}$ of $44
35. $\frac{2}{13}$ of £5200
36. $\frac{1}{16}$ of $\frac{1}{4}$ mile

Exercise 2.4

1. Copy and complete the multiplication square.

	$\frac{1}{4}$	$\frac{2}{3}$	$\frac{3}{5}$	$\frac{3}{4}$	2	$\frac{5}{6}$
$\frac{1}{4}$						
$\frac{2}{3}$						
$\frac{3}{5}$						
$\frac{3}{4}$				$\frac{9}{16}$		
2		$1\frac{1}{3}$			4	
$\frac{5}{6}$						

2. Copy and complete the multiplication square.

	$\frac{1}{3}$	$\frac{5}{3}$	$\frac{2}{5}$	3	$\frac{1}{7}$	$\frac{5}{8}$
$\frac{1}{3}$				1		
$\frac{5}{3}$						
$\frac{2}{5}$						
3						
$\frac{1}{7}$					$\frac{1}{49}$	
$\frac{5}{8}$						

Dividing fractions

(a) $2 \div \frac{1}{4}$ means 'how many $\frac{1}{4}$'s are there in 2?'

We know the answer is 8.

Notice that $2 \div \frac{1}{4} = \frac{2}{1} \times \frac{4}{1}$
$= 8$

General rule:

To divide by a fraction, turn the fraction you are dividing by upside down and then multiply.

Examples

(a) $\frac{3}{5} \div \frac{1}{4} = \frac{3}{5} \times \frac{4}{1}$
$= \frac{12}{5}$
$= 2\frac{2}{5}$

(b) $\frac{5}{6} \div \frac{3}{4} = \frac{5}{6} \times \frac{4}{3}$
$= \frac{20}{18} = \frac{10}{9}$
$= 1\frac{1}{9}$

Exercise 2.5
Do the following calculations.

1. $\frac{1}{2} \div \frac{1}{4}$
2. $\frac{1}{3} \div \frac{1}{2}$
3. $\frac{3}{4} \div \frac{1}{3}$
4. $\frac{2}{3} \div \frac{1}{2}$
5. $\frac{1}{5} \div \frac{1}{2}$
6. $\frac{1}{2} \div \frac{1}{5}$
7. $\frac{3}{4} \div \frac{4}{5}$
8. $\frac{1}{1} \div \frac{1}{6}$
9. $\frac{5}{6} \div \frac{1}{3}$
10. $\frac{2}{5} \div \frac{2}{3}$
11. $\frac{5}{7} \div \frac{9}{10}$
12. $\frac{5}{12} \div \frac{1}{8}$
13. $\frac{3}{7} \div \frac{3}{5}$
14. $\frac{9}{14} \div \frac{6}{7}$
15. $\frac{11}{15} \div \frac{1}{10}$
16. $\frac{4}{3} \div \frac{8}{1}$
17. $\frac{2}{5} \div \frac{2}{1}$
18. $\frac{5}{7} \div \frac{6}{1}$
19. $\frac{4}{9} \div 6$
20. $\frac{5}{11} \div 3$
21. $\frac{7}{9} \div 3$
22. $\frac{4}{1} \div 3$
23. $\frac{6}{1} \div 5$
24. $\frac{8}{1} \div 5$
25. $\frac{3}{7} \div \frac{9}{14}$
26. $\frac{5}{6} \div 7$
27. $\frac{2}{3} \div \frac{1}{12}$
28. $\frac{9}{10} \div \frac{9}{10}$
29. $\frac{5}{9} \div \frac{5}{9}$
30. $\frac{4}{15} \div 1$
31. $1 \div \frac{4}{15}$
32. $1 \div \frac{7}{2}$
33. $2 \div \frac{3}{4}$
34. $90 \div \frac{1}{2}$
35. $10 \div \frac{1}{5}$
36. $200 \div \frac{1}{10}$
37. $15 \div \frac{1}{6}$
38. $\frac{7}{8} \div \frac{14}{15}$
39. $\frac{5}{6} \div \frac{25}{36}$
40. $\frac{4}{7} \div \frac{4}{7}$

Multiplying and dividing mixed numbers

Examples

(a) $2\frac{1}{2} \times 1\frac{1}{5} = \frac{5}{2} \times \frac{6}{5}$
$= \frac{30}{10}$
$= 3$

(b) $3\frac{1}{2} \div 1\frac{1}{4} = \frac{7}{2} \div \frac{5}{4}$
$= \frac{7}{2} \times \frac{4}{5}$
$= \frac{28}{10}$
$= \frac{14}{5}$
$= 2\frac{4}{5}$

When dealing with mixed numbers always convert them to top-heavy fractions before you add, subtract, multiply or divide.

Exercise 2.6
Calculate the following

1. $1\frac{1}{2} \times 2\frac{1}{4}$
2. $2\frac{2}{3} \times 1\frac{1}{2}$
3. $1\frac{1}{4} \times 1\frac{1}{5}$
4. $2\frac{1}{3} \times 1\frac{5}{7}$
5. $1\frac{1}{8} \times 1\frac{1}{3}$
6. $1\frac{3}{5} \times 2\frac{1}{2}$
7. $2\frac{2}{3} \times 2\frac{1}{4}$
8. $1\frac{1}{3} \times 1\frac{1}{2}$
9. $1\frac{1}{7} \times 1\frac{3}{4}$
10. $2\frac{1}{5} \times 1\frac{1}{4}$
11. $1\frac{1}{6} \times 1\frac{1}{2}$
12. $\frac{7}{9} \times 1\frac{5}{7}$
13. $1\frac{1}{3} \div 2\frac{2}{3}$
14. $2\frac{1}{2} \div 1\frac{2}{3}$
15. $2\frac{1}{2} \div 1\frac{1}{3}$
16. $2\frac{1}{3} \div 1\frac{1}{4}$
17. $2\frac{1}{4} \div 1\frac{1}{2}$
18. $1\frac{3}{7} \div 1\frac{2}{3}$
19. $4\frac{1}{2} \div 1\frac{1}{5}$
20. $3\frac{2}{3} \div 2\frac{1}{2}$
21. $1\frac{3}{4} \div 2\frac{2}{5}$
22. $1\frac{3}{5} \div \frac{1}{2}$
23. $3\frac{3}{4} \div 3\frac{1}{3}$
24. $1\frac{1}{4} \div 1\frac{1}{4}$
25. $2\frac{2}{7} \div 2\frac{2}{7}$
26. $9\frac{1}{4} \div 9\frac{1}{4}$
27. $3\frac{2}{5} \times 3\frac{1}{3}$
28. $2\frac{3}{4} \times \frac{4}{11}$
29. $4 \div 3\frac{1}{2}$
30. $6 \div 2\frac{1}{4}$
31. $4\frac{1}{2} \div 6$
32. $4\frac{1}{4} \div 2$
33. $5 \div 1\frac{3}{7}$
34. $1\frac{1}{3} \times 1\frac{1}{2} \times 2\frac{1}{2}$
35. $1\frac{1}{3} \times 1\frac{1}{4} \times 2\frac{2}{5}$
36. $1\frac{1}{2} \times 2\frac{1}{3} \times 1\frac{1}{7}$
37. $1\frac{1}{5} \times 1\frac{2}{3} \times 4\frac{1}{2}$
38. $2\frac{3}{4} \times 1\frac{1}{3} \times 2$
39. $2\frac{1}{3} \times 4\frac{1}{2} \times 1\frac{3}{7}$
40. $1\frac{1}{3} \times 1\frac{1}{3} \times 1\frac{1}{3}$

Arithmetic with fractions

Here is a quick reminder of the methods of addition, subtraction, multiplication and division.

Example

(a) $\frac{4}{5} + \frac{1}{3}$
$= \frac{12}{15} + \frac{5}{15}$
$= \frac{17}{15}$
$= 1\frac{2}{15}$

(b) $\frac{4}{5} - \frac{1}{3}$
$= \frac{12}{15} - \frac{5}{15}$
$= \frac{7}{15}$

(c) $\frac{4}{5} \times \frac{1}{3} = \frac{4}{15}$

(d) $\frac{4}{5} \div \frac{1}{3}$
$= \frac{4}{5} \times \frac{3}{1}$
$= \frac{12}{5}$
$= 2\frac{2}{5}$

Fractions

Exercise 2.7

Copy and complete the table. Leave room for the working.

+	−	×	÷
1. $\frac{3}{4} + \frac{2}{3} = 1\frac{5}{12}$	$\frac{3}{4} - \frac{2}{3} = \frac{1}{12}$	$\frac{3}{4} \times \frac{2}{3} = \frac{1}{2}$	$\frac{3}{4} \div \frac{2}{3} = 1\frac{1}{8}$
2. $\frac{4}{5} + \frac{1}{2} = 1\frac{3}{10}$	$\frac{4}{5} - \frac{1}{2} =$	$\frac{4}{5} \times \frac{1}{2} =$	$\frac{4}{5} \div \frac{1}{2} =$
3. $\frac{7}{8} + \frac{2}{3} =$	$\frac{7}{8} - \frac{2}{3} =$	$\frac{7}{8} \times \frac{2}{3} =$	$\frac{7}{8} \div \frac{2}{3} =$
4. $\frac{3}{5} + \frac{1}{3} =$	$\frac{3}{5} - \frac{1}{3} =$	$\frac{3}{5} \times \frac{1}{3} =$	$\frac{3}{5} \div \frac{1}{3} =$
5. $\frac{6}{7} + \frac{1}{8} =$	$\frac{6}{7} - \frac{1}{8} =$	$\frac{6}{7} \times \frac{1}{8} =$	$\frac{6}{7} \div \frac{1}{8} =$
6. $\frac{11}{12} + \frac{2}{3} =$	$\frac{11}{12} - \frac{2}{3} =$	$\frac{11}{12} \times \frac{2}{3} =$	$\frac{11}{12} \div \frac{2}{3} =$
7. $\frac{5}{9} + \frac{1}{3} =$	$\frac{5}{9} - \frac{1}{3} =$	$\frac{5}{9} \times \frac{1}{3} =$	$\frac{5}{9} \div \frac{1}{3} =$
8. $\frac{3}{8} + \frac{1}{5} =$	$\frac{3}{8} - \frac{1}{5} =$	$\frac{3}{8} \times \frac{1}{5} =$	$\frac{3}{8} \div \frac{1}{5} =$
9. $\frac{7}{10} + \frac{2}{3} =$	$\frac{7}{10} - \frac{2}{3} =$	$\frac{7}{10} \times \frac{2}{3} =$	$\frac{7}{10} \div \frac{2}{3} =$
10. $\frac{3}{5} + \frac{7}{12} =$	$\frac{3}{5} - \frac{7}{12} =$	$\frac{3}{5} \times \frac{7}{12} =$	$\frac{3}{5} \div \frac{7}{12} =$
11. $\frac{5}{9} + \frac{1}{4} =$	$\frac{5}{9} - \frac{1}{4} =$	$\frac{5}{9} \times \frac{1}{4} =$	$\frac{5}{9} \div \frac{1}{4} =$
12. $\frac{6}{7} + \frac{1}{2} =$	$\frac{6}{7} - \frac{1}{2} =$	$\frac{6}{7} \times \frac{1}{2} =$	$\frac{6}{7} \div \frac{1}{2} =$
13. $1\frac{3}{4} + \frac{2}{3} =$	$1\frac{3}{4} - \frac{2}{3} =$	$1\frac{3}{4} \times \frac{2}{3} =$	$1\frac{3}{4} \div \frac{2}{3} =$
14. $2\frac{2}{3} + 1\frac{1}{5} =$	$2\frac{2}{3} - 1\frac{1}{5} =$	$2\frac{2}{3} \times 1\frac{1}{5} =$	$2\frac{2}{3} \div 1\frac{1}{5} =$
15. $3\frac{1}{2} + 2\frac{3}{5} =$	$3\frac{1}{2} - 2\frac{3}{5} =$	$3\frac{1}{2} \times 2\frac{3}{5} =$	$3\frac{1}{2} \div 2\frac{3}{5} =$
16. $2\frac{3}{5} + 1\frac{7}{8} =$	$2\frac{3}{5} - 1\frac{7}{8} =$	$2\frac{3}{5} \times 1\frac{7}{8} =$	$2\frac{3}{5} \div 1\frac{7}{8} =$
17. $3\frac{3}{4} + 2\frac{1}{2} =$	$3\frac{3}{4} - 2\frac{1}{2} =$	$3\frac{3}{4} \times 2\frac{1}{2} =$	$3\frac{3}{4} \div 2\frac{1}{2} =$
18. $2\frac{2}{5} + 1\frac{1}{4} =$	$2\frac{2}{5} - 1\frac{1}{4} =$	$2\frac{2}{5} \times 1\frac{1}{4} =$	$2\frac{2}{5} \div 1\frac{1}{4} =$

Calculate the following.

19. $\dfrac{\frac{1}{2} - \frac{1}{3}}{\frac{1}{2} + \frac{1}{3}}$

20. $\dfrac{\frac{5}{6} + \frac{1}{4}}{\frac{5}{6} - \frac{1}{4}}$

21. $(\frac{3}{4} - \frac{1}{3}) \times 2\frac{1}{2}$

22. $(2\frac{1}{4} + 1\frac{1}{2}) \div \frac{2}{3}$

23. $\dfrac{2\frac{1}{2} \times 1\frac{1}{5}}{2\frac{1}{2} - 1\frac{1}{5}}$

24. $\dfrac{5\frac{1}{2} \times 2\frac{2}{3}}{1\frac{4}{9} \times \frac{11}{16}}$

25. $\dfrac{\frac{1}{5}}{2\frac{1}{2} - 2\frac{1}{3}}$

26. $(5\frac{1}{4} + 1\frac{1}{3}) \times 1\frac{5}{7}$

27. $\dfrac{3\frac{1}{3} \div 2\frac{1}{2}}{1\frac{3}{4} + 2\frac{2}{3}}$

28. $\dfrac{\frac{3}{4} \times \frac{1}{2}}{\frac{3}{4} \div \frac{1}{2}}$

29. $3 + \dfrac{3}{5 + \frac{2}{5}}$

30. $2 - \dfrac{1}{3 + \frac{1}{4}}$

Multiplying fractions by decimals

Example

(a) $\frac{2}{5}$ of $4.8 = \frac{2}{5} \times \frac{4.8}{1}$

$= \dfrac{9.6}{5}$

$1.\ 9\ 2$
$5)9.^46\ ^10$ answer $= 1.92$

Exercise 2.8

Work out

1. $\frac{2}{5}$ of 3.6
2. $\frac{1}{4}$ of 8.4
3. $\frac{2}{3}$ of 4.8
4. $\frac{4}{5}$ of 3.2
5. $\frac{5}{8}$ of 1.2
6. $\frac{1}{3}$ of 0.693

12 Fractions

7. $\frac{3}{4}$ of 0·15
8. $\frac{4}{7}$ of 2·8
9. $\frac{3}{10}$ of 0·71
10. $\frac{5}{9}$ of 0·333
11. $\frac{6}{7}$ of 2·38
12. $\frac{1}{6}$ of 31·38
13. $\frac{2}{3}$ of 11·4
14. $\frac{5}{8}$ of 0·1
15. $\frac{1}{8}$ of 1·1
16. $\frac{3}{4}$ of 0·042
17. $\frac{3}{5}$ of 4·2 kg
18. $\frac{5}{12}$ of 8·4 km
19. $\frac{7}{10}$ of 0·31 seconds
20. $\frac{4}{9}$ of 1·53 cm
21. $\frac{4}{5}$ of £3·20
22. $\frac{3}{5}$ of £7·50
23. $\frac{9}{10}$ of £6·30
24. $\frac{7}{10}$ of £81·10
25. $\frac{2}{5}$ of $4·85
26. $\frac{3}{8}$ of $50
27. $\frac{1}{8}$ of 0·6 kg
28. $\frac{5}{7}$ of 0·014 cm
29. $\frac{5}{12}$ of 2·4 miles
30. $\frac{7}{100}$ of 2·2 tonnes
31. $\frac{5}{11}$ of 13·2 km
32. $\frac{3}{8}$ of £10
33. $\frac{3}{7}$ of 21·7 seconds
34. $\frac{7}{9}$ of £15·30
35. $\frac{7}{11}$ of 58·3 m
36. $\frac{5}{12}$ of 7·62 cm
37. $\frac{2}{9}$ of 0·0414 cm
38. $\frac{11}{100}$ of $582
39. $\frac{4}{7}$ of £33·32
40. $\frac{10}{11}$ of $64·46

Word questions: fractions

When a problem is given in words always give the final answer in words.

Example

On each bounce a ball rises to $\frac{3}{5}$ of its previous height. How high will a ball bounce if it is dropped from a height of 10 m?

We need to work out $\frac{3}{5}$ of 10 m.

$\frac{3}{5}$ of $10 = \frac{3}{5} \times \frac{10}{1}$

$\qquad = \frac{30}{5}$

$\qquad = 6$ m

The ball bounces to a height of 6 m.

Exercise 2.9

1. On each bounce a ball rises to $\frac{3}{4}$ of its previous height. How high will a ball bounce if it is dropped from a height of 6 m?
2. A piece of card is $\frac{2}{3}$ mm thick. How thick is a pile of 30 pieces of card?
3. In an examination full marks were 85. How many marks did Sarah get if she had $\frac{3}{5}$ of full marks?
4. A glass holds $\frac{5}{8}$ of a litre of liquid. How much liquid is contained in 16 glasses?
5. A television is bought for £287 and is later sold at $\frac{3}{7}$ of this price. What is the selling price?
6.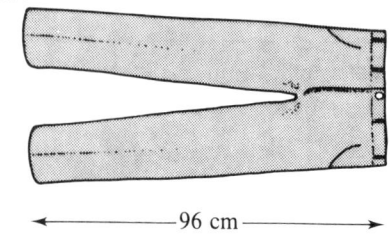

   ←——— 96 cm ———→

   Paul's new jeans are shown above. After washing they shrink to $\frac{11}{12}$ of their previous length. What is the new length of the jeans?
7. The petrol tank of a car holds 56 litres. How much petrol is in the tank when it is $\frac{5}{8}$ full?
8. A small container has a volume of 5 cm^3. How many times can it be filled from a container whose volume is 1000 cm^3?
9. An ink bottle has a volume of 12 cm^3. How many times can it be filled from a large ink bottle which contains 384 cm^3 of ink?
10. A fountain pen contains $\frac{7}{8}$ cm^3 of ink when full. How many times can the pen be filled from an ink bottle which contains 42 cm^3 of ink?
11. A wine glass holds $\frac{1}{7}$ of a litre of wine. How many times can the glass be filled from a bottle which contains 2 litres of wine?
12. A mug has a capacity of $\frac{3}{8}$ of a litre. How many times can the mug be filled from a large tea-pot which contains 3 litres of tea?
13. The gear box of a car has a capacity of $\frac{5}{8}$ of a gallon. How many gear boxes can be filled with oil from a large oil drum which contains 50 gallons?
14. How many pieces of wood, each $5\frac{1}{2}$ cm long, can be cut from a plank 132 cm long?
15. An unfortunate motorist has to fill a five litre petrol can using a mug which takes only $\frac{5}{8}$ of a litre each time. How many times does he have to use the mug?
16. A sum of £20 is divided between several people so that each receives $\frac{2}{5}$ of a pound. How many people receive a share?
17. A sheet of paper is $\frac{1}{10}$ mm thick. How thick is a pad containing 360 sheets of paper?
18. Five people share a prize of £11·20. How much does each person receive?
19. In a sale a book is reduced to $\frac{2}{5}$ of its original price. What is the sale price if it originally cost £2·25?
20. Which is the greater: $\frac{5}{6}$ of £7·86 or $\frac{5}{8}$ of £10·24?

Example

48 pages

A book has 48 pages, each $\frac{1}{80}$ cm thick, and two covers, each $\frac{1}{6}$ cm thick. What is the total thickness of the book?

The thickness of all the pages

$$= 48 \times \frac{1}{80}$$

$$= \frac{48}{1} \times \frac{1}{80}$$

$$= \frac{48}{80}$$

$$= \frac{3}{5} \text{ cm}$$

The total thickness of the book is found by adding the thickness of the pages to the thickness of the two covers.

$$\text{Thickness of book} = \frac{3}{5} + \frac{1}{6} + \frac{1}{6}$$

$$= \frac{18}{30} + \frac{5}{30} + \frac{5}{30}$$

$$= \frac{28}{30}$$

$$= \frac{14}{15} \text{ cm.}$$

The book is $\frac{14}{15}$ cm thick.

Exercise 2.10

1. Which is greater: $\frac{3}{5} \times \frac{4}{3}$ or $\frac{3}{5} + \frac{4}{3}$?
2. A mug contains $\frac{3}{8}$ of a litre, a cup contains $\frac{3}{16}$ of a litre and a glass contains $\frac{3}{4}$ of a litre. How much is contained in:
   (a) a mug and a cup?
   (b) a glass and a mug?
   (c) $\frac{5}{6}$ of a glass?
   (d) half a mug and half a cup?
   (e) 2 mugs and 3 cups?
   (f) $\frac{8}{9}$ of a cup and a glass?

3. Look at the three containers below. How much is contained in:
   (a) a jar and a tin?
   (b) $\frac{2}{3}$ of a jar and a drum?
   (c) 3 jars and 8 tins?
   (d) a jar a tin and a drum?
   (e) $\frac{3}{4}$ of a drum?
   (f) $\frac{9}{10}$ of a jar and $\frac{3}{4}$ of a tin?

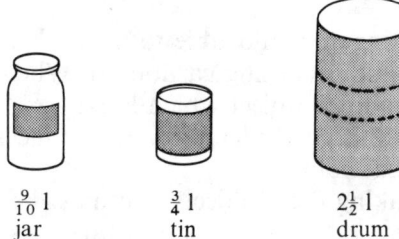

$\frac{9}{10}$ l jar $\quad$ $\frac{3}{4}$ l tin $\quad$ $2\frac{1}{2}$ l drum

4. A book has 440 pages, each $\frac{1}{100}$ cm thick, and two covers, each $\frac{3}{10}$ cm thick. What is the total thickness of the book?
5. A book has 250 pages, each $\frac{1}{150}$ cm thick, and two covers, each $\frac{1}{4}$ cm thick. What is the total thickness of the book?
6. A book has 340 pages, each $\frac{1}{120}$ cm thick, and two covers, each $\frac{1}{5}$ cm thick. What is the total thickness of the book?
7. An centipede is born with 60 legs. It loses $\frac{1}{5}$ of its legs falling downstairs and a further $\frac{1}{3}$ of the remainder following an argument with a blackbird. How many legs has it left?
8. Deidre spends $\frac{1}{2}$ of her money on Saturday and $\frac{3}{4}$ of what was left on Monday. What fraction of her money is still left?
9. An alloy is composed of $\frac{1}{9}$ iron, $\frac{5}{8}$ lead and the rest copper. What fraction of the alloy is copper?
10. When a number is divided by $3\frac{1}{4}$ the answer is $4\frac{1}{2}$. What is the number?
11. Which is the greater: $3\frac{1}{2}$ added to $1\frac{1}{3}$ or $3\frac{1}{2}$ multiplied by $1\frac{1}{3}$?
12. A cake contains the following ingredients: $\frac{1}{5}$ kg flour, $\frac{1}{8}$ kg butter, $\frac{1}{4}$ kg fruit and $\frac{1}{10}$ kg milk. How much does the cake weigh? After cooking the weight falls to $\frac{1}{2}$ kg. What weight was lost during cooking?
13. In her will a woman leaves $\frac{1}{2}$ of her money to her son, $\frac{1}{4}$ to her daughter, $\frac{1}{8}$ to her dog, $\frac{1}{16}$ to her cat, $\frac{1}{32}$ to her canary and the rest is divided equally between her three goldfish. What fraction does each goldfish receive?
14. An exercise book is $\frac{2}{5}$ cm thick. How many books are there in a pile which is $10\frac{2}{5}$ cm high?
15. Arrange the fractions $\frac{8}{9}, \frac{11}{12}, \frac{5}{6}$ and $\frac{17}{18}$ in order of size. Divide the sum of the two largest fractions by the sum of the two smallest fractions.

3 Nets

Three-dimensional shapes: nets

It is interesting and enjoyable to make three-dimensional objects using cardboard. When you have made an object which looks attractive it is a good idea to paint the faces using different colours.

When making these objects you must be particularly *careful* and work accurately. Use a sharp pencil, a good pair of compasses and a sharp pair of scissors. Take your time over each object and produce something you can be proud of.

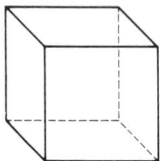

If the cube above was made of cardboard, and you cut along some of the edges and laid it out flat, you would have the *net* of the cube.

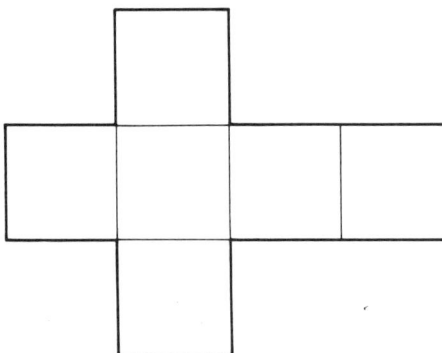

Draw the net of a cube on a piece of thin cardboard. Make each square 5 cm by 5 cm. Cut out the net and make sharp folds along the lines using the point of a pair of compasses. Fold the card to make a cube and stick it together.

Tetrahedron

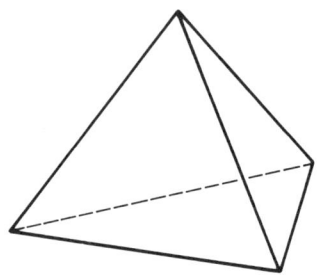

The net for a tetrahedron consists of four equilateral triangles

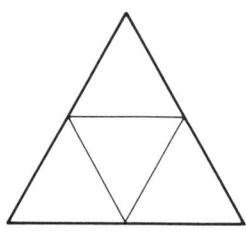

Square-based pyramid

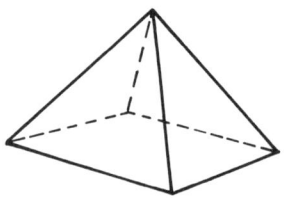

The net for a square-based pyramid is a square and four equilateral triangles.

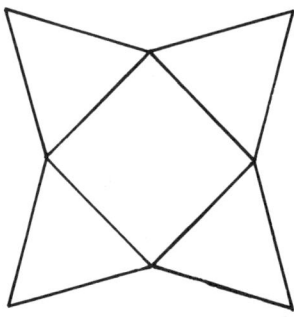

Constructing and using nets

We are going to use equilateral triangles for several different objects so it is worth spending some time on a method for constructing a whole series of equilateral triangles all at once.

(a) Draw the line AB. Use a pair of compasses to draw a pattern of circles as shown. Make the radius of the circles 3 cm. The centres of the circles are marked with an O.

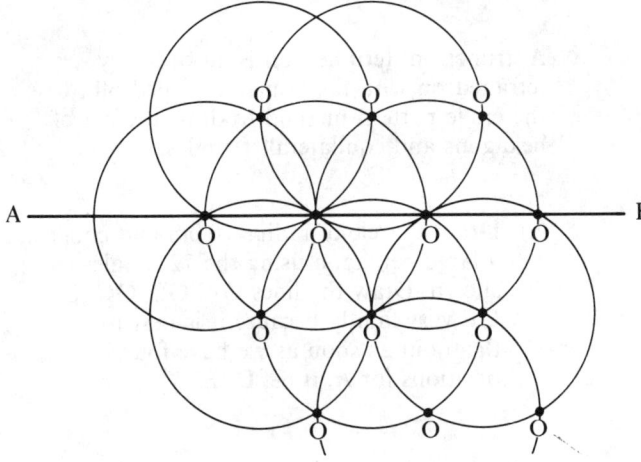

(b) Draw the lines to produce a series of equilateral triangles.

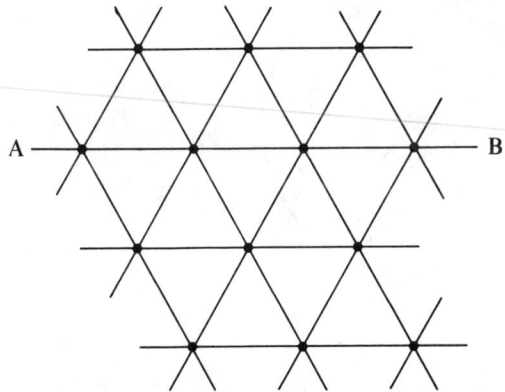

We can also use this method to produce a series of regular hexagons.

Exercise 3.1

Several objects are shown together with the net which will produce them. Draw the net on a piece of cardboard, cut it out, and fold it to make the object. Remember: Be careful! You will not be able to make the shape if your net is not accurate.

1. Tetrahedron

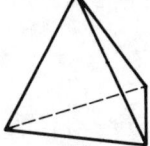   net: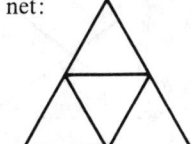

2. Octahedron

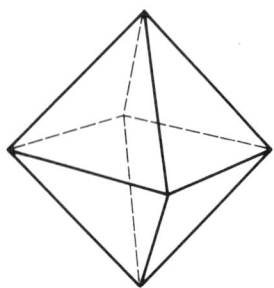

net:

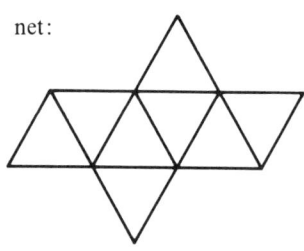

3. Icosahedron (an object with 20 faces)

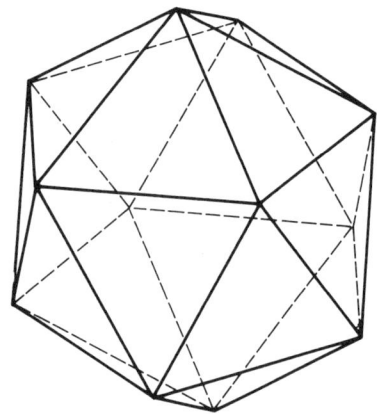

net:

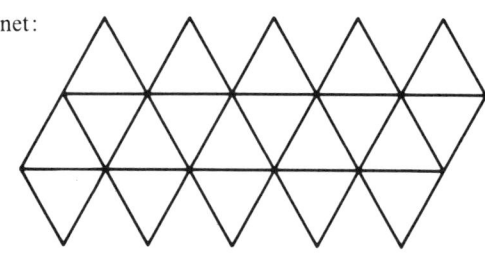

4. Truncated tetrahedron

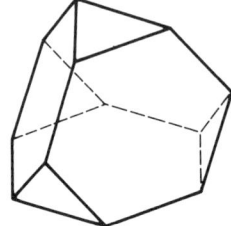

net:

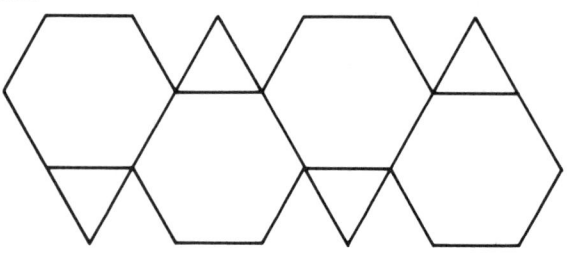

A 'truncated' tetrahedron is an ordinary tetrahedron with the points 'chopped off'. Use the circle pattern method to draw the net of hexagons and equilateral triangles.

5. (a) Draw a circle of radius 10 cm and construct a large pentagon using the 72° angles as shown. Draw the lines OA, OB, OC, OD, OE very faintly because it is best to rub them out as soon as we have found the positions for A, B, C, D, E.

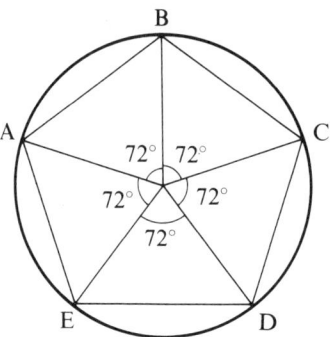

(b) Join A to C and A to D.
Join B to E and B to D.
Join C to E.
Mark the points V, W, X, Y, Z.

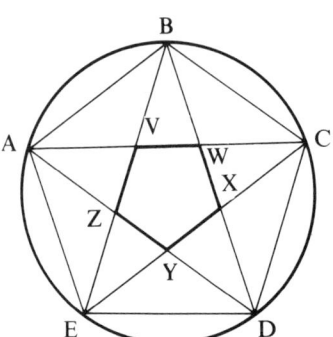

(c) Draw a line through Z and W.
   Draw a line through V and X.
   Draw a line through W and Y.
   Draw a line through Z and X.
   Draw a line through V and Y.

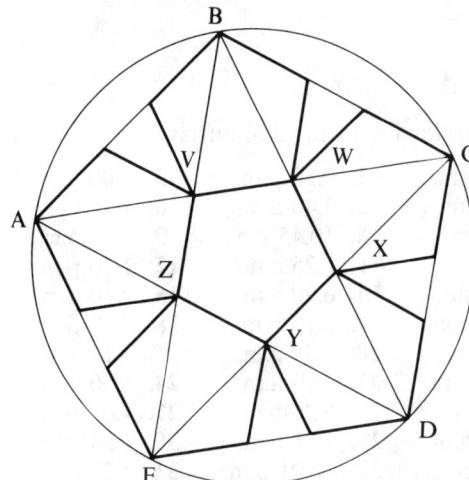

This pattern forms a series of regular pentagons shown by the thick lines.

6. Dodecahedron (12 faces)

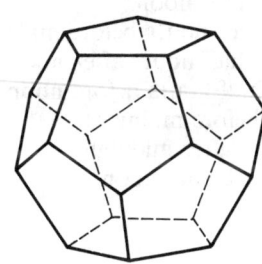

net:

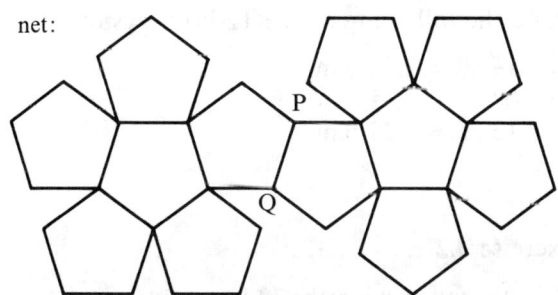

Draw the pattern of regular pentagons twice, as shown in question 5, and join them along the line PQ.

7. (For the enthusiast!)
Cuboctahedron

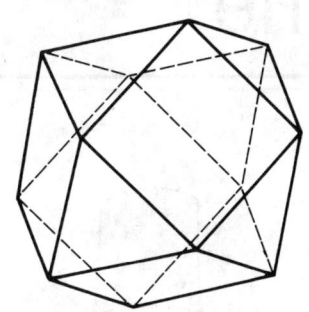

net:

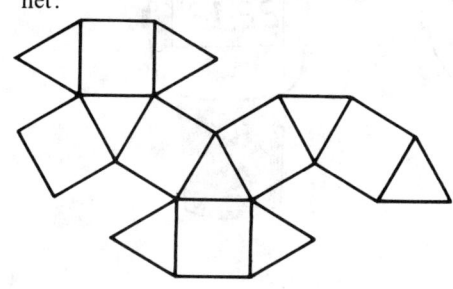

8. Truncated octahedron

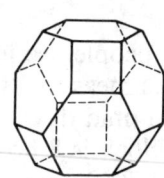

net:

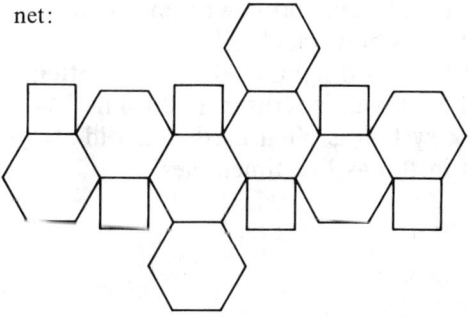

4 Time

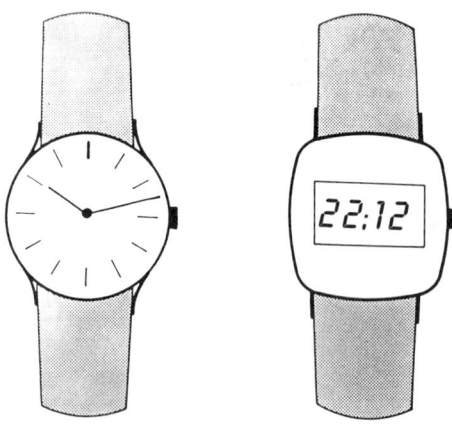

24-hour clock

The times which most people use in their everyday lives are times measured from midnight or from noon (mid-day).

In the morning 8 o'clock is 8 hours after midnight and is written 8.00 a.m.

In the afternoon 5 o'clock is 5 hours after noon (after mid-day) and is written 5 p.m.

Using the 24-hour clock all times are measured from midnight. 8.00 a.m. is written 08.00 and 5.00 p.m. is written 17.00. The 24-hour clock system is often used to avoid confusion in things like timetables.

Examples

Write each of the following times in the 24-hour system.

(a) 7.00 a.m. = 07.00
(b) 10.30 p.m. = 22.30
(c) 5.15 p.m. = 17.15

Remember:

'a.m. is morning'
'p.m. is afternoon'.

Exercise 4.1

Write the following in the 24-hour system.

1. 8.00 a.m. 2. 9.30 p.m. 3. 6.00 p.m.
4. 5.30 a.m. 5. 7.40 a.m. 6. 10.00 p.m.
7. 7.15 p.m. 8. 10.45 p.m. 9. 8.30 a.m.
10. 4.15 a.m. 11. 2.25 a.m. 12. 1.30 p.m.
13. 7.20 p.m. 14. 6.50 a.m. 15. 7.10 a.m.
16. 11.50 a.m. 17. 6.10 p.m. 18. 4.09 p.m.
19. 7.06 p.m. 20. 3.54 a.m. 21. 9.11 a.m.
22. 11.17 p.m. 23. 9.09 a.m. 24. 1.00 a.m.
25. Noon 26. 5.26 p.m. 27. 7.07 p.m.
28. 10.10 a.m. 29. 1.01 a.m. 30. 12.45 p.m.
31. 12.20 p.m. 32. 12.01 p.m. 33. 5.27 a.m.
34. Midnight 35. 4.40 p.m. 36. 8.11 a.m.
37. 12.06 p.m. 38. 1.59 a.m. 39. 12.59 p.m.
40. Two minutes before midnight.
41. Five minutes before noon.
42. One hour after midnight.
43. Twenty minutes after midnight.
44. Six minutes after noon.
45. Two and a half hours before midnight.
46. Three and a half hours after noon.
47. One and a half hours before noon.
48. Five hours before midnight.
49. Fifty minutes after midnight.
50. Half an hour before noon.

Examples

Write the following in the 12-hour system.

(a) 19.30 = 7.30 p.m.
(b) 08.45 = 8.45 a.m.
(c) 13.25 = 1.25 p.m.

Exercise 4.2

Write the following in the 12-hour system.

1. 07.00 2. 19.30 3. 11.20 4. 04.45
5. 20.30 6. 21.15 7. 09.10 8. 11.45
9. 23.10 10. 20.00 11. 12.00 12. 01.40
13. 04.00 14. 07.07 15. 13.13 16. 12.15
17. 12.30 18. 15.45 19. 16.20 20. 05.16
21. 00.40 22. 00.04 23. 09.09 24. 12.01
25. 00.30 26. 23.50 27. 23.59 28. 16.01
29. 07.59 30. 11.39

Time intervals

Example

Find how many hours and minutes there are between the following times:

17.40 and 19.05
From 17.40 until 18.00 there are 20 minutes. From 18.00 until 19.05 there is 1 hour 5 minutes. Altogether there is 1 hour 25 minutes between the two times.

Exercise 4.3

Find the number of hours and minutes between the following.

1. 20.10 and 21.20
2. 21.40 and 23.50
3. 22.15 and 23.10
4. 19.30 and 20.05
5. 20.16 and 23.36
6. 11.25 and 13.10
7. 09.40 and 12.00
8. 21.17 and 23.10
9. 23.04 and 23.57
10. 17.45 and 23.10
11. 05.15 and 07.05
12. 11.26 and 14.40
13. 9.50 a.m. and 11.05 a.m.
14. 11.10 a.m. and 1.30 p.m.
15. 10.40 a.m. and 12.40 p.m.
16. 11.55 a.m. and 3.10 p.m.
17. 9.30 a.m. and 2.05 p.m.
18. 7.30 a.m. and 7.30 p.m.
19. 5.40 a.m. and 1.00 p.m.
20. 1.35 a.m. and 8.40 a.m.
21. 22.30 on Monday to 03.30 on Tuesday
22. 21.00 on Thursday to 01.40 on Friday
23. 17.30 on Monday to 02.00 on Tuesday
24. 23.45 on Saturday to 02.10 on Sunday
25. 22.50 on Thursday to 07.00 on Friday
26. 07.00 on Friday to 02.00 on Saturday
27. 09.30 on Monday to 04.30 on Tuesday
28. 09.15 on Wednesday to 02.45 on Thursday
29. 22.10 on Friday to 07.35 on Saturday
30. 06.30 on Friday to 16.30 on Saturday

Timetables

Exercise 4.4

Here is a railway timetable for three trains, A, B and C.

	train A	train B	train C
Swansea	07.10	09.25	11.00
Cardiff	08.15	10.27	11.55
Newport	08.35	10.42	12.15
Swindon	09.00	11.05	12.38
Reading	09.40	11.40	13.15

We will ignore the waiting times at the stations.

1. Which train arrives in Reading in the afternoon?
2. Which train arrives in Swindon at 09.00?
3. Which train arrives in Cardiff just before 10.30?
4. Which train will I catch if I get to Cardiff station at 11.00?
5. How long will I have to wait for a train if I arrive at Newport station at 11.30?
6. Which train takes 2 hours 30 minutes for the journey from Swansea to Reading?
7. Between which two stations is train B at 10.00?
8. Between which two stations is train C at noon?
9. Between which two stations is train A at 08.10?
10. Which train takes the shortest time between Swansea and Cardiff?
11. Which train takes only 15 minutes to travel between Cardiff and Newport?
12. If I leave home at 08.30 and arrive at Swansea station 40 minutes later, how long will I have to wait for the next train?
13. If it takes 25 minutes to walk from home to Cardiff station, when should I leave so that I can catch the first train?
14. If it takes 3 hours 10 minutes to drive from Swansea to Reading, how much quicker is the journey using train A?

In questions **15** to **25** find the time taken for each of the journeys below.

15. Swansea to Cardiff on train C.
16. Newport to Swindon on train A.
17. Cardiff to Newport on train B.
18. Swindon to Reading on train C.
19. Swansea to Newport on train A.
20. Cardiff to Reading on train A.
21. Swansea to Swindon on train B.
22. Swansea to Newport on train B.
23. Cardiff to Reading on train C.
24. Newport to Reading on train A.
25. Swansea to Swindon on train C.

Exercise 4.5

Here is another railway timetable.

	train W	train X	train Y	train Z
Kings Cross	09.10	15.25	21.30	00.30
Cambridge	10.13	16.30	22.25	01.30
York	11.12	17.27	23.36	02.25
Newcastle	12.05	18.15	00.30	03.20
Dundee	15.20	21.55	03.40	06.00

In questions **1** to **15** find the time taken for each of the journeys below.

1. Kings Cross to York on train W.
2. Cambridge to Newcastle on train Z.
3. York to Dundee on train W.
4. Kings Cross to Newcastle on train Y.
5. Cambridge to Dundee on train X.
6. York to Newcastle on train Z.
7. Kings Cross to Dundee on train Z.
8. York to Dundee on train Z.
9. Cambridge to York on train W.
10. Newcastle to Dundee on train Y.
11. Kings Cross to Dundee on train Y.
12. Cambridge to Dundee on train Y.
13. York to Newcastle on train W.
14. Newcastle to Dundee on train Z.
15. Cambridge to Newcastle on train X.
16. Between which two stations is train W at 14.30?
17. Between which two stations is train Z at 01.00?
18. Between which two stations is train X at 17.20?
19. Between which two stations is train Y at midnight?
20. Between which two stations is train W at noon?
21. Which train takes the shortest time between Kings Cross and Cambridge?
22. Which train takes the longest time between York and Dundee?
23. If train Y is one hour late at every station when does it arrive at York?
24. If train W is 30 minutes late at every station when does it arrive at Dundee?
25. Which train takes less than six hours to travel from Kings Cross to Dundee?

Revision exercises 1

Quick tests

Test 1
1. Write 5.15 p.m. in the 24-hour system.
2. Write 9.20 a.m. in the 24-hour system.
3. Write 8.40 p.m. in the 24-hour system.
4. Write 23.30 in the 12-hour system.
5. Write 08.15 in the 12-hour system.
6. Write 15.45 in the 12-hour system.
7. $77 + 9$
8. $65 + 19$
9. $73 + 19$
10. $84 - 19$
11. $27 - 12$
12. $100 - 63$
13. $200 - 47$
14. $\frac{1}{2} \times \frac{1}{2}$
15. $\frac{1}{2} \times \frac{1}{3}$
16. $\frac{2}{3} \times \frac{2}{3}$
17. $\frac{3}{4} \times \frac{1}{2}$
18. $\frac{1}{10} \times \frac{1}{4}$
19. $\frac{1}{7} \times \frac{5}{12}$
20. $\frac{1}{2} + \frac{1}{3}$

Test 2
1. $61 + 17$
2. $65 + 14$
3. $80 - 27$
4. 15×9
5. 17×9
6. $53 - 19$
7. $85 - 29$
8. How many lines of symmetry has a rectangle (oblong)?
9. How many lines of symmetry has a square?
10. How many lines of symmetry has an equilateral triangle?
11. Cancel down $\frac{4}{12}$
12. Cancel down $\frac{15}{18}$
13. Cancel down $\frac{24}{30}$
14. Cancel down $\frac{18}{30}$
15. What is next? 5, 8, 11, 14 . . .
16. What is next? 3, 7, 11 . . .
17. What is next? 19, 14, 9, . . .
18. What is the next prime number after 7?
19. What is the next prime number after 19?
20. What is the next prime number after 47?

Whole numbers

Revision exercise 1.1

Calculate the following
1. Six hundred and thirty-four multiplied by six.
2. Five hundred and seventy-three multiplied by four.
3. Nine hundred and sixty-five multiplied by two.
4. Eight thousand five hundred and eleven divided by three.
5. Three thousand seven hundred and four divided by four.
6. Four thousand and fifty-five multiplied by seven.
7. 433×8
8. 272×6
9. 3448×3
10. $2625 \div 3$
11. 6104×9
12. $3568 \div 8$
13. 5359×4
14. 3571×7
15. $6012 \div 6$
16. $14130 \div 2$
17. A flower-seller earns £18 every day from Monday to Friday inclusive. He earns £29 on Saturday, but does not work on Sunday. How much does he earn in a week?
18. A man wishes to divide £434 equally between his seven grandchildren. How much does each grandchild receive?
19. A worker earns £375 every month. How much does she earn in six months?
20. £2149 is to be shared equally between you and six other people. How much will you get?
21. In a school assembly hall there are 51 rows of boys with 9 boys in each row, and 53 rows of girls with 8 girls in each row. How many more boys are there than girls?
22. In a school term there are 72 school days with 8 lessons in each day. How many lessons are there during that term?
23. 63×24
24. 87×16
25. 432×14
26. 613×25
27. 72×43
28. 226×31
29. 39×39
30. 146×52
31. $832 \div 13$
32. $690 \div 15$
33. $391 \div 17$
34. $1012 \div 23$
35. $1728 \div 24$
36. $6099 \div 19$
37. 234×16
38. $2236 \div 43$
39. 417×243
40. $9618 \div 21$

Angle

Revision exercise 1.2

In *each question* draw a set of axes with x and y both going from 0 to 15.

1. Copy the diagram below and measure the angles of the triangle as accurately as you can.

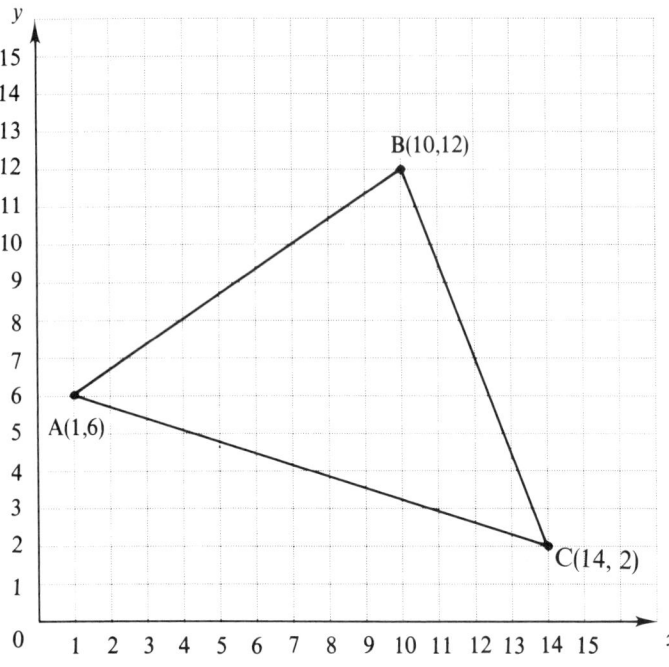

2. Copy the diagram below and measure the angles of the triangle as accurately as you can.

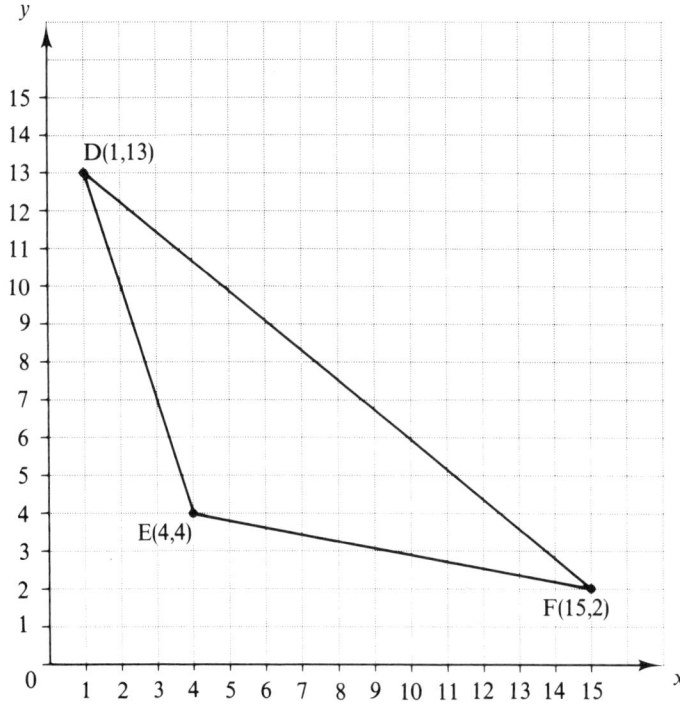

3. Plot and label A(0, 0), B(15, 0), C(10, 12). Join the points A, B and C to form a triangle and then measure its angles as accurately as you can.
4. Plot and label C(0, 0), D(10, 0), E(15, 10). Measure the angles of the triangle CDE.
5. Plot and label P(0, 0), Q(5, 10), R(12, 6). Measure the angles of the triangle PQR.
6. Plot and label L(0, 10), M(5, 0), N(12, 6). Measure the angles of the triangle LMN.
7. Plot and label H(12, 5), J(5, 3), K(2, 10). Measure the angles of the triangle HJK.
8. Plot and label R(2, 10), S(8, 1), T(15, 4). Measure the angles of the triangle RST.
9. Plot and label A(2, 5), P(9, 3), W(14, 8). Measure the angles of the triangle APW.
10. Plot and label A(1, 14), B(4, 1), C(15, 15). Measure the angles of the triangle ABC.

Number patterns

Revision exercise 1.3

Reminders

(a) The *factors* of 8 are 1, 2, 4, 8.
(b) The first four *multiplies* of 5 are 5, 10, 15, 20.
(c) The first five *prime* numbers are 2, 3, 5, 7, 11.
(d) Four is a *square* number

1. Write down all the factors of the following numbers:

   (a) 10 (b) 12 (c) 18
   (d) 9   (e) 13 (f) 24

2. Write down the common factors for each of the following pairs of numbers:

   [For example for 12 and 18: 1, 2, 3, 6 divide into both numbers.]

   (a) 8, 12   (b) 15, 24 (c) 18, 30
   (d) 24, 40 (e) 21, 36 (f) 6, 35
   (g) 35, 42 (h) 22, 88

3. Write down the first four multiples of the following numbers:

   (a) 4 (b) 6   (c) 7
   (d) 9 (e) 12 (f) 15

4. Write down all the prime numbers

   (a) between 10 and 20
   (b) between 30 and 40
   (c) between 70 and 80
   (d) between 90 and 100
   (e) between 100 and 110.

5. Draw a factor tree to find the prime factors of the following numbers.

   For example:

   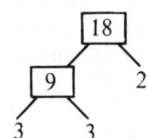

   $18 = 2 \times 3 \times 3$.

   (a) 24   (b) 40   (c) 90
   (d) 150   (e) 72   (f) 630
   (g) 1800 (h) 1890 (i) 6468

6. From the set
   A = {2, 3, 4, 5, 6, 7, 8, 9, 10, 11, 12, 13}, write down:

   (a) all the prime numbers,
   (b) all the square numbers,
   (c) all the factors of 10,
   (d) all the factors of 12.

7. From the set
   B = {2, 4, 8, 9, 15, 16, 21, 25, 33, 36}, write down:

   (a) all the square numbers,
   (b) all the prime numbers,
   (c) all the factors of 36,
   (d) all the multiples of 4,
   (e) all the multiples of 3.

8. From the set
   C = {3, 5, 8, 9, 14, 16, 21, 59, 65, 81, 100}, write down:

   (a) all the prime numbers,
   (b) all the square numbers,
   (c) all the multiples of 5,
   (d) all the multiples of 3,
   (e) all the factors of 6500.

In questions **9** to **30** write down the next three numbers in the sequence.

9. 3, 6, 9, 12, ...
10. 1, 5, 9, 13, ...
11. 2, 9, 16, 23, ...
12. 3, 14, 25, 36, ...
13. 27, 24, 21, 18, ...
14. 36, 31, 26, 21, ...
15. 100, 93, 86, 79, ...
16. 2, 14, 26, 38, ...
17. 59, 50, 41, 32, ...
18. 1, 8, 15, 22, ...
19. 100, 88, 76, 64, ...
20. 5, 6, 8, 11, ...
21. 11, 13, 17, 23, ...
22. 2, 4, 8, 16, ...
23. 7, 9, 12, 16, ...
24. 60, 59, 57, 54, ...
25. 48, 24, 12, 6, ...
26. 243, 81, 27, 9, ...
27. 15, 16, 14, 17, 13, ...
28. 1, 2, 6, 24, ...
29. 10, 12, 9, 13, ...
30. 0, 1, 1, 2, 3, 5, ...

In questions **11** to **20**, change the top-heavy fraction to a mixed number.

11. $\frac{9}{2}$ 12. $\frac{4}{3}$ 13. $\frac{7}{5}$ 14. $\frac{10}{7}$ 15. $\frac{11}{3}$
16. $\frac{13}{2}$ 17. $\frac{22}{9}$ 18. $\frac{12}{5}$ 19. $\frac{21}{2}$ 20. $\frac{19}{8}$

In questions **21** to **30**, change the mixed number to a top-heavy fraction.

21. $1\frac{1}{2}$ 22. $3\frac{3}{4}$ 23. $1\frac{3}{4}$ 24. $2\frac{4}{5}$ 25. $3\frac{1}{7}$
26. $10\frac{1}{3}$ 27. $6\frac{1}{4}$ 28. $7\frac{1}{2}$ 29. $3\frac{5}{6}$ 30. $4\frac{2}{11}$

In questions **31** to **50**, calculate the answer.

31. $\frac{3}{11} + \frac{4}{11}$ 32. $\frac{5}{9} - \frac{1}{9}$ 33. $\frac{3}{5} - \frac{1}{5}$
34. $\frac{6}{13} + \frac{2}{13}$ 35. $\frac{6}{7} - \frac{2}{7}$ 36. $\frac{5}{11} + \frac{4}{11}$
37. $\frac{2}{3} + \frac{1}{2}$ 38. $\frac{3}{4} - \frac{1}{2}$ 39. $\frac{4}{5} - \frac{1}{2}$
40. $\frac{5}{6} - \frac{1}{4}$ 41. $\frac{2}{9} + \frac{1}{3}$ 42. $\frac{2}{3} + \frac{1}{6}$
43. $\frac{1}{5} + \frac{2}{3}$ 44. $\frac{2}{3} - \frac{5}{9}$ 45. $\frac{2}{3} + \frac{1}{2} - \frac{3}{4}$
46. $\frac{4}{5} + \frac{1}{4} - \frac{1}{3}$ 47. $\frac{3}{4} + \frac{2}{5} - \frac{1}{2}$ 48. $\frac{1}{2} - \frac{3}{7}$
49. $\frac{2}{11} + \frac{1}{2}$ 50. $\frac{5}{9} + \frac{2}{3} - \frac{3}{4}$

Fractions

Revision exercise 1.4

In questions **1** to **10**, copy down the shape and shading and write down the fraction of the shape that is shaded, *giving your answer in its simplest form.*

1.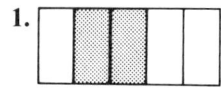
2.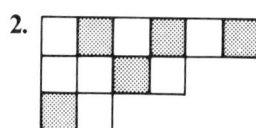
3.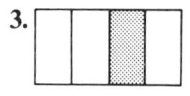
4.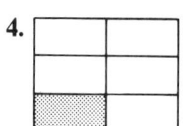
5.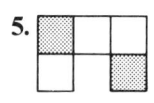
6.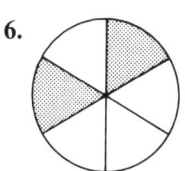
7.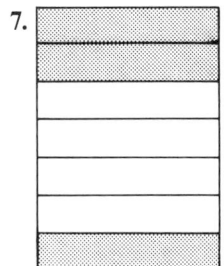
8.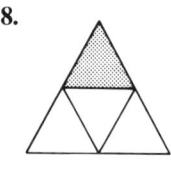
9.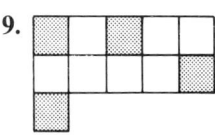
10.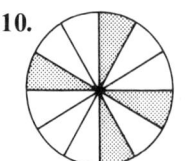

5 Decimal numbers

Adding and subtracting decimals

When adding and subtracting decimals we set out the question so that the decimal points are in a vertical line, one below the other.

Example

Work out $2.74 + 13.6 + 0.025$

```
    2.74
   13.6
 + 0.025
 ───────
   16.365
 ───────
     1
```

Exercise 5.1

Calculate the following

1. $34.6 + 11.32$
2. $746.84 + 103.7$
3. $42.73 - 19.2$
4. $71.36 - 2.18$
5. $37.64 + 12.03$
6. $4.02 - 1.8$
7. $3.7 - 1.23$
8. $4.43 - 1.06$
9. $6.41 + 13.068 + 1.32$
10. $38.6 + 29.0 + 6.25$
11. $13.26 + 74.8$
12. $6.28 + 45$
13. $22.7 - 8.9$
14. $4.7 - 2.34$
15. $6.78 + 0.097$
16. $62.3 - 0.2$
17. $41.6 - 0.09$
18. $11.64 + 153.2$
19. $97.6 + 1.052$
20. $48 - 0.2$
21. $6.69 + 2.38$
22. $15.061 + 9.509$
23. $36 - 0.34$
24. $14.972 - 2.39$
25. $7.31 + 0.455 + 16$
26. $27.2 + 1.36 + 2.154$
27. $10.22 + 12 - 3.31$
28. $11.6 - 0.42 + 17.6$
29. $15.3 + 22.8 - 0.3$
30. $62.6 + 5.37 + 102.07$

31. Mr Lovell travels 7·4 km by bus and then 16·7 km by train. How far has he travelled altogether?
32. The distance between two railway stations is 5·6 km. A train leaves one station but after travelling 1·9 km it has to stop at a signal. Find how far it still has to go to the next station.
33. Mrs Brown buys two dresses costing £12·45 and £23·16. How much does she spend altogether?
34. Mr Kahn buys three tools costing £4·60, £3·37 and £11·99 respectively. Find the total cost of the tools.
35. Donna buys a record for £3·79. How much change should she get from £5?
36. A boy buys two items for his train set. If they cost £5·42 and £2·73, how much change should he get from £10?
37. Three lengths of wood are joined end to end. If their individual lengths are 19·4 cm, 26·7 cm and 32 cm, what is their combined length?
38. Find the total weight of the three objects below.

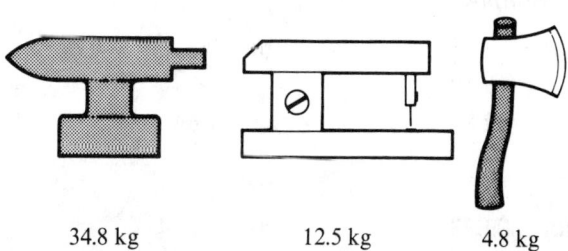

34.8 kg   12.5 kg   4.8 kg

39. Two objects together weigh 74·3 kg. One of the objects is known to weigh 55·5 kg. Find the weight of the other object.
40. A man buys three shirts costing £7·20, £9·50 and £8·35 respectively. If he pays for them with three £10 notes, how much change should he receive?

Multiplying decimals by whole numbers

Examples

(a) $5.71 \times 10 = 57.1$
(b) $0.332 \times 100 = 33.2$
(c) $0.053 \times 1000 = 53$
(d) $4.2 \times 1000 = 4200$

Exercise 5.2

Do the following calculations.

1. 4.23×10
2. 5.63×10
3. 0.427×100
4. 4.63×100
5. 0.075×10
6. 0.0063×100
7. 1.147×1000
8. 10.7×1000
9. 6.33×100
10. $0.00714 \times 10\,000$
11. 6.36×100
12. 8.142×10
13. $0.71 \times 10\,000$
14. 8.9×1000
15. 12×100
16. 13×10
17. 7×1000
18. $9.2 \times 10\,000$
19. 0.7×100
20. $0.5 \times 100\,000$
21. 0.01×10
22. 5.2×100
23. 14×1000
24. 0.1×10
25. $0.2 \times 10\,000$
26. $8.31 \times 100\,000$
27. 9.2×1 million
28. 8.34×1 million
29. 0.71×1 million
30. 8.6×100
31. 27×1000
32. 53×100
33. 0.0084×10
34. $0.74 \times 10\,000$
35. 91×100
36. 0×1000
37. $5.6 \times 10 \times 10$
38. $2.14 \times 10 \times 10$
39. $0.0634 \times 10 \times 100$
40. $0.1111 \times 100 \times 100$
41. $8 \times 100 \times 10$
42. $7.24 \times 100 \times 100$
43. $0.12 \times 1000 \times 10$
44. $0.1434 \times 100 \times 10$
45. 3.21×10 million

Examples

(a) 8.21
    $\underline{\times 4}$
    32.84

(b) 0.82
    $\underline{\times 2}$
    1.64
    ${}_1$

(c) 0.073
    $\underline{\times 9}$
    0.657
    ${}_{62}$

(d) 8.04
    $\underline{\times 7}$
    56.28
    ${}_2$

In each case the answer has the same number of figures to the right of the decimal point as there are in the numbers being multiplied.

Exercise 5.3

Do the following calculations.

1. 1.3×3
2. 2.4×2
3. 5.1×4
4. 6.11×5
5. 7.21×4
6. 1.23×6
7. 0.71×7
8. 1.33×3
9. 0.84×4
10. 1.63×5
11. 0.314×3
12. 0.114×6
13. 11.7×7
14. 2.14×8
15. 1.732×5
16. 1.917×9
17. 0.832×8
18. 0.014×7
19. 0.037×9
20. 0.004×8
21. 0.009×6
22. 9.666×4
23. 82.72×3
24. 8.63×10
25. 0.747×10
26. 0.841×10
27. 3.707×9
28. 2.13×11
29. 3.34×12
30. 0.415×12
31. 0.775×3
32. 1.45×7
33. 50.1×4
34. 70.7×7
35. 11.9×2
36. 0.07×9
37. 0.0063×6
38. 1.14×11
39. 2.007×5
40. 3.008×6
41. 0.761×10
42. 7.421×100

Example

(a) $2.3 \times 20 = 2.3 \times 10 \times 2$
$ = 23 \times 2$
$ = 46$

(b) $0.31 \times 500 = 0.31 \times 100 \times 5$
$ = 31 \times 5$
$ = 155$

Exercise 5.4

Calculate the following

1. 4.2×30
2. 3.1×20
3. 2.1×60
4. 8.21×40
5. 6.33×300
6. 1.21×70
7. 0.23×200
8. 0.322×400
9. 0.031×80
10. 1.211×500
11. 0.214×60
12. 0.07×400
13. 0.012×3000
14. 11.2×20
15. 3.12×110
16. $0.71 \times 10\,000$
17. 0.00034×100
18. 2.6×1000
19. 2.04×700
20. 4.31×2000
21. 0.001×5000
22. 2.74×90
23. 8.13×120
24. 27.4×110
25. 3.333×1200
26. 3.201×9000
27. 8.17×500
28. 29.1×600
29. 0.007×70
30. $0.33 \times 40\,000$
31. 3.62×300
32. 6.29×50
33. 21.3×40
34. 14.6×100
35. 1.64×700
36. 4.35×6000
37. 0.27×80
38. 0.025×40
39. 4.6×2000
40. 0.74×300

41. 13·8 × 40
42. 5·82 × 200
43. 12·5 × 700
44. 0·124 × 5000
45. 0·037 × 8000
46. 6·7 × 80
47. 0·024 × 20
48. 0·042 × 700
49. 4·403 × 500
50. 1·345 × 3000
61. £4 − £1·47
62. £3 − £0·27
63. £10 − £5·53
64. £1 − 73p
65. £2·50 − 79p
66. £11 − £2·07
67. £1·60 − 65p
68. £2 − £1·19
69. £10 − £2·43
70. £0·73 − 27p

Money

Examples

(a) Write 75p in pounds.
    75p = £0·75

(b) Write £2·35 in pence
    £2·35 = 235p

(c) Work out 45p + £1·16 + £2·09
```
   0·45
   1·16
 +2·09
 ─────
   3·70
```
    Answer = £3·70

Exercise 5.5

Write in pounds

1. 47p
2. 33p
3. 59p
4. 175p
5. 214p
6. 300p
7. 250p
8. 17p
9. 29p
10. 7p
11. 5p
12. 100p
13. 4p
14. 2145p
15. 6130p
16. 9p
17. 11p
18. 1p
19. 200p
20. 4000p

Write in pence

21. £1·15
22. £2·44
23. £0·15
24. £0·29
25. £2·15
26. £10·10
27. £9·80
28. £0·55
29. £0·08
30. £0·02
31. £8·02
32. £0·95
33. £0·03
34. £12
35. £7
36. £5·50
37. £50
38. £0·17
39. £13·13
40. £400

Work out

41. £2·40 + £1·35 + £0·63
42. £0·75 + £3·40 + £0·19
43. £6·50 + £1·24 + 20p
44. £2·14 + £5·65 + 75p
45. £1·74 + £0·74 + 59p + 12p
46. £2·59 + £3·76 + 45p + 6p
47. £6·31 + £4 + 95p
48. £3 + £7·15 + 9p + 72p
49. £4 + £7 + 71p + 58p
50. £6·07 + 55p + £0·73 + 8p
51. £1·15 + £3·27 + 63p + 29p + £3
52. £2·40 + £1·65 + 77p + £0·08
53. £3·15 − 75p
54. £1·95 − 80p
55. £2·50 − 67p
56. £3·16 − £1·24
57. £4·15 − £1·99
58. £2·17 − £1·90
59. £8·90 − 55p
60. £3·05 − 27p

Exercise 5.6

Find the total cost.

1. 2 jars at £1·75 each
   4 boxes at £0·40 each
   1 bottle at £1·25

2. 3 tins at £0·51 each
   5 packets at £1·10 each
   2 pints of milk at 22p per pint.

3. 6 tins at £0·75 each
   3 bags at £0·69 each
   4 packets at 21p each

4. 3 loaves at 42p each
   2 cauliflowers at 45p each
   4 cans at £1·50 each

5. 12 eggs at 45p per dozen
   7 bottles at £0·37 each
   3 oranges at 10p each

6. 2 lb of meat at £1·60 per lb
   5 cans at 63p each
   3 packets at £2·11 each

7. 6 eggs at 46p per dozen
   3 litres at 95p per litre
   10 bags at £0·54 each

8. $\frac{1}{2}$ kg of rice at 76p per kg
   7 cans at £0·84 each
   3 loaves at 35p each

9. $1\frac{1}{2}$ lb of meat at £1·20 per lb
   6 eggs at 44p per dozen
   4 grapefruit at 16p each
   3 tins at £0·65 each

10. 5 lb of potatoes at 11p per lb
    3 packets at £2·95 each
    1 loaf at 37p
    6 cans at £0·24 each

11. $2\frac{1}{2}$ lb of carrots at 8p per lb
    5 oranges at 12p each
    3 jars at £1·65 each
    4 kg of sugar at £0·49 per kg

12. 4 litres of oil at 97p per litre
    6 bags at £0·33 each
    3 lb of meat at £2·12 per lb
    1 cauliflower at 42p

13. 18 eggs at 50p per dozen
    $\frac{1}{2}$ lb of cheese at £1·30 per lb
    3 lb of leeks at 18p per lb
    2 packets at £2·30 each

14. 1½ lb of meat at £1·80 per lb
    3 kg of flour at 44p per kg
    15 packets at £0·22 each
    10 oranges at 12p each

15. 25 litres of petrol at 41p per litre
    2½ lb of meat at £1·40 per lb
    6 eggs at 40p per dozen
    13 tins at 31p each

16. 25 kg of potatoes at 21p per kg
    11 boxes at £0·52 each
    2 loaves at £0·35 each
    5 pens at £0·22 each

17. 24 eggs at 44p per dozen
    1½ lb of cheese at 90p per lb
    13 packets at £0·51 each
    3 grapefruit at 9p each

18. 35 litres of petrol at 39p per litre
    5 m of cloth at £4·20 per m
    15 bottles at £0·46 each
    1¼ lb of meat at £1·60 per lb

19. 15 jars at £0·63 each
    4 bags at £2·17 each
    22 m of cloth at £2·30 per m
    3½ lb of meat at £3·50 per lb
    1 cauliflower at 46p

20. 30 eggs at 40p per dozen
    55 litres of fuel at £0·43 per litre
    5 packets at £1·17 each
    13 cans at 23p each
    1 calculator at £6·45.

Multiplying decimals together

When we multiply two decimal numbers together, the answer has the same number of figures to the right of the decimal point as the total number of figures to the right of the decimal points in the question.

Examples

(a) $0·3 \times 0·4$
    $(3 \times 4 = 12)$
    $0·3 \times 0·4 = 0·12$

(b) $0·7 \times 0·05$
    $(7 \times 5 = 35)$
    $0·7 \times 0·05 = 0·035$

Exercise 5.7

Calculate the following

1. $0·7 \times 0·3$
2. $0·7 \times 0·03$
3. $0·07 \times 0·03$
4. $0·07 \times 0·3$
5. $0·7 \times 3$
6. $0·4 \times 0·03$
7. $0·3 \times 0·2$
8. $0·02 \times 4$
9. $0·04 \times 0·08$
10. $0·5 \times 0·06$
11. $0·005 \times 0·1$
12. $0·05 \times 0·003$
13. $0·7 \times 0·7$
14. $0·001 \times 0·7$
15. $0·3 \times 0·05$
16. $0·8 \times 0·4$
17. $0·08 \times 0·02$
18. $0·4 \times 0·04$
19. $0·7 \times 0·04$
20. $0·05 \times 0·4$
21. $4 \times 0·06$
22. $0·3 \times 0·3$
23. $0·5 \times 0·005$
24. $0·0005 \times 0·8$
25. $0·7 \times 0·02$
26. $0·07 \times 0·04$
27. $0·06 \times 0·004$
28. $0·008 \times 0·006$
29. $0·6 \times 0·06$
30. $0·00003 \times 6$
31. $0·002 \times 0·7$
32. $0·004 \times 0·8$
33. $0·6 \times 0·2$
34. $8 \times 0·09$
35. $0·8 \times 0·8$
36. $0·02 \times 0·02$
37. $0·07 \times 0·2$
38. $0·004 \times 0·003$
39. $0·009 \times 0·009$
40. $0·003 \times 0·03$
41. $0·8 \times 0·08$
42. $0·04 \times 0·004$
43. $0·8 \times 0·3$
44. $0·05 \times 6$
45. $0·7 \times 0·08$
46. $0·009 \times 0·9$
47. $0·9 \times 0·06$
48. $7 \times 0·9$
49. $0·08 \times 0·07$
50. $0·3 \times 0·9$

Example

$3·1 \times 0·6$ First work out 31×6

$$\begin{array}{r} 31 \\ \times 6 \\ \hline 186 \end{array}$$ So $3·1 \times 0·6 = 1·86$

Exercise 5.8

Do the following calculations.

1. $1·2 \times 0·3$
2. $3·2 \times 0·2$
3. $1·4 \times 0·4$
4. $2·1 \times 0·5$
5. $3·61 \times 0·3$
6. $2·11 \times 0·6$
7. $0·31 \times 0·7$
8. $0·42 \times 0·02$
9. $0·33 \times 0·02$
10. $3·24 \times 0·04$
11. $8·11 \times 0·07$
12. $16·2 \times 0·8$
13. $24·3 \times 0·9$
14. $35·3 \times 0·001$
15. $20·6 \times 0·08$
16. $30·4 \times 0·9$
17. $5·06 \times 0·005$
18. $0·704 \times 0·06$
19. $1·21 \times 0·7$
20. $0·77 \times 0·009$
21. $251·3 \times 0·08$
22. $100 \times 0·7$
23. $1000 \times 0·0004$
24. $100 \times 0·007$
25. $2000 \times 0·0006$
26. $400 \times 0·008$
27. $300 \times 0·0008$
28. $2000 \times 0·5$
29. $2·75 \times 0·04$
30. $8·93 \times 0·07$
31. $0·75 \times 0·6$
32. $0·34 \times 0·2$

33. 0·83 × 0·8
34. 0·043 × 0·5
35. 0·071 × 0·7
36. 0·0421 × 0·3
37. 0·83 × 0·06
38. 0·95 × 0·04
39. 0·93 × 0·07
40. 4·6 × 0·005
41. 51·3 × 0·004
42. 65·04 × 0·06
43. 200 × 0·06
44. 500 × 0·004

Example

2·4 × 0·21 First work out 24 × 21

```
     24
   × 21
   ----
     24
    480
   ----
    504    So 2·4 × 0·21 = 0·504
```

Exercise 5.9

Do the following calculations.

1. 1·7 × 3·1
2. 1·5 × 2·2
3. 1·8 × 2·3
4. 2·1 × 0·41
5. 1·9 × 0·24
6. 24·1 × 0·15
7. 35·2 × 5·3
8. 23·4 × 1·7
9. 31·4 × 0·37
10. 4·12 × 0·021
11. 0·71 × 0·032
12. 0·63 × 0·72
13. 2·31 × 4·2
14. 12·5 × 0·031
15. 6·01 × 0·013
16. 29 × 4·2
17. 35 × 7·1
18. 211 × 8·2
19. 0·073 × 0·95
20. 0·034 × 0·59
21. 9·6 × 0·014
22. 0·88 × 0·16
23. 1·24 × 24
24. 71·5 × 31
25. 0·072 × 25
26. 1·08 × 36
27. 3·07 × 43
28. 101·2 × 16
29. 0·0043 × 0·43
30. 2·5 × 0·0025
31. 1·16 × 0·21
32. 0·31 × 0·42
33. 3·02 × 0·25
34. 11·4 × 1·5
35. 0·073 × 3·1
36. 4·23 × 0·045
37. 6·42 × 0·033
38. 12·7 × 3·7
39. 17·24 × 0·75
40. 18·76 × 0·86
41. 0·68 × 19
42. 1·72 × 23
43. 8·07 × 32
44. 0·006 14 × 35

We have seen how to multiply by:

(a) tens, hundreds, thousands etc.
(b) ordinary whole numbers
(c) one figure decimal numbers
(d) two figure decimal numbers.

The next exercise contains a mixture of these.

Exercise 5.10

Calculate the following

1. 2·06 × 1000
2. 3·12 × 7
3. 3·21 × 0·7
4. 0·63 × 0·05
5. 0·714 × 100
6. 31·2 × 5
7. 0·84 × 2·1
8. 0·65 × 0·32
9. 0·032 × 50
10. 0·0072 × 40
11. 1·71 × 300
12. 21·4 × 10 000
13. 7·23 × 0·01
14. 9·6 × 0·001
15. 2·41 × 9
16. 3·7 × 3·7
17. 1000 × 0·021
18. 400 × 0·033
19. 0·07 × 100
20. 0·0095 × 100 000
21. 4·02 × 11
22. 0·701 × 12
23. 0·301 × 43
24. 1·04 × 26
25. 0·021 × 700
26. 0·11 × 4000
27. 0·1 × 0·052
28. 100 × 0·0071
29. 7·2 × 100
30. 11·3 × 30
31. 11 × 60
32. 9 × 440
33. 0·21 × 510
34. 1000 × 0·83
35. 7·24 × 1000
36. 514·1 × 0·02
37. 0·63 × 67
38. 200 × 0·71
39. 0·0005 × 2·3
40. 1·3 × 40 000

Word questions: multiplying

Exercise 5.11

1. A woman buys five books, each costing £2·13. What is the total cost?
2. Mohammed buys 100 stamps each costing £0·15. What is the total cost?
3. Find the cost of 15 articles at £3·04 each.
4. Multiply 2·3 by itself and then multiply the answer by 10.
5. Ann buys 400 articles at £0·11 each. What is the total cost?
6. Javid buys four records at £1·95 each and three books at £1·75 each. What is the total cost?
7. Mrs Wood buys five tins of beans at £0·33 each and two bottles of vinegar at £0·53 each. What is the total cost?
8. Find the total cost of all the items below.

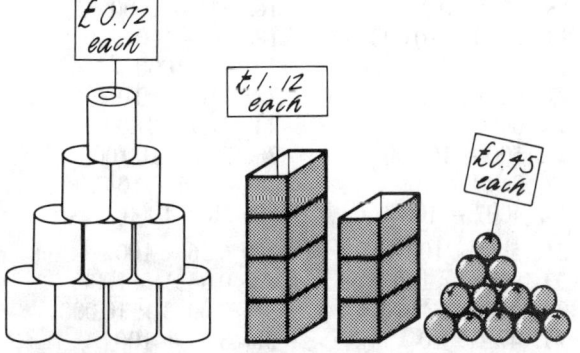

9. Multiply 0·37 by 400 and then multiply the answer by 0·063.
10. A teacher gives each of the 32 children in his form a Christmas treat of £0·15. What is the total cost?

30 Decimal numbers

11. Winston buys 400 pencils at 4·1 pence each. What change does he receive from £20?
12. A shopowner buys twelve footballs for a total of £42·50. What is her profit if she sells them all at £6·52 each?
13. At a restaurant seven people each pay £7·15 for food and £2·30 for drinks. What is the total bill for the seven people?
14. A newsagent buys 300 magazines at £0·453 each and 2000 newspapers at £0·072 each. What is the total cost?
15. Every day at school James buys a roll for 27p, crisps for 11p and a drink for 13p. How much does he spend in the whole school year of 200 days? (Answer in pounds.)

Dividing decimals by whole numbers

Examples

(a) $56·7 \div 10 = 5·67$
(b) $6·24 \div 100 = 0·0624$
(c) $0·314 \div 10 = 0·0314$
(d) $58 \div 1000 = 58·0 \div 1000 = 0·058$.

Exercise 5.12

Do the following calculations.

1. $57·2 \div 10$
2. $89·2 \div 10$
3. $5·3 \div 10$
4. $47·1 \div 100$
5. $141·2 \div 100$
6. $19·3 \div 10$
7. $151·8 \div 100$
8. $4·7 \div 100$
9. $25·2 \div 1000$
10. $0·63 \div 10$
11. $47·2 \div 100$
12. $27·9 \div 1000$
13. $6·2 \div 1000$
14. $198·7 \div 100$
15. $47 \div 10$
16. $416 \div 1000$
17. $2400 \div 10\,000$
18. $89 \div 100$
19. $63 \div 100$
20. $7 \div 1000$
21. $0·86 \div 10$
22. $516 \div 10\,000$
23. $0·077 \div 100$
24. $21·9 \div 1000$
25. $500 \div 10\,000$
26. $260 \div 100\,000$
27. $0·051 \div 100$
28. $890·4 \div 10$
29. $4007 \div 100$
30. $20 \div 1000$
31. $5·14 \times 10$
32. $6·26 \times 100$
33. $0·414 \times 100$
34. $0·0631 \times 1000$
35. $0·005 \times 100$
36. $0·0063 \times 10\,000$
37. $47·4 \div 10$
38. $8·97 \div 100$
39. $54·2 \div 1000$
40. 63×100
41. 47×10
42. $0·84 \times 10\,000$
43. $0·7 \div 100$
44. $6·2 \div 10$
45. $4·73 \times 10$
46. $0·001 \times 1000$
47. $47 \div 100$
48. 47×100
49. $9 \div 10$
50. $0·0075 \times 100\,000$

Examples

(a) $8·44 \div 4$

$$\begin{array}{r} 2·11 \\ 4\overline{)8·44} \end{array}$$

(b) $13·86 \div 6$

$$\begin{array}{r} 2·\,31 \\ 6\overline{)13·^186} \end{array}$$

(c) $21·28 \div 7$

$$\begin{array}{r} 3·0\ \ 4 \\ 7\overline{)21·2\ ^28} \end{array}$$

(d) $4·3 \div 5$

$$\begin{array}{r} 0·\,8\ \ 6 \\ 5\overline{)4·^43\ ^30} \end{array}$$

Exercise 5.13

Do the following calculations.

1. $8·4 \div 4$
2. $9·6 \div 3$
3. $8·42 \div 2$
4. $6·7 \div 5$
5. $22·48 \div 4$
6. $205·2 \div 6$
7. $75·3 \div 3$
8. $251·4 \div 6$
9. $18·52 \div 4$
10. $1·57 \div 5$
11. $4·984 \div 7$
12. $27·0 \div 6$
13. $18·93 \div 3$
14. $3·078 \div 6$
15. $0·504 \div 8$
16. $236·0 \div 5$
17. $327·6 \div 4$
18. $3·12 \div 4$
19. $0·329 \div 7$
20. $49·92 \div 8$
21. $487·26 \div 9$
22. $1·9884 \div 6$
23. $1·1075 \div 5$
24. $24·964 \div 4$
25. $165·2 \div 4$
26. $4298 \div 7$
27. $1953 \div 9$
28. $890 \div 10$
29. $0·45 \div 10$
30. $0·2198 \div 7$
31. $60·6 \div 10$
32. $12·42 \div 6$
33. $161·6 \div 4$
34. $144·9 \div 7$
35. $2·754 \div 9$
36. $0·032\,56 \div 8$
37. $2380 \div 5$
38. $766·8 \div 9$
39. $31\,500 \div 5$
40. $24\,100 \div 10$
41. $991·1 \div 11$
42. $144·12 \div 12$
43. $4477 \div 11$
44. $3·768 \div 12$
45. $6·894 \div 9$

Examples

We change each of the following questions to another one which has the same answer but is easier to work out.

(a) $62·8 \div 20 = 6·28 \div 2$
$ = 3·14$

(b) $125·2 \div 40 = 12·52 \div 4$
$ = 3·13$

(c) $2160 \div 500 = 21·60 \div 5$
$ = 4·32$

Exercise 5.14

Do the following calculations.

1. $42·8 \div 20$
2. $97·2 \div 30$
3. $98·0 \div 40$
4. $468·0 \div 30$
5. $6·86 \div 20$
6. $27·1 \div 50$

7. 22·02 ÷ 60
8. 13·56 ÷ 30
9. 124 ÷ 200
10. 312 ÷ 400
11. 2·07 ÷ 50
12. 5·856 ÷ 80
13. 85·77 ÷ 900
14. 194·4 ÷ 300
15. 0·618 ÷ 20
16. 175·6 ÷ 40
17. 125·4 ÷ 3000
18. 85·05 ÷ 70
19. 37 760 ÷ 800
20. 15 390 ÷ 300
21. 2904 ÷ 600
22. 0·834 ÷ 20
23. 0·906 ÷ 2000
24. 68·22 ÷ 90
25. 4·459 ÷ 700
26. 23·9 ÷ 5000
27. 3648 ÷ 80
28. 0·7415 ÷ 100
29. 1824 ÷ 300
30. 12 984 ÷ 60
31. 0·63 ÷ 80
32. 450 ÷ 9000
33. 1·16 ÷ 400
34. 9·114 ÷ 3000
35. 0·0749 ÷ 70
36. 120 ÷ 8000
37. 18 ÷ 40 000
38. 0·063 ÷ 400
39. 13·5 ÷ 900
40. 0·61 ÷ 1000

Word questions: dividing

Exercise 5.15

1. A father shares £4·56 between his 6 children. How much does each receive?
2. The stick below is cut into seven equal lengths. How long is each piece?

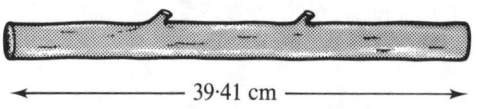

← 39·41 cm →

3. An angle of 271·7° is divided into eleven equal sectors. What is the angle of each sector?
4. The tip of the hour hand of a clock moves a distance of 47·16 cm in 9 hours. How far does it move in 1 hour?
5. A coach carrying 30 passengers charges £34·50 for the journey. How much should each passenger pay?
6. The total bill for a meal for nine people is £76·23. How much does each person pay?
7. A man leaves a total of £450 in his will. He leaves £260 to his wife and his four children share the rest equally. How much does each child receive?
8. A wedding cake of weight 51·12 kg is divided equally between 60 guests. How much does each guest receive?
9. Six hundred packets of sugar weigh a total of 1326 kg. Find the weight of one packet.
10. 7000 people share a prize of £94 920. How much does each receive?
11. An athlete runs 30 laps of a track in 34 minutes 21 seconds.
    (a) How many seconds does it take to run 30 laps?
    (b) On average, how long does it take to run one lap?
12. A car takes 210 minutes 5 seconds to travel 50 km.
    (a) How many seconds does it take to go 50 km?
    (b) On average, how long does it take to go 1 km?
13. A total of £23 400 is raised from the sale of 4000 tickets. What was the price of one ticket?
14. A school buys 200 rulers for £17·14. How much does one ruler cost?
15. A pile of 400 sheets of paper is 8·5 cm thick. What is the thickness of one sheet of paper?

Dividing decimals by decimals

Take extra care when dividing *by* a decimal number.

Examples

(a) 6·54 ÷ 0·2 = 65·4 ÷ 2

```
   32· 7
2)65·¹4
```

answer: 32·7

(b) 1·944 ÷ 0·6 = 19·44 ÷ 6

```
   3· 2 4
6)19·¹4 ²4
```

answer: 3·24

(c) 0·228 ÷ 0·04 = 22·8 ÷ 4

```
   5· 7
4)22·²8
```

answer: 5·7

(d) 0·0635 ÷ 0·005 = 63·5 ÷ 5

```
   1 2· 7
5)6 ¹3·³5
```

answer: 12·7

Exercise 5.16

Calculate the following

1. 1·48 ÷ 0·2
2. 2·52 ÷ 0·4
3. 0·942 ÷ 0·3
4. 0·712 ÷ 0·2
5. 0·375 ÷ 0·5
6. 0·522 ÷ 0·6
7. 0·7304 ÷ 0·8
8. 0·010 52 ÷ 0·02
9. 0·1368 ÷ 0·04
10. 0·1683 ÷ 0·03

11. $0.498 \div 0.06$
12. $5.04 \div 0.7$
13. $3.744 \div 0.09$
14. $0.1685 \div 0.005$
15. $0.1684 \div 0.2$
16. $0.05859 \div 0.09$
17. $0.0257 \div 0.005$
18. $1.872 \div 0.08$
19. $0.268 \div 0.4$
20. $0.39 \div 0.006$
21. $0.42 \div 0.03$
22. $7.041 \div 0.01$
23. $0.2632 \div 0.001$
24. $15.33 \div 0.07$
25. $0.0996 \div 0.12$
26. $0.08701 \div 0.11$
27. $1.05 \div 0.6$
28. $0.000386 \div 0.0001$
29. $4.006 \div 0.002$
30. $3.05 \div 0.08$
31. $1.701 \div 0.09$
32. $0.0333 \div 0.9$
33. $0.00611 \div 0.50$
34. $26.16 \div 0.60$
35. $0.333 \div 0.40$
36. $4.101 \div 0.30$
37. $0.093888 \div 0.012$
38. $5.9004 \div 0.11$
39. $0.20312 \div 0.008$
40. $0.00705 \div 0.1$

Examples

(a) $0.735 \div 0.21 = 73.5 \div 21$

$$21 \overline{)73.^{10}5} \quad \begin{array}{c} 3.5 \end{array}$$

(b) $8.64 \div 0.032 = 8640 \div 32$

$$32 \overline{)86^{22}40} \quad \begin{array}{c} 270 \end{array}$$

Exercise 5.17

Do these calculations.

1. $0.357 \div 0.17$
2. $0.276 \div 0.12$
3. $0.416 \div 0.13$
4. $0.375 \div 0.15$
5. $8.5 \div 0.25$
6. $3.68 \div 0.16$
7. $7.35 \div 0.21$
8. $0.0682 \div 0.22$
9. $0.063 \div 0.15$
10. $0.0561 \div 0.11$
11. $0.252 \div 0.14$
12. $4.08 \div 1.2$
13. $41.4 \div 1.8$
14. $8.61 \div 2.1$
15. $1188 \div 3.3$
16. $86.1 \div 0.41$
17. $2.783 \div 0.023$
18. $0.1271 \div 0.031$
19. $0.006354 \div 0.018$
20. $0.009968 \div 0.016$
21. $0.01143 \div 0.045$
22. $14.784 \div 3.2$
23. $990 \div 4.5$
24. $113.04 \div 0.36$
25. $9.88 \div 0.038$
26. $13260 \div 3.9$
27. $5.25 \div 0.0021$
28. $0.19127 \div 0.0031$
29. $0.4459 \div 0.0013$
30. $0.007353 \div 0.0043$

Word questions

Exercise 5.18

1. A pie weighing 2.43 kg is divided into 9 equal pieces. How much does each piece weigh?
2. A cake weighing 7.2 kg is divided into several pieces each weighing 0.6 kg. How many pieces are there?
3. A rod of length 2.86 m is divided into 11 equal pieces. How long is each piece?
4. A rod of length 1.36 m is divided into several pieces each of length 0.08 m. How many pieces are there?
5. Twenty-five pebbles, each weighing 0.14 kg, are put into a bag. What is the total weight of the pebbles?
6. Twelve articles each weighing 0.32 kg are added to seven articles each weighing 0.53 kg. What is the total weight of the nineteen articles?
7. How many times will the jub below have to be filled and emptied to completely empty the drum?

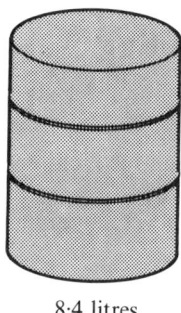

8.4 litres   0.6 litres

8. A bird initially weighs 0.31 kg and a worm weighs 0.008 kg. How much does the bird weigh after eating 9 worms?
9. Water evaporates from a shallow tray at the rate of 0.002 kg every half hour. A metal tray weighs 1.4 kg and it contains 0.344 kg of water at 10.00 h. How much will the tray and water weigh at 16.00 h?
10. A phone call costs £0.04. How many calls can I make if I have £3.52?

Example

The weight of 2000 bricks is 1856 kg. Find the weight of one brick.

If 2000 bricks weigh 1856 kg

1 brick weighs $1856 \div 2000$ kg.

$1856 \div 2000 = 1.856 \div 2$

$$2 \overline{)1.85^{1}6} \quad \begin{array}{c} 0.928 \end{array}$$

One brick weighs 0.928 kg.

Decimal numbers

Exercise 5.19

1. A man buys five articles at £0·71 each and seven articles at £0·09 each. What is the total cost?
2. Five people share the fuel cost of a car journey which amounts to £18·65. How much does each person pay?
3. A manufacturer sells 4000 pencils at 1·2 pence each and 700 rulers at 8·32 pence each. What is the total money received from the sales? (Give the answer in pounds.)
4. A prison chef makes 90·4 kg of stew for 200 prisoners. How much does each prisoner receive?
5. A builder buys wood in lengths of 5 m. How many pieces of length 75 cm can be cut from each 5 m length? How much is left over?
6. A pile of nine ceramic tiles is 4·05 cm thick. What is the thickness of each tile?
7. A newsagent buys 2000 magazines at 13·2 pence each and sells them all at 25 pence each. What is her total profit in pounds?
8. An athlete runs every 400 m lap in 67·3 seconds.
   (a) How many laps of the track does he run in a race of 10 000 m?
   (b) How long does he take to run 10 000 m?
9. A man spends £1·73 in the first shop, £5·18 in the second shop and £11·13 in the third shop. How much has he left if he started with £20?
10. When a joint of meat weighing 5 kg is cooked, its weight is reduced to only 3·78 kg. How much weight is 'lost' in the cooking?
11. A cyclist takes 822·8 seconds to go 20 times around a track. How long does he take for each lap if he cycles at the same speed all the time?
12. Forty-five passengers on a coach each pay a fare of £5·60.
    (a) How much money is raised in this way?
    (b) If the running costs of the coach are £145·50, how much profit does the coach owner make?
13. A pile of 600 sheets of paper is 10·44 cm thick. How thick is each sheet of paper?
14. A cake of weight 4·6 kg is divided into small pieces each weighing 0·2 kg. Into how many pieces is the cake divided?
15. Hao spends £1·15 in the first shop and twice as much in the second shop. How much is left of the £5 he started with?
16. On a school outing the 33 members of a class each pay £0·75 for food, £2·15 for transport and £0·40 for tickets to a zoo. What is the total cost of the trip for the whole class?
17. The monthly rental for a television set is £8·65. How much rent is paid over a period of three years?
18. A herd of 60 cows produces a total of 338·4 litres of milk each day. How much does an average cow produce?
19. Twenty children visit the Science Museum and each pays £1·12 for travel, 75p for refreshments and 15p for a museum guide. What is the total cost for the whole group?
20. The weight of 100 000 ball bearings is 254 kg. How much does each ball bearing weigh?

Exercise 5.20

State whether the following are 'True' or 'False'.

1. $4·2 \times 1000 = 4200$
2. $0·61 \times 100 = 0·6100$
3. $5 + 8·9 = 13·9$
4. $7·44 \div 6 = 1·24$
5. $13·6 + 3 = 13·9$
6. $0·844 \div 10 = 8·44$
7. $7·41 - 1·9 = 5·51$
8. $4·2 \times 50 = 210$
9. $7 - 3·64 = 3·36$
10. $8 \div 100 = 0·8$
11. $1·41 + 13·5 = 14·91$
12. $8·75 + 19 = 26·75$
13. $2·14 \times 1000 = 2140$
14. $4 - 0·65 = 3·35$
15. $25·6 \div 50 = 0·512$
16. £5 − £4·12 = £1·88
17. £10 − £7·34 = £2·66
18. £7 − £2·45 = £5·45
19. $4·2 \div 0·2 = 21$
20. $1·944 \div 0·6 = 3·24$
21. $6·9 \div 0·05 = 3·45$
22. $3·6 \times 2·1 = 7·56$
23. $4·5 \times 0·17 = 0·755$
24. $0·007 \times 10 = 0·7$
25. $11 - 2·95 = 8·05$
26. $1·2 + 14 = 15·2$
27. $0·01456 \div 0·04 = 0·364$
28. $0·1 \div 100 = 0·001$
29. $45·7 \times 0·07 = 3·198$
30. $6·279 \div 0·7 = 8·97$

Quick tests

Test 1
1. $4·2 \times 10$
2. $0·63 \times 10$
3. $5·3 + 4$
4. $6·2 - 5$
5. $4·8 \div 4$
6. $73·6 \div 10$
7. $213 \div 100$
8. $8·6 \times 10$
9. $0·71 \times 10$
10. $1·3 + 0·6$
11. $2·7 - 0·5$
12. $5·4 + 5$
13. Write 'five pounds 40p' in figures
14. Write 'five pounds 4p' in figures
15. Write '1207·09' in words
16. $0·6 \times 100$
17. $3·6 \div 3$
18. $0·09 \div 9$
19. $1·2 + 2·1$
20. £5 − £2·75

Test 2
1. $3·2 + 6$
2. $2·9 \div 10$
3. $2·9 \times 10$
4. £3 − £1·20
5. £6·50 − £4·20
6. $0·73 \times 10$
7. $0·123 \times 100$
8. $444 \div 10$
9. $444 \div 1000$
10. Write 'seventeen pounds 17p' in figures
11. Write 'seven pounds 7p' in figures
12. $3·2 + 2·3$
13. $5 - 1·6$
14. $14·7 - 10$
15. $0·95 \times 100$
16. $0·12 \div 6$
17. £8 − £3·65
18. £10 − £7·15
19. $1 + 1·1 + 2·2$
20. $0·1 \times 0·1$

6 Charts and graphs

Bar charts

It is often much easier to understand information when it is given in the form of a table or a graph than when it is given as a series of numbers.

Example

The number of cars of different makes in a car park is shown in the chart below. Answer the questions which follow.

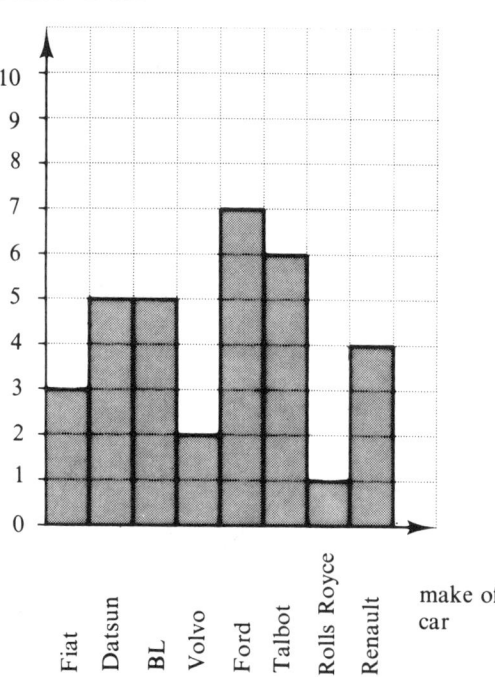

(a) How many Renaults are there?
There are four Renaults.
(b) How many BL cars are there?
There are five BL cars.
(c) Of which make are there most cars?
There are more Fords than any other car.
(d) How many cars are there in the car-park altogether?
There are 33 cars altogether.
(e) How many Japanese cars are there?
There are five Japanese cars.

Exercise 6.1

Copy each chart before answering the questions.

1. The number of cars of different makes which visited a petrol station is shown below.

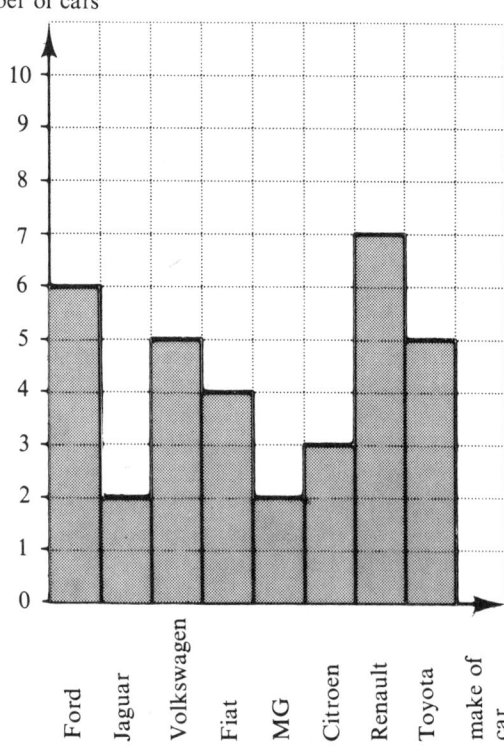

(a) How many Jaguars were there?
(b) How many Toyotas were there?
(c) Of which make were there most cars?
(d) How many cars visited the petrol station altogether?
(e) How many Italian cars were there?
(f) How many German cars were there?

2. The number of flights by various airlines into Heathrow during one afternoon is shown below.

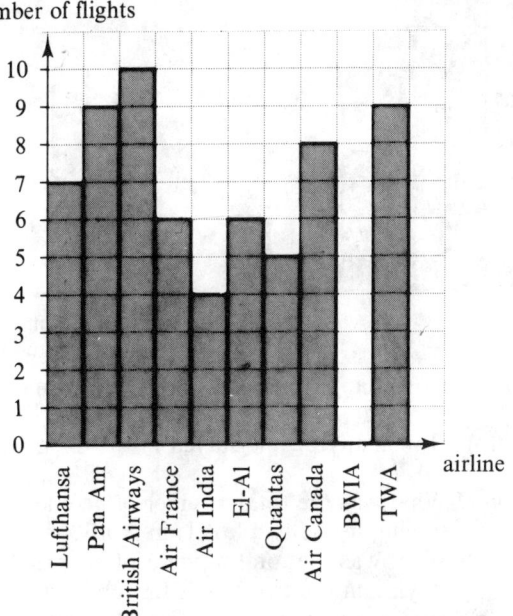

(a) How many TWA flights were there?
(b) How many Lufthansa flights were there?
(c) Which airline had the most arrivals?
(d) Which airline had the fewest arrivals?
(e) How many flights were there altogether?
(f) How many Australian flights were there?

3. The number of marks gained by the pupils in a class test is shown below.

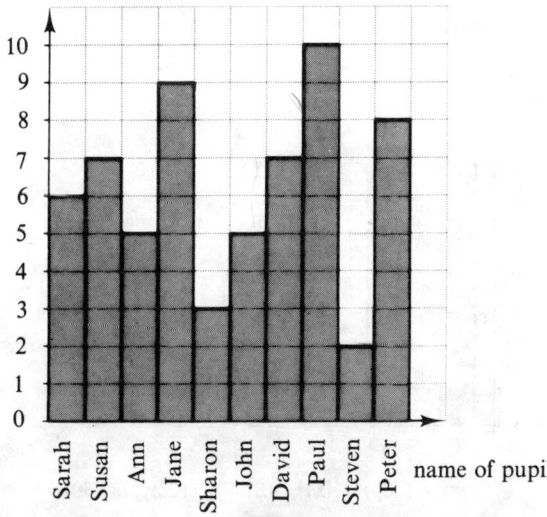

(a) How many marks did Ann get?
(b) Who came top of the class?
(c) Who came second?
(d) Who was bottom of the class?
(e) Who got the most marks altogether; the girls or the boys?

4. The monthly rainfall in Seathwaite (in the Lake District) is shown below.

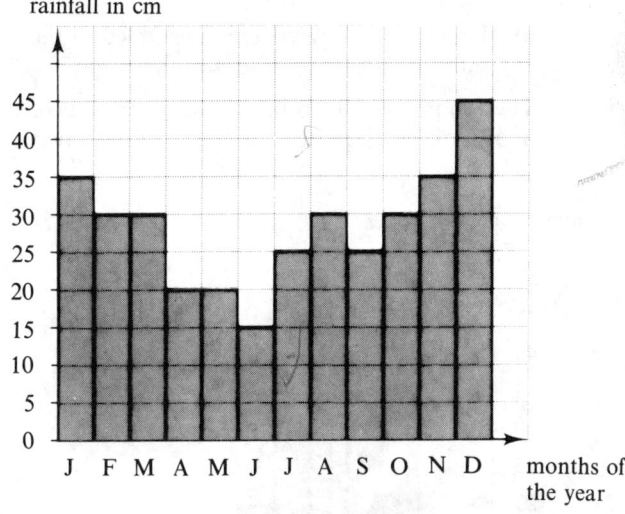

(a) How much rain fell in August?
(b) Which was the driest month in the year?
(c) Which was the wettest month in the year?
(d) In which months did 25 cm of rain fall?
(e) How much rain fell in the whole year?
(f) In which months did 30 cm of rain fall?

5. In a poll people were asked what method of transport they used to get to work; the results are shown below.

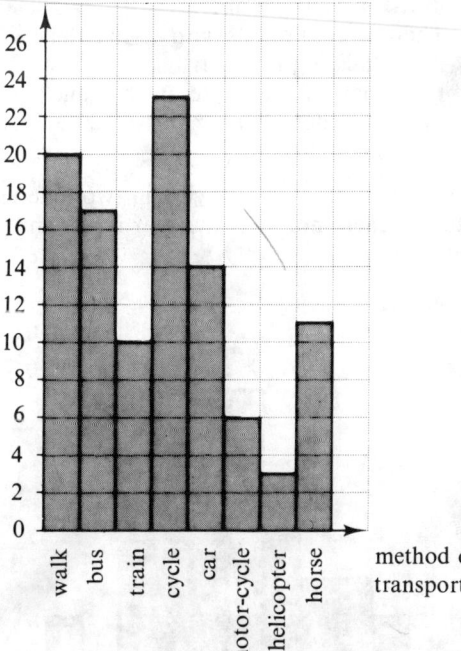

(a) How many people went by bus?
(b) How many people went by horse?

(c) What method was used by 14 people?
(d) What method was used by 3 people?
(e) What was the most common method of transport?
(f) How many people were questioned in the poll?

6. The number of letters in the words on a page of a book was counted; the results are shown below.

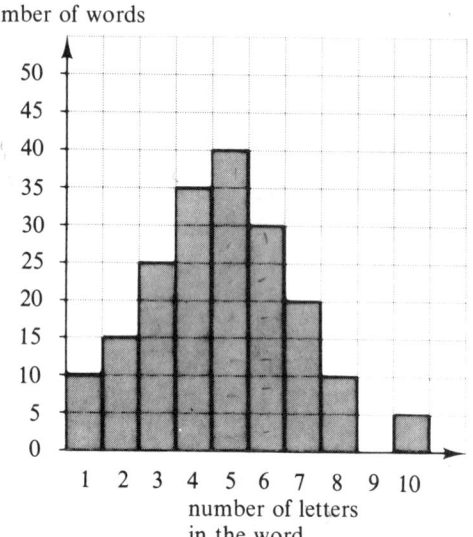

(a) How many words had three letters?
(b) How many words had six letters?
(c) There were 35 words with ____ letters. Fill in the missing number.
(d) There were 0 words with ____ letters. Fill in the missing number.
(e) How many words were on the page?
(f) (Much harder.) How many letters were on the page?

7. The number of people staying in two different hotels in each month of the year is shown below.

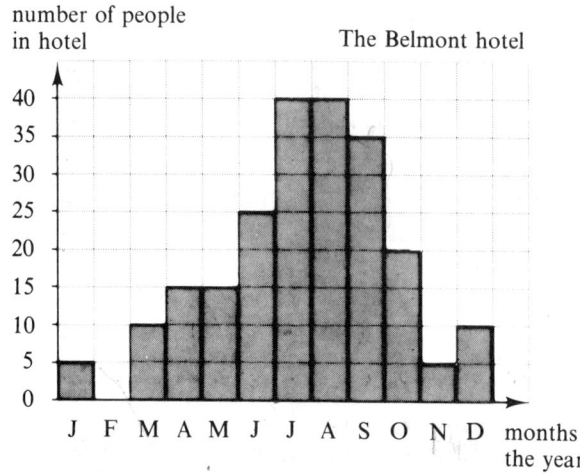

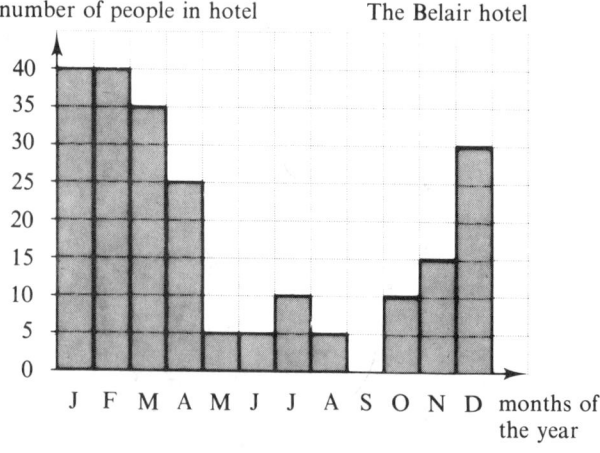

(a) How many people stayed in the 'Belmont' in July?
(b) How many people stayed in the 'Belair' in July?
(c) What was the total number of people staying in the two hotels in April?
(d) What was the total number of people staying in the two hotels in February?
(e) How many people stayed in the 'Belmont' during the whole year?
(f) In which month was the total number of people staying in the two hotels the highest?
(g) One hotel is in a ski resort and the other is by the seaside. Which hotel is in the ski resort?

8. In a restaurant there are six meals on the menu: A, B, C, D, E and F. The number of people choosing each meal on a certain day is shown below.

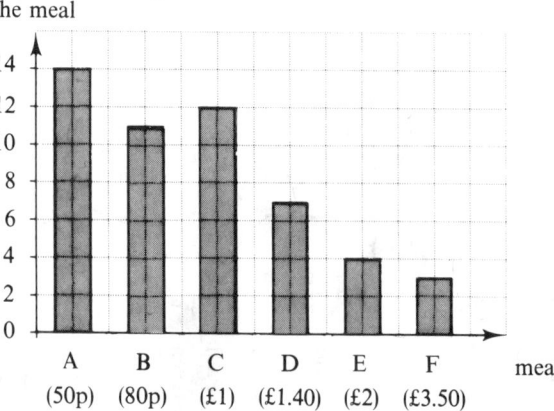

The price for each meal is shown in brackets.

(a) How many people had meal C?
(b) How many people had meal D?
(c) How many meals were served altogether?
(d) How much money did the restaurant receive for the sales of meal A?

(e) How much money did the restaurant receive for the sales of meal F?
(f) (Much harder.) How much money did the restaurant receive altogether?

9. A pet shop owner sells six kinds of dog food: 'Blaze', 'Bruno', 'Bark', 'Growl', 'Bite' and 'Munch'. He records the number of tins of each kind which he sells in one week; the results are shown below together with the price for each kind of dog-food.

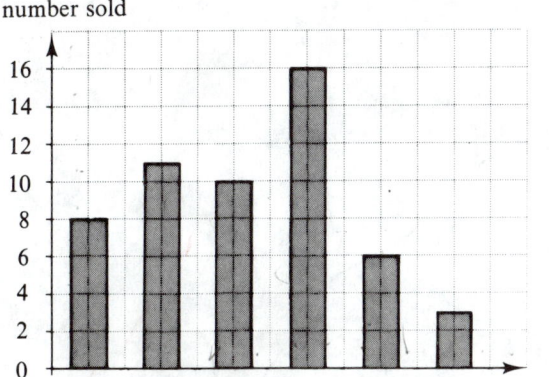

number sold

'Blaze' 'Bruno' 'Bark' 'Growl' 'Bite' 'Munch' Dog food
(40p)   (45p)   (49p) (50p)   (60p) (65p)

(a) How many tins of 'Bark' did he sell?
(b) How many tins of 'Bite' did he sell?
(c) Which was the most popular brand?
(d) How many tins did he sell altogether?
(e) How much money did he receive from the sale of 'Bark'?
(f) How much money did he receive from the sale of 'Bruno'?
(g) (Harder.) How much money did he receive altogether from the sale of dog food?

10. The monthly rainfall for one year in Darwin (Australia) is shown in the table below.

Month	Rainfall (cm)
January	40
February	35
March	25
April	15
May	5
June	2·5
July	2.5
August	0
September	5
October	15
November	15
December	25

Draw a chart to show this information. Use a scale of 1 cm to 5 cm of rain on the vertical axis. The start of the chart is shown.

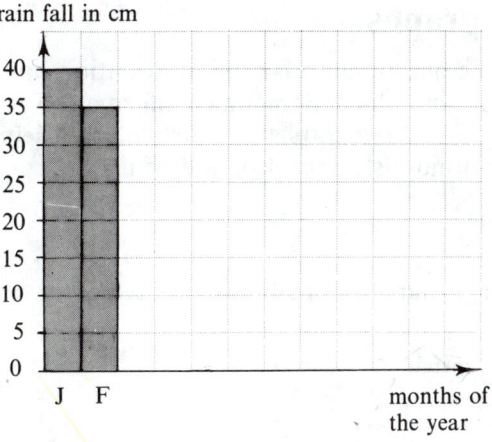

rain fall in cm

months of the year

Use the chart to answer the following questions.

(a) In how many months did more than 20 cm of rain fall?
(b) Which was the wettest month in the year?
(c) How much rain fell altogether in the three driest months of the year?
(d) How much rain fell altogether in the two wettest months of the year?

11. In a survey 30 people were asked to state which was their favourite colour. The answers they gave are shown below.

[R = red, B = blue, G = green, Y = yellow, P = pink, M = mauve, O = orange.]

G B Y R G R R G Y M
R B G G M O O Y G B
M P O Y G R B R Y G

Count the preferences for each colour and then display the information on a chart.

(a) Which was the most popular colour?
(b) Which was the least popular colour?
(c) How many people said that either blue or green was their favourite colour?

Line graphs

In all the questions so far the information has been given in the form of a bar chart. Sometimes information is given in the form of a *line graph*. Line graphs are particularly useful when quantities vary continuously over a period of time.

Example

The temperature in a house was recorded every two hours for a whole day; the results are shown below.

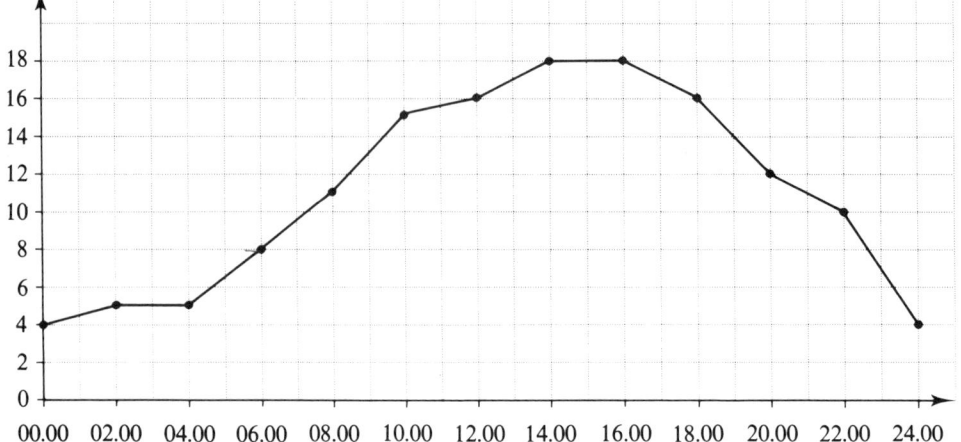

Note: We join up the measurements with straight lines.

(a) What was the temperature at 06.00 h?
The temperature was 8°C at 06.00 h.

(b) At what two times was the temperature 16°C?
The temperature was 16°C at 12.00 h and at 18.00 h.

(c) How much did the temperature fall between 22.00 h and 24.00 h?
The temperature fell by 6°C between 22.00 h and 24.00 h.

(d) What was the difference between the highest and the lowest temperatures during the day?
The difference between the highest and the lowest temperatures was 14°C [18°C − 4°C].

(e) *Estimate* the temperature at 17.00 h.
The temperature was *about* 17°C at 17.00 h.

(f) *Estimate* the temperature at 09.00 h.
The temperature was *about* 13°C at 09.00 h.

Exercise 6.2

Make a neat copy of each graph before answering the questions which follow.

1. The temperature in a house was recorded every two hours for a whole day; the results are shown below.

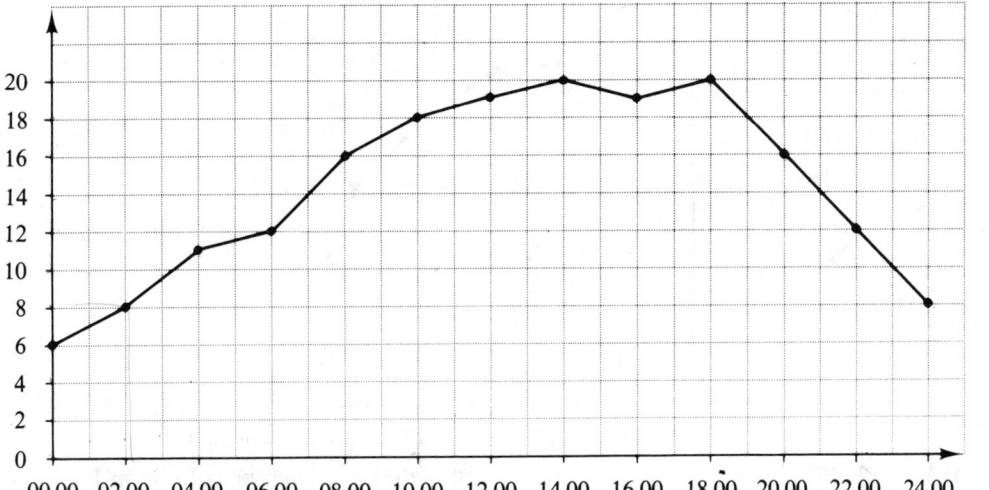

(a) What was the temperature at 10.00 h?
(b) What was the temperature at 20.00 h?
(c) What was the temperature at 02.00 h?
(d) At which two times was the temperature 16°C?
(e) At which two times was the temperature 20°C?
(f) *Estimate* the temperature at 07.00 h.
(g) *Estimate* the temperature at 23.00 h.

2. The temperature in a centrally heated house is recorded every hour from 12.00 till 24.00 h; the results are shown below.

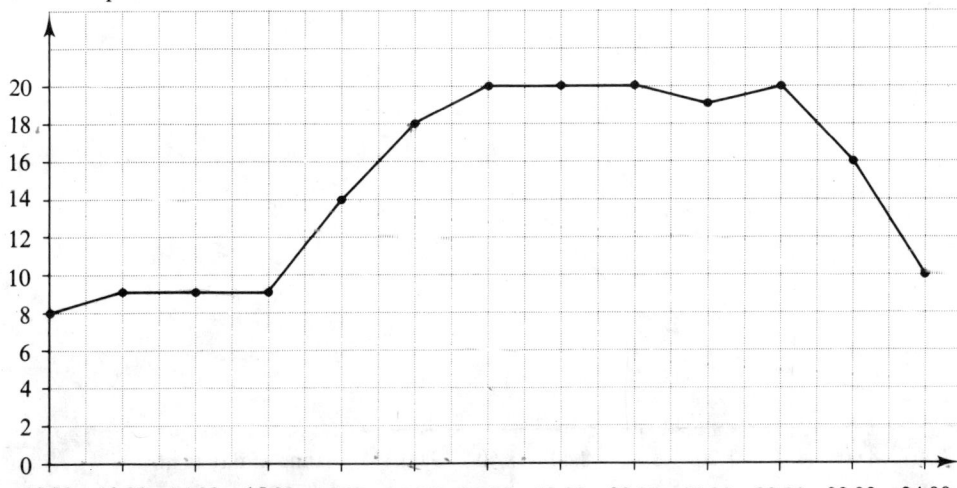

(a) What was the temperature at 20.00 h?
(b) What was the temperature at 13.00 h?
(c) Estimate the temperature at 16.30 h.
(d) Estimate the temperature at 22.30 h.
(e) Estimate the two times when the temperature was 18°C.
(f) Estimate the two times when the temperature was 16°C.
(g) When do you think the central heating was switched on?
(h) When do you think the central heating was switched off?

40 Charts and graphs

3. A car went on a five hour journey starting at 12.00 h with a full tank of petrol. The volume of petrol in the tank was measured after every hour; the results are shown below.

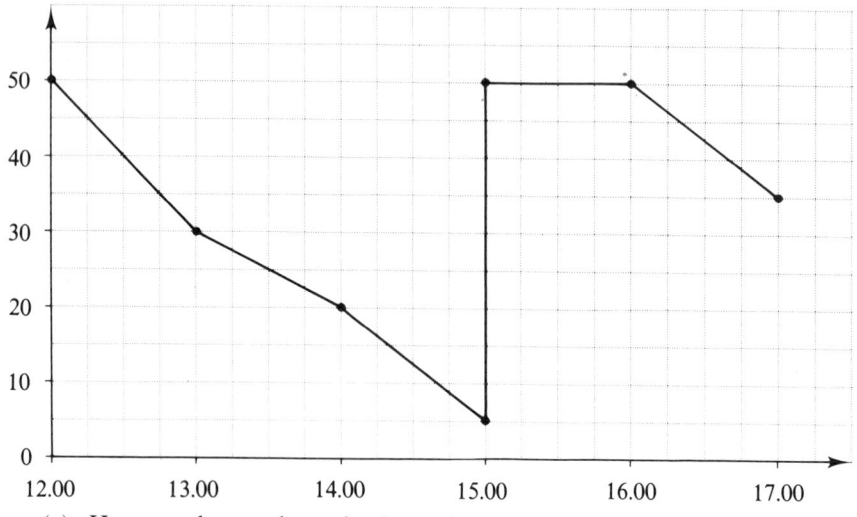

(a) How much petrol was in the tank at 13.00 h?
(b) How much petrol was in the tank at 16.00 h?
(c) At what time was there 5 litres in the tank?
(d) How much petrol was used in the first hour of the journey?
(e) Estimate how much petrol was in the tank at 13.30 h.
(f) Estimate how much petrol was in the tank at 12.45 h.
(g) What happened at 15.00 h?
(h) What do you think happened between 15.00 h and 16.00 h?

4. The number of children inside a school is counted every ten minutes from 7.30 a.m. until 9.00 a.m., when the bell rings; the results are shown below.

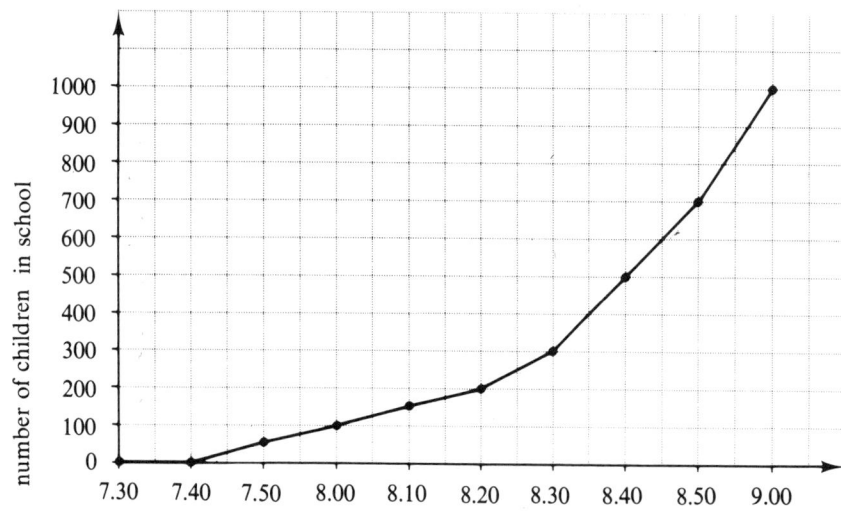

(a) How many children were inside the school at
    (i) 8.00 a.m.?   (ii) 8.35 a.m.?
    (iii) 8.45 a.m.?   (iv) 8.55 a.m.?
(b) How many children arrived between 7.30 a.m. and 8.30 a.m.?
(c) Estimate when the first children arrived.
(d) How many children arrived during the last 10 minutes before the bell rang at 9.00 a.m.?
(e) At what time were there 250 children in school?
(f) At what time were there 75 children in school?

5. A man climbing a mountain measures his height above sea level after every 30 minutes; the results are shown below.

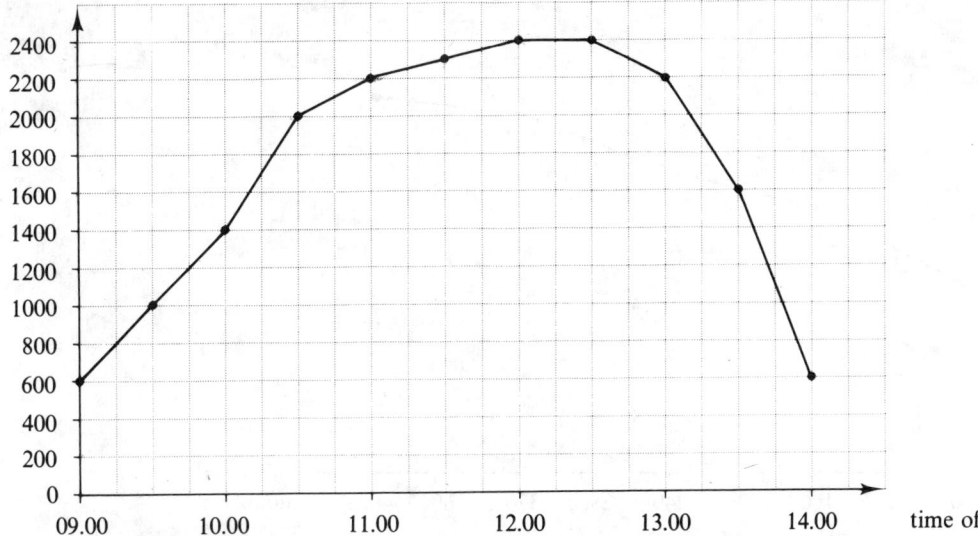

(a) At what height was he at 10.00 h?
(b) At what height was he at 13.30 h?
(c) Estimate his height above sea level at 09.45 h.
(d) Estimate his altitude at 10.45 h.
(e) Estimate his height above sea level at 13.45 h.
(f) At what two times was he 2200 m above sea level?
(g) How high was the mountain? (He got to the top!)
(h) How long did he rest at the summit?
(i) How long did he take to reach the summit?

6. The cost of making a telephone call depends on the duration of the call as shown below.

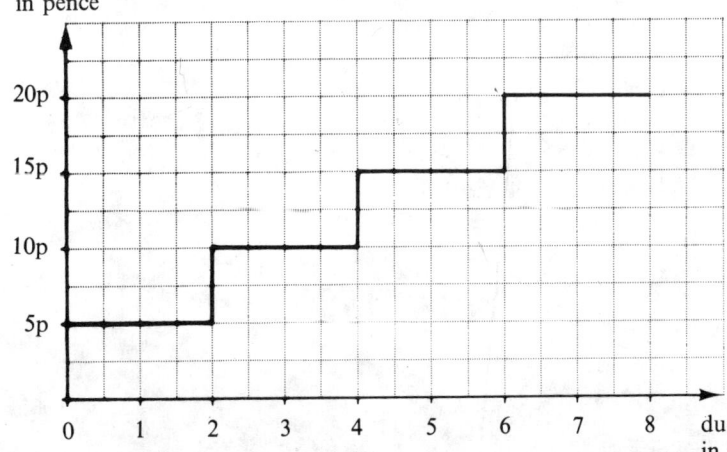

(a) How much is a call lasting 1 minute?
(b) How much is a call lasting 1 minute 30 seconds?
(c) How much is a call lasting 5 minutes?
(d) How much is a call lasting 6 minutes 30 seconds?
(e) How much is a call lasting 2 minutes 10 seconds?
(f) How much is a call lasting 4 minutes 27 seconds?
(g) What is the minimum charge for a call?
(h) A call costing 15p is between ____ minutes and ____ minutes in length. Fill in the spaces.

42 Charts and graphs

7. The cost of printing a book depends on the number of pages in the book as shown below.

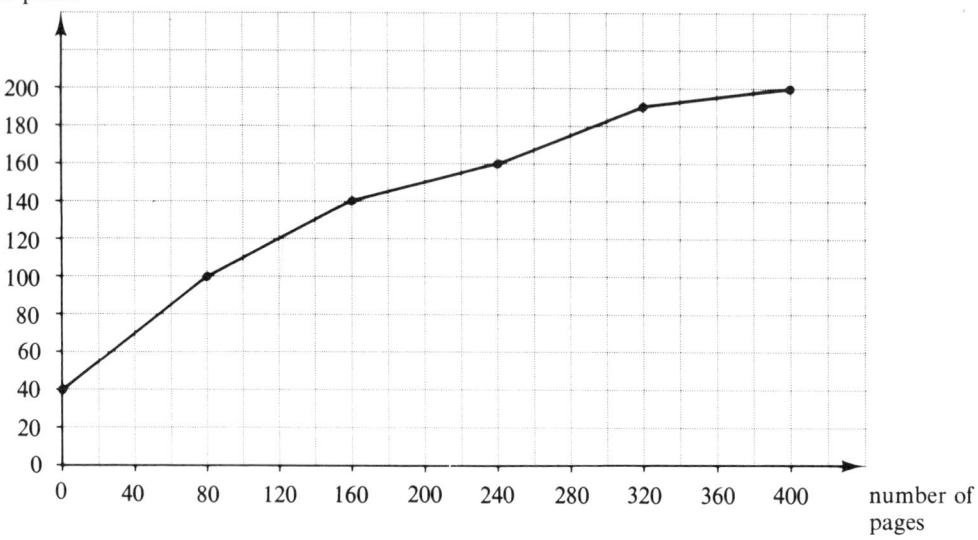

(a) What is the cost of printing a book with 240 pages?
(b) What is the cost of printing a book with 120 pages?
(c) What is the cost of printing a book with 40 pages?
(d) What is the cost of printing a book with 200 pages?
(e) How many pages has a book which costs 100p to print?
(f) How many pages has a book which costs 190p to print?
(g) How many pages has a book which costs £1·20 to print?
(h) How much do the printing costs rise when the number of pages in a book increases from 160 to 240?

8. The number of people sitting down in a cinema was recorded every quarter of an hour; the results are shown below.

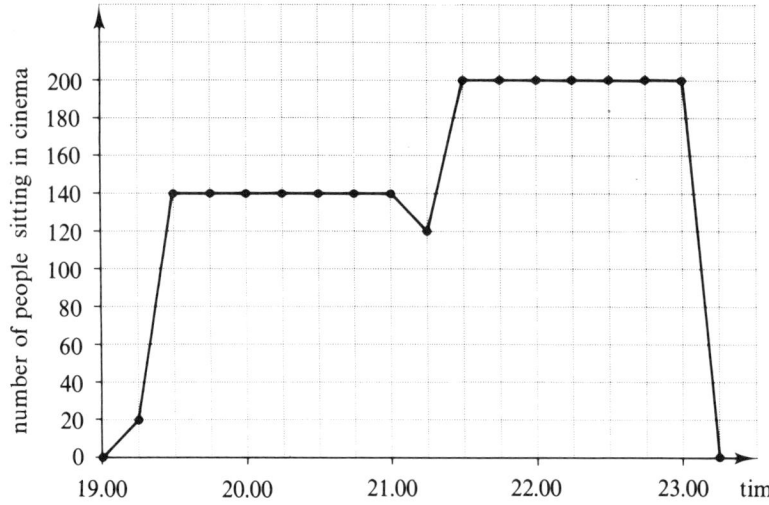

(a) How many people were sitting down at 20.00 h?
(b) How many people were sitting down at 21.15 h?
(c) When do you think the first film started?
(d) When do you think the first film ended?
(e) How long was the interval between the two films?
(f) Which film was more popular?

9. The temperature in a room is measured every hour between 12.00 h and 22.00 h; the results are given in the table below.

Time of day (h)	Temperature (°C)
12.00	6
13.00	7
14.00	7
15.00	8
16.00	12
17.00	16
18.00	22
19.00	22
20.00	22
21.00	20
22.00	10

Draw a line graph to illustrate this information. Use a scale of 1 cm to 1 hour on the horizontal axis and 1 cm to 4°C on the vertical axis.

The beginning of the graph is shown below.

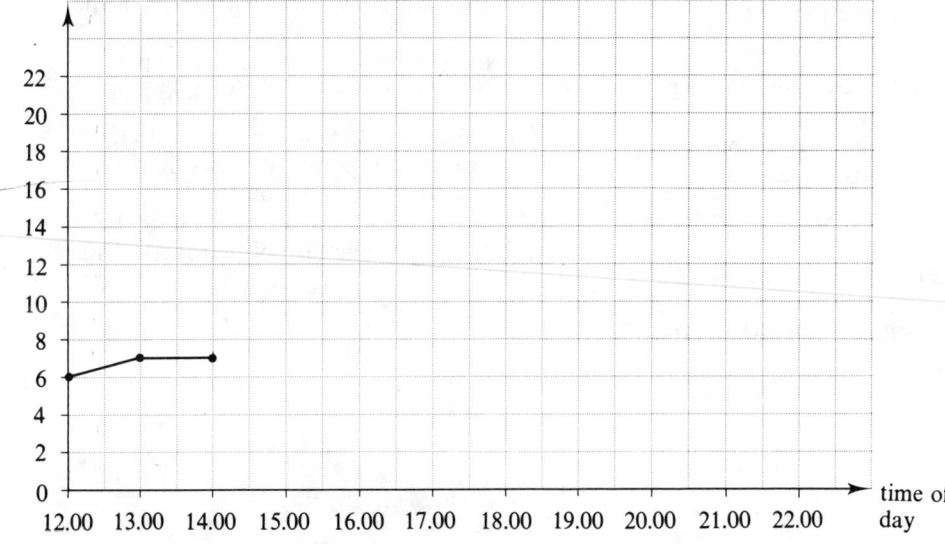

(a) Estimate the room temperature at
(i) 15.30 h (ii) 19.30 h
(iii) 20.30 h (iv) 17.30 h

(b) At which two times was the temperature 10°C?

(c) During which hour-long period did the temperature rise most steeply?

(d) During which hour-long period did the temperature fall most steeply?

(e) For how long was the temperature above 10°C?

44 Charts and graphs

10. An athlete runs along a straight road for three minutes. His distance from the starting point is measured after every 20 seconds; the results are given in the table below.

Time (seconds)	Distance from start (m)
0	0
20	100
40	200
60	400
80	550
100	600
120	600
140	700
160	800
180	1000

Draw a line graph to illustrate this information. Use a scale of 1 cm to 10 seconds on the horizontal axis and 1 cm to 100 m on the vertical axis.

Use the graph to answer the following questions.

(a) Estimate his distance from the starting point after:
   (i) 50 seconds   (ii) 110 seconds
   (iii) 150 seconds   (iv) 5 seconds

(b) After what time was he 650 m from the start?

(c) During which 20 second period did he stop?

(d) During which two 20 second periods did he run the furthest?

(e) How long did he take to run the *last* 600 m?

11. A motorist set out on a five-hour drive with a full tank of petrol. The volume of petrol in the tank was measured after every hour; the results are shown below.

Time of day	Volume of petrol in tank (litres)
1.00 p.m.	50
2.00 p.m.	35
3.00 p.m.	25
4.00 p.m.	10
5.00 p.m.	10
6.00 p.m.	5

Draw a line graph to illustrate this information. Use a scale of 2 cm to 1 hour on the horizontal axis and 1 cm to 5 litres on the vertical axis.

Use the graph to answer the following questions.

(a) Estimate how much petrol was in the tank at:
   (i) 2.30 p.m.   (ii) 1.30 p.m.
   (iii) 4.15 p.m.   (iv) 5.30 p.m.

(b) When was the engine switched off?

(c) How much petrol was used in the first three hours of the journey?

(d) What was the cost of petrol for the whole journey if one litre of petrol costs 40p?

7 Angles

Angles and straight lines

The angles at the four corners of this book are all right angles. In other words they are each 90°.

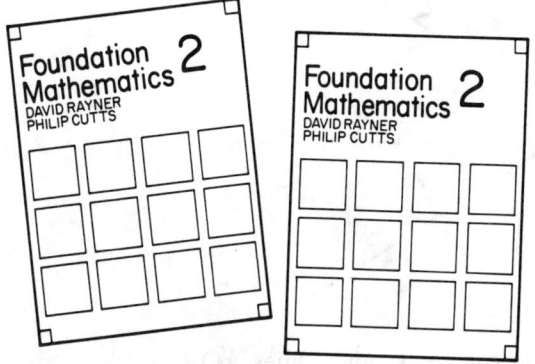

If two books are placed next to each other we see that two right angles make a straight line.

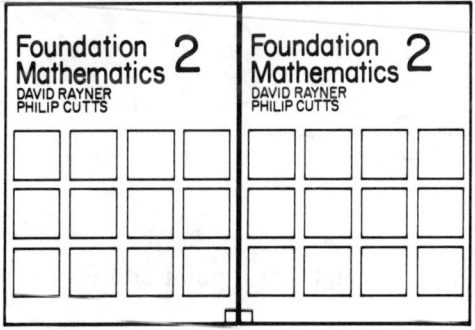

Remember:
The angles on a straight line add up to 180°.

Examples
Find the angles marked with letters.

(a)

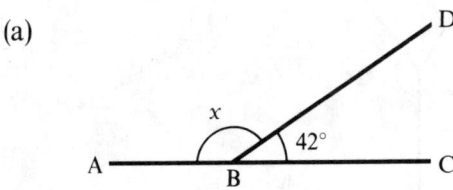

ABC is a straight line

$$\therefore \quad x + 42 = 180$$
$$x = 138°$$

(b)

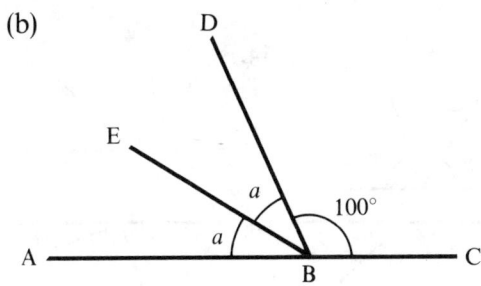

ABC is a straight line

$$\therefore \quad a + a + 100 = 180$$
$$a = 40°$$

Exercise 7.1

Copy the diagrams into your book and then find the angles marked with letters. (Do not draw the angles with a protractor.)

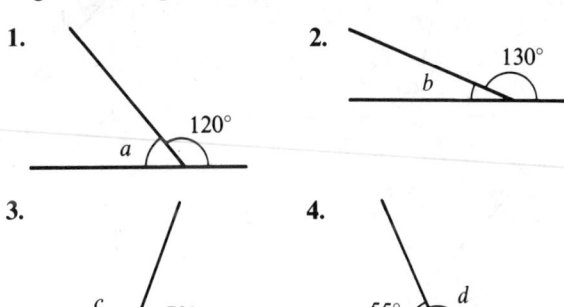

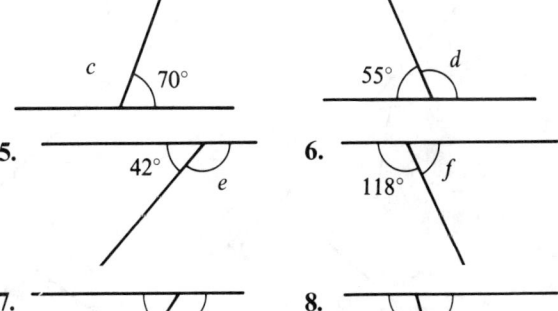

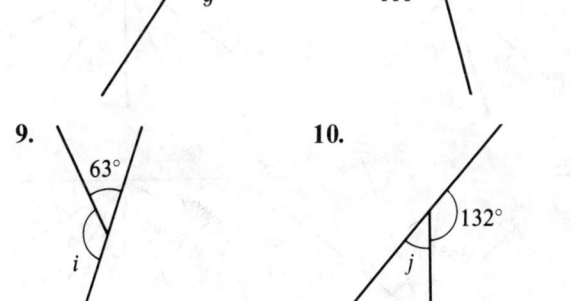

46 Angles

11.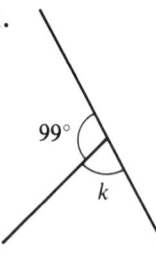

12.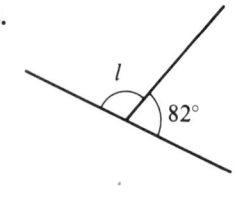

27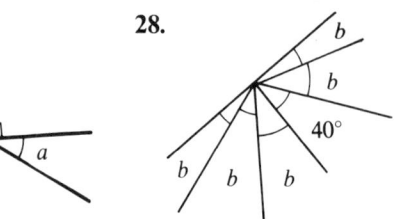

28.

13.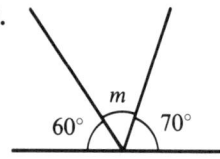

14.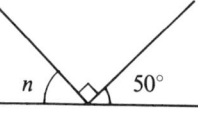

Angles at a point

15.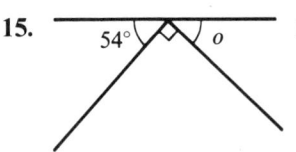

16.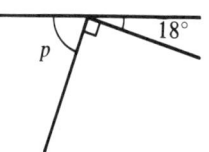

17.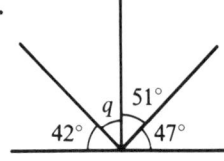

18.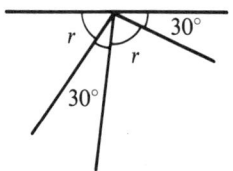

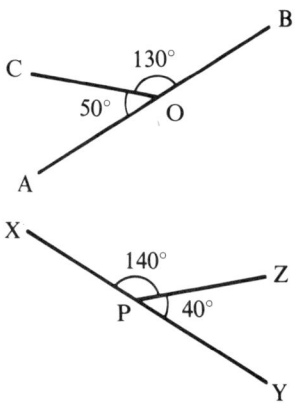

19.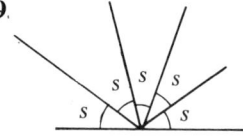

20.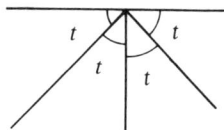

Suppose the straight lines AOB and XPY are brought together so that O and P cover the same point

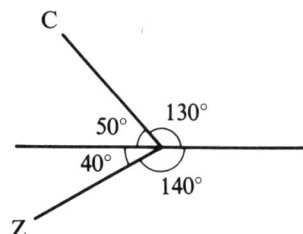

21.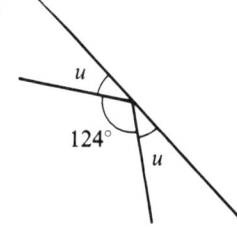

22.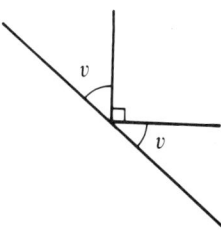

We see that the angles at a point add up to 360°.

Examples

Find the angles marked with letters

(a)

23.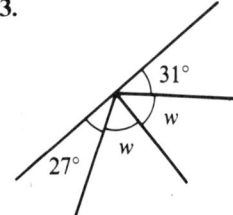

24.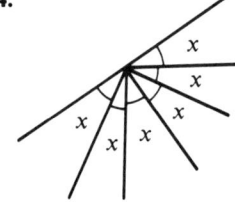

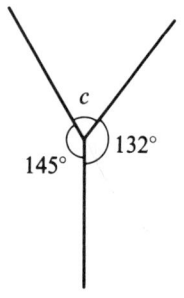

25.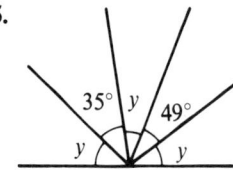

26.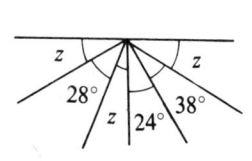

$c + 145° + 132° = 360°$
$c = 83°$

Angles 47

(b)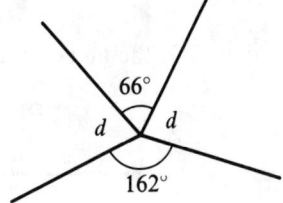

$2d + 66 + 162 = 360$

```
   66            3 5̷ ¹0
+ 162          − 2 2 8
  ───           ───────
  228            1 3 2
```

$2d = 132$
$d = 66°$

Exercise 7.2

Copy the diagrams and then find each of the angles marked with letters.

1.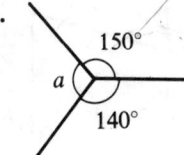

2.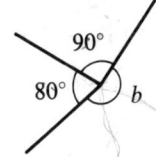

3.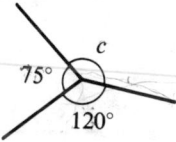

4.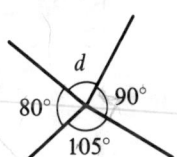

5.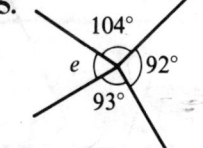

6.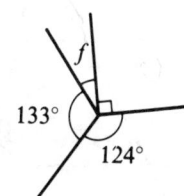

7.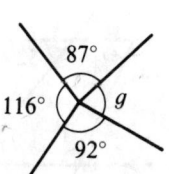

8.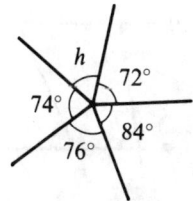

9.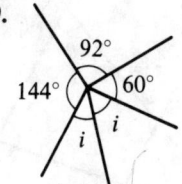

10.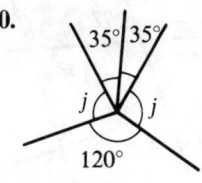

11.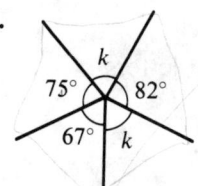

12.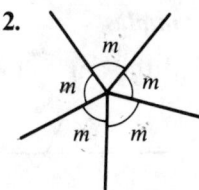

13.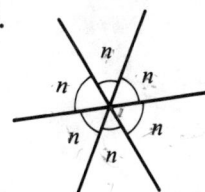

14.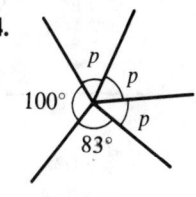

15.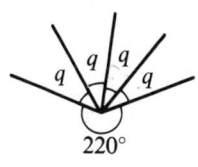

16.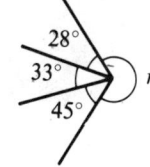

17.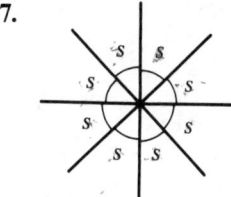

18.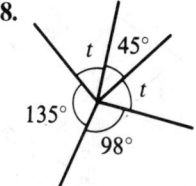

19.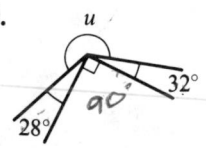

20.

Angles and parallel lines

Two straight lines are *parallel* if they never meet. They are always the same distance apart.

In the diagram, lines AB and CD are parallel. Lines which are parallel are marked with arrows. The line XY cuts AB and CD.

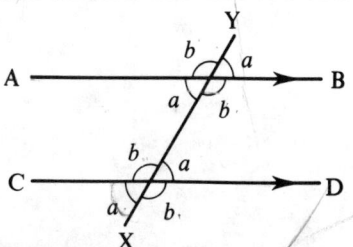

All the angles marked a are equal.
All the angles marked b are equal.
Remember:
All the acute angles are equal and all the obtuse angles are equal.

48 Angles

Examples

Find the angles marked with letters.

(a)
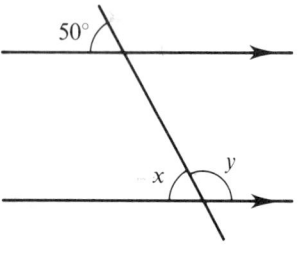

$x = 50°$
$y = 130°$

(b)
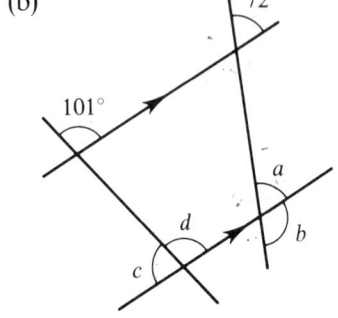

$a = 72°$
$b = 108°$
$c = 79°$
$d = 101°$

Intersecting lines

When two lines intersect, the opposite angles are equal.
In the diagram below, $a = 36°$ and $b = 144°$

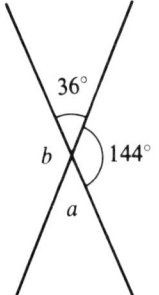

Exercise 7.3

Copy the diagram and then find the angles marked with letters.

1. 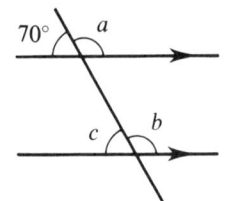 2.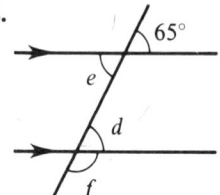

3. 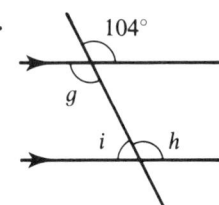 4.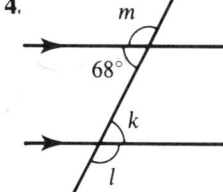

5. 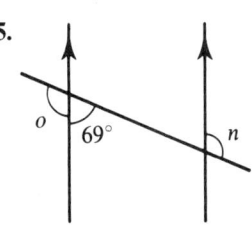 6.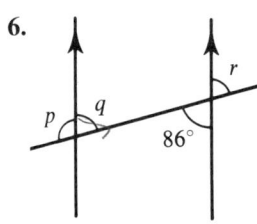

7. 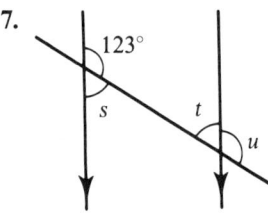 8.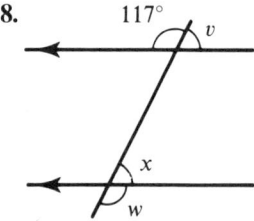

9. 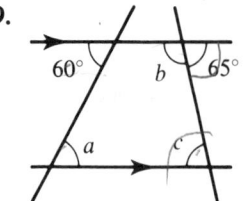 10.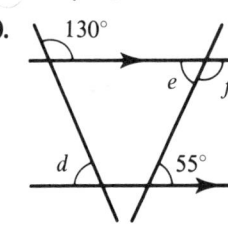

11. 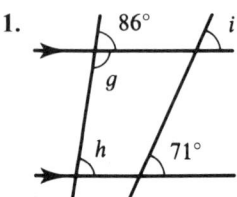 12.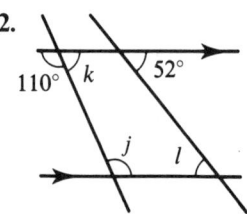

13. 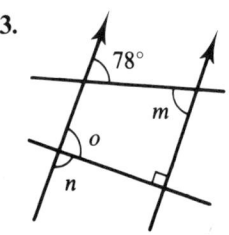 14.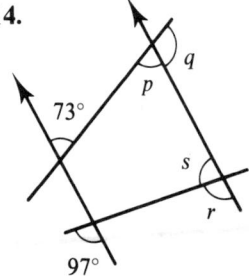

Angles 49

15.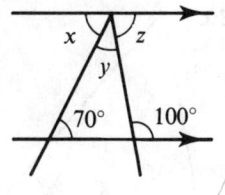
16.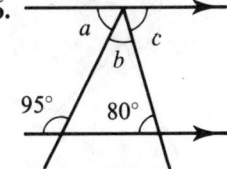

When the angles a, b and c are placed together they form a straight line.

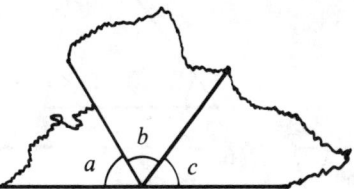

17.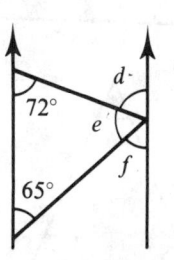
18.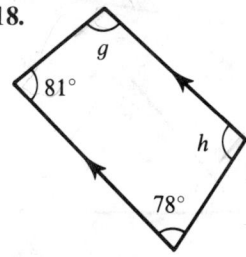

Again we see that the angles in a triangle add up to 180° (angles on a straight line).

Examples

Find the angles marked with letters.

(a)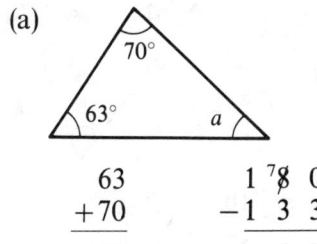

19.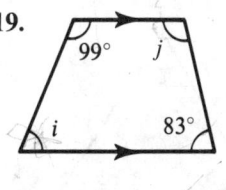
20.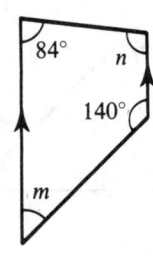

```
  63         1 ⁷8 0
+ 70       − 1  3 3
────       ───────
 133          4 7
```

$a = 47°$

Angles in triangles

(a) In the diagram below, the line XBY is parallel to AC.

(b)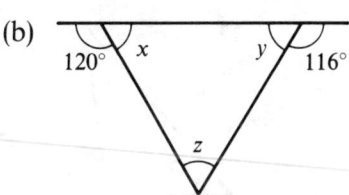

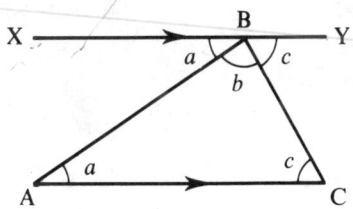

$X\hat{B}A = a$ and $Y\hat{B}C = c$ (parallel lines)

But XBY is a straight line.
So $a + b + c = 180°$
a, b and c are the angles of the triangle ABC.

∴ The angles of a triangle add up to 180°.

(b) Draw a triangle of any shape on a piece of card and cut it out accurately. Now tear off the three corners as shown.

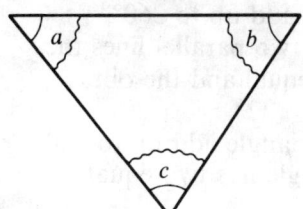

$x = 60°$ (angles on a straight line)
$y = 64°$ (angles on a straight line)
$z + 60 + 64 = 180$

```
  60        1 ⁷8 ¹0
+ 64      − 1  2 4
────      ────────
 124          5 6
```

$z = 56°$.

Exercise 7.4

Copy the diagram and then find the angles marked with letters.

1.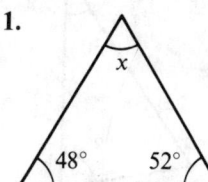
2.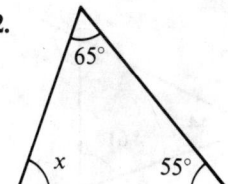

3. 58°, 44°, x

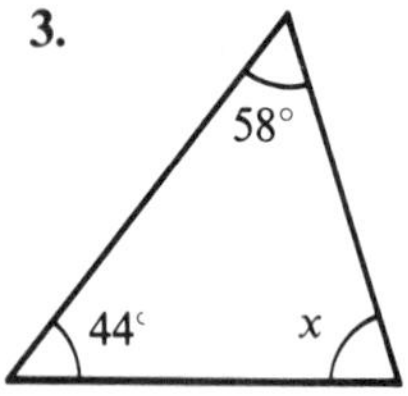

4. 50°, a, 75°

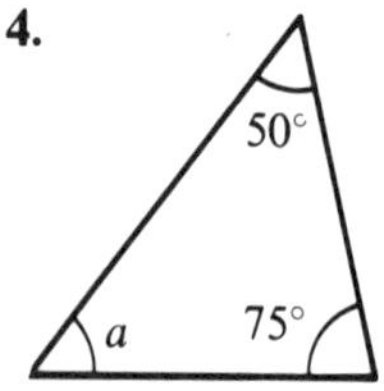

5. 41°, 60°, b

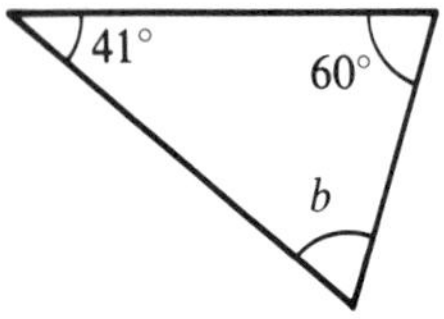

6. c, 37°, 74°

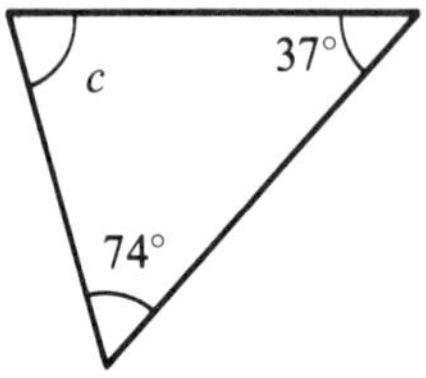

7. d, 91°, 38°

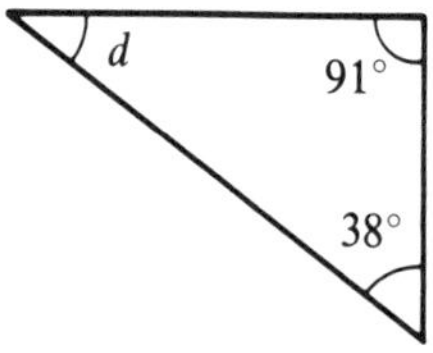

8. 62°, 56°, e

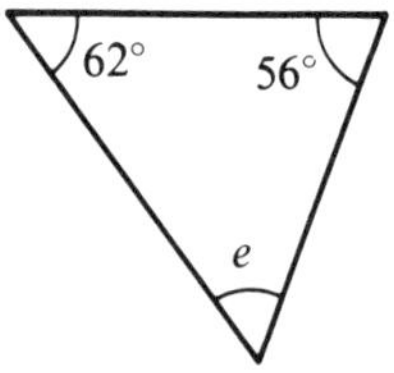

9. 120°, f, 70°

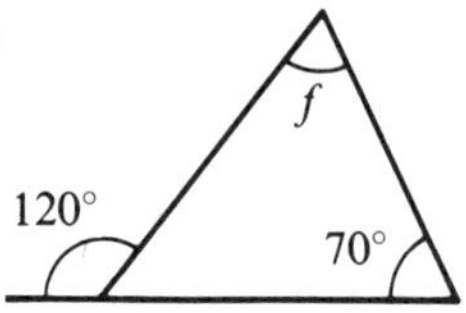

10. g, 82°, 105°

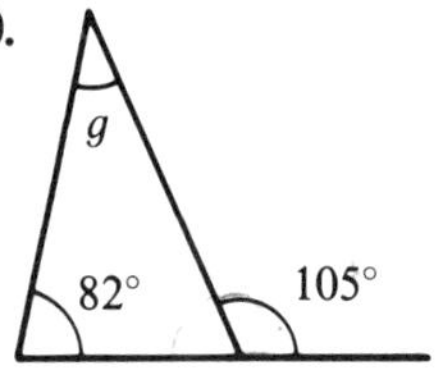

11. 30°, 75°, h

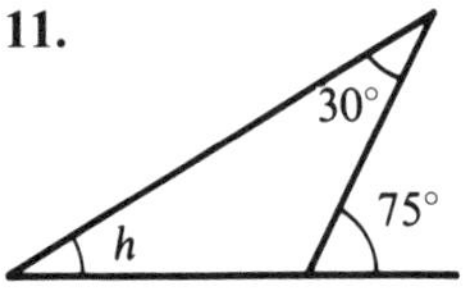

12. i, 42°, 82°

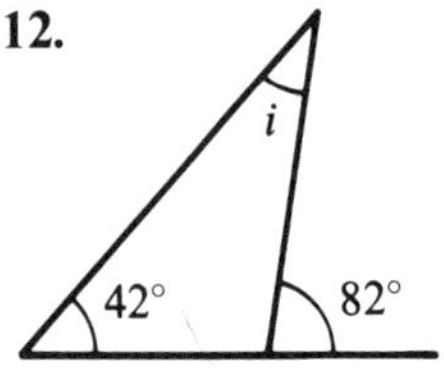

13. 59°, 102°, a

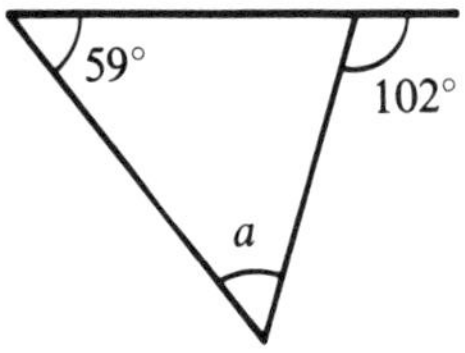

14. 35°, b, 41°

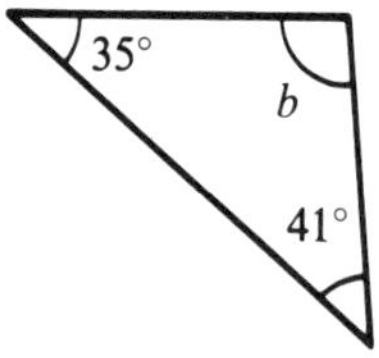

15. 32°, c, 27°

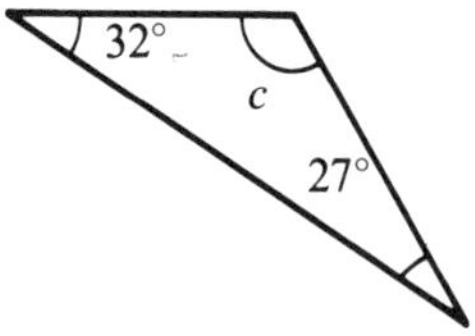

16. 62°, d, 58°

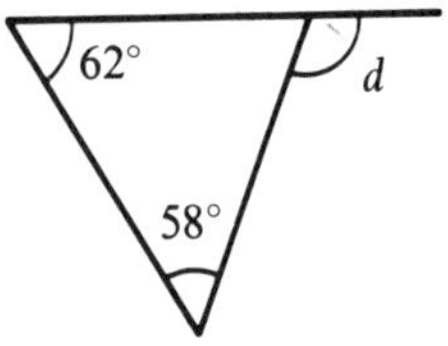

17. 44°, e, 61°

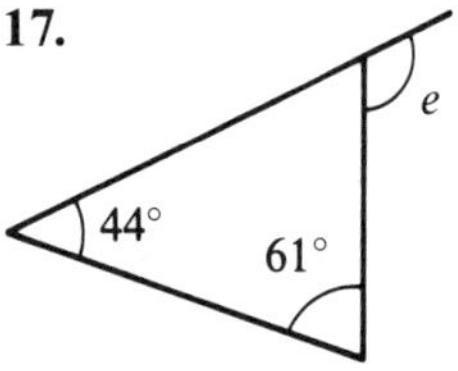

18. 30°, f, 68°

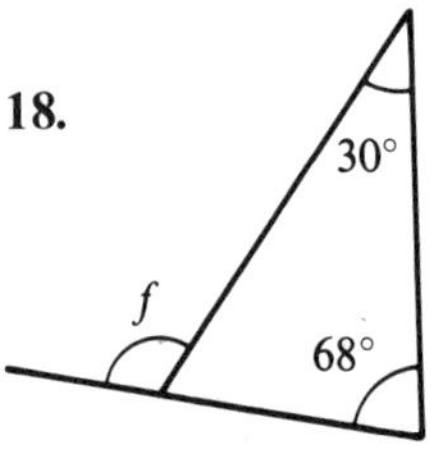

19. 107°, 57°, g

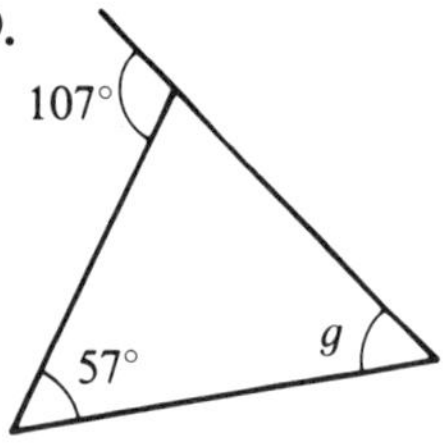

20. x, 80°, x

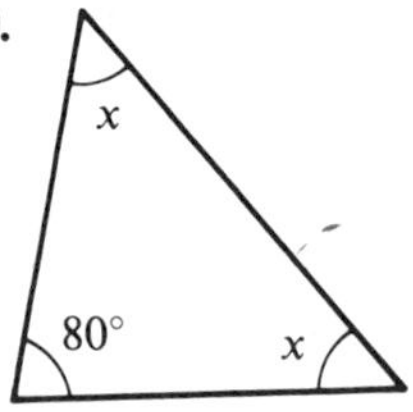

21. 84°, y, y

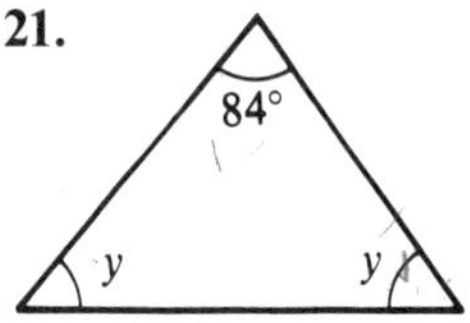

22. 46°, z, z

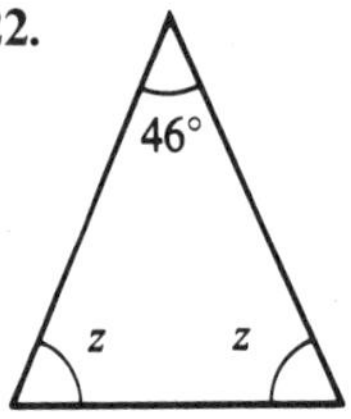

23. a, a, 55°

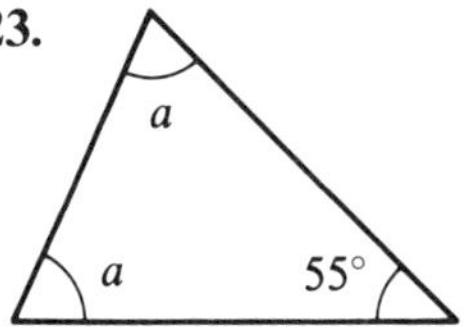

24. b, b, b

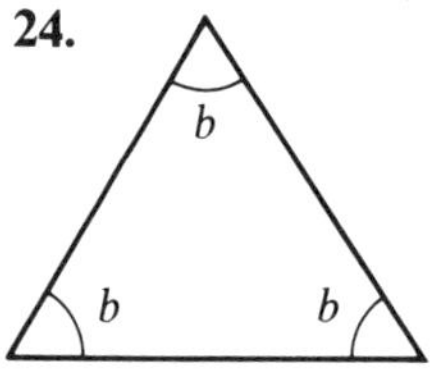

Isosceles and equilateral triangles

An *isosceles* triangle has two equal sides and two equal angles.

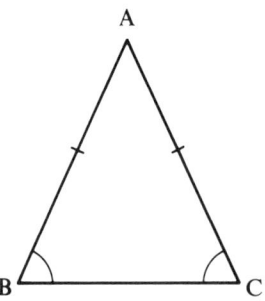

The sides AB and AC are equal (marked with a dash) so angles $A\hat{B}C$ and $A\hat{C}B$ are also equal.

An *equilateral* triangle has three equal sides and three equal angles (all 60°).

In the next exercise you will need to remember:
(a) Angles on a straight line add up to 180°.
(b) Angles at a point add up to 360°.
(c) When a line cuts two parallel lines the acute angles are equal and the obtuse angles are equal.
(d) The angles in a triangle add up to 180°.
(e) An isosceles triangle has two equal angles.

Angles 51

Exercise 7.5

Copy each diagram and then find the angles marked with letters.

1.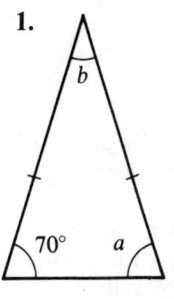
2.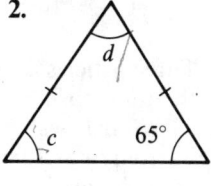
3.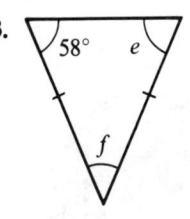
4.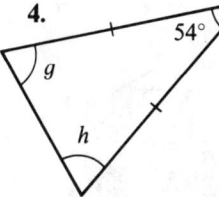
5.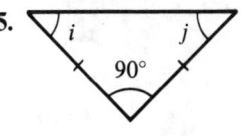
6.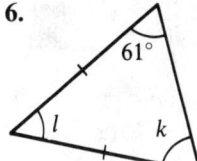
7.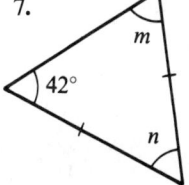
8.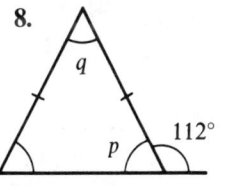
9.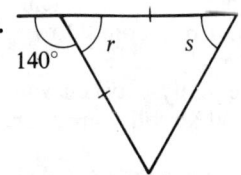
10.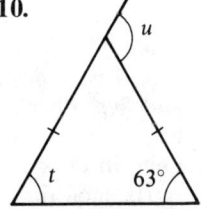
11.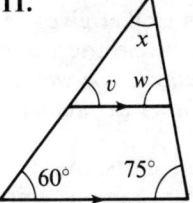
12.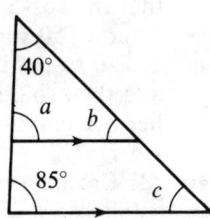
13.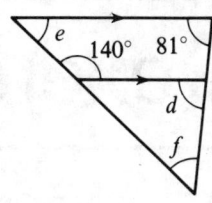
14.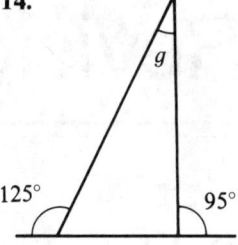
15.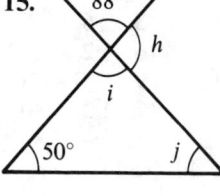
16.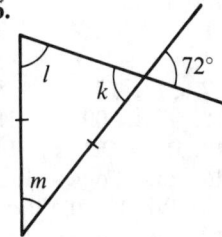
17.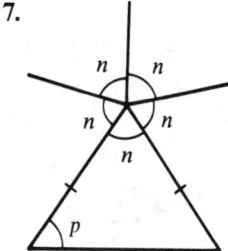
18.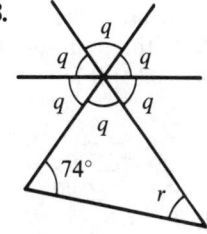
19.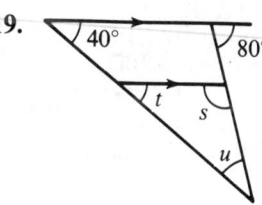
20.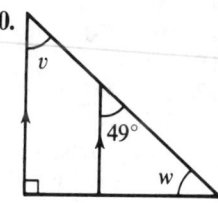
21.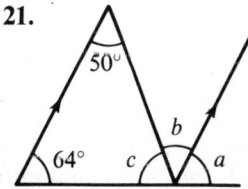
22.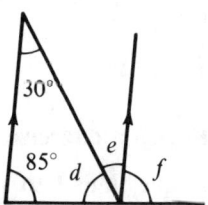
23.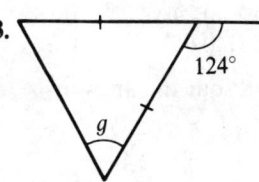
24.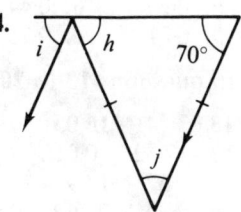

Revision exercises 2

Quick tests

Test 1
1. 0.35×100
2. 0.4×100
3. $2.6 \div 10$
4. $5.3 \div 100$
5. 4.1×10
6. 6.2×100
7. $57 \div 10$
8. $63 \div 100$
9. $400 \div 10$
10. $97 \div 100$
11. 2.1×20
12. 1.3×30
13. 0.1×0.2
14. 0.3×6
15. 0.4×8
16. Two angles of a triangle are 40° and 60°. What is the third?
17. Two angles of a triangle are 50° and 70°. What is the third?
18. Two angles of a triangle are 45° and 65°. What is the third?
19. Is the point (4, 0) on the x-axis or the y-axis?
20. 0.02×0.1

Test 2
1. £5 − £2·30
2. £6 − £1·40
3. £10 − £5·80
4. £2 − 55p
5. £3 − 74p
6. $2 + 3 + 4$
7. $1 + 2 + 3 + 4$
8. $3 \times 4 \times 5$
9. $65 + 99$
10. $53 + 99$
11. $200 - 54$
12. 0.3×10
13. 0.6×100
14. 0.71×1000
15. $0.4 \div 10$
16. $0.7 \div 100$
17. Two angles of a triangle are 72° and 48°. What is the third?
18. Two angles of a triangle are 57° and 10°. What is the third?
19. Is the point (0, 5) on the x-axis or the y-axis?
20. $15 - 3.6$

Decimals

Revision exercise 2.1

In questions **1** to **12**, change the given decimal into the equivalent fraction (in its simplest form).

1. 0·5
2. 0·6
3. 0·8
4. 0·15
5. 0·25
6. 0·44
7. 0·24
8. 0·18
9. 0·21
10. 0·75
11. 0·65
12. 0·02

In questions **13** to **20**, work out the answer.

13. $3.24 + 16.051$
14. $5.72 - 2$
15. $17.32 + 0.018$
16. $6 - 2.4$
17. $3.57 - 1.09$
18. $16.307 + 204.92$
19. $6.34 + 2.562 + 15$
20. $6.3 - 4.18$

21. Three articles cost £7·26, £4·40 and £9. Find the total cost.
22. Mrs Jones wishes to buy a coat costing £76·40. She only has £38·74. How much more money does she need to save?
23. Mr Cohen buys three small books costing £2·45, £3·55 and 95p respectively. Find how much change he should get from £10.
24. Find the difference in price between the two dresses below.

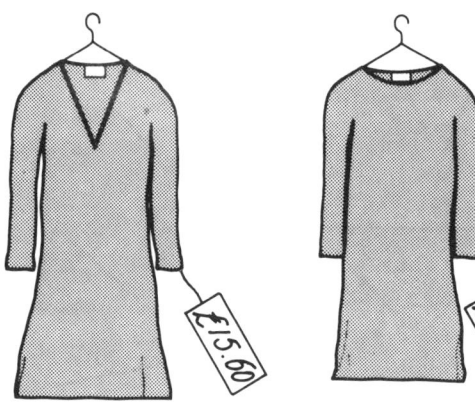

25. 2.35×3
26. $21.15 \div 5$
27. 42.7×4
28. $35.1 \div 3$
29. $1.17 \div 9$
30. 104.2×6
31. 0.253×8
32. $82.6 \div 7$
33. A bottle of a new brand of wine costs £3·24. Find the cost of 3 bottles of that wine.
34. £14·36 is to be shared equally between 4 people. How much will each person receive?
35. Rolls of a vinyl wallpaper cost £4·30 each. Julie needs 7 rolls for her bedroom. How much will she have to pay?
36. £83·04 is to be shared equally between you and five other people. What will your share be?
37. One tin of biscuits costs £1·16. Find the cost of six such tins.
38. Find the cost of 7 tins of baked beans, given that the cost of one tin is 23p.
39. After a £50 win at bingo, Mrs Collier gives £23·20 to her husband for a new electric razor and then shares out the rest equally between her five children. How much does each child receive?
40. Mr Freeman buys six identical shirts, the total cost is £84·90. Find the price of one shirt.

Revision exercise 2.2

1. 2·4 × 5
2. 3·2 × 7
3. 2·63 × 10
4. 0·416 × 100
5. 3·1 × 0·6
6. 13·7 × 0·8
7. 1·82 × 1·3
8. 28·5 × 1·5
9. 18·6 × 0·04
10. 7·04 × 2·1

11. If 1 kg of beef costs £3·40, find the cost of:
    (a) 2 kg of beef (b) 5 kg of beef
    (c) 1·5 kg of beef (d) 0·4 kg of beef.

12. If 1 kg of pork costs £2·25, find the cost of:
    (a) 3 kg of pork (b) 10 kg of pork
    (c) 0·8 kg of pork (d) 1·8 kg of pork

13. If 1 kg of cheese costs £3·12, find the cost of:
    (a) 4 kg of cheese (b) 100 kg of cheese
    (c) 20 kg of cheese (d) 1·5 kg of cheese.

In questions **14** to **20** use the following prices to find the total cost.

Lamb: £3·20 per kg
Cod: £2·80 per kg
Mince: £2·60 per kg
Lemonade: 55p per litre
Eggs: 90p per dozen
Butter: 56p per ¼ kg
Potatoes: 20p per kg
Lettuce: 22p each

14. 2 kg of lamb
    ½ kg of butter
    Half a dozen eggs
    Two lettuces

15. 3 kg of mince
    4 kg of potatoes
    1 litre of lemonade
    12 eggs

16. 1½ kg of cod
    1 kg of butter
    2 kg of potatoes
    Three lettuces

17. 2 kg of lamb
    1·4 kg of mince
    Two litres of lemonade
    2½ kg of potatoes

18. 0·8 kg of cod
    1·2 kg of mince
    Half a dozen eggs
    ¾ kg of butter
    10 lettuces

19. 1·7 kg of lamb
    3 litres of lemonade
    3·5 kg of potatoes
    0·9 kg of cod
    12 eggs

20. 2·3 kg of mince
    0·9 kg of lamb
    1·1 kg of cod
    0·5 kg of butter
    3 litres of lemonade
    1 lettuce.

Angles

Revision exercise 2.3

Make an accurate full size drawing of each shape using a ruler, a protractor and a *sharp* pencil. Measure and record all the sides and angles marked with letters.

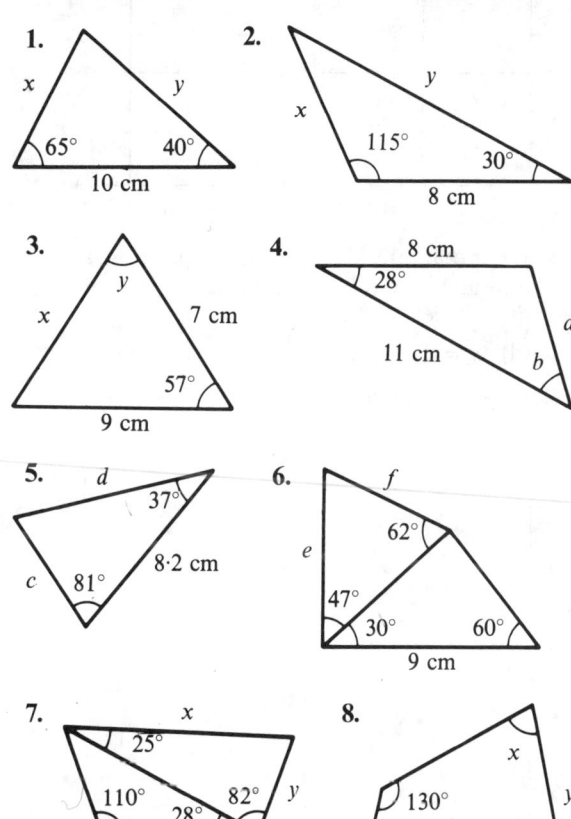
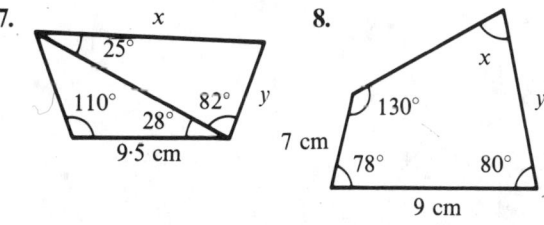
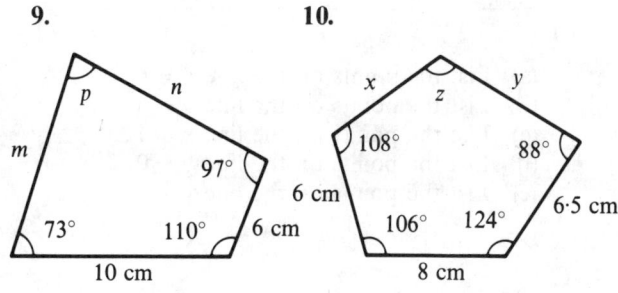

Coordinates

Revision exercise 2.4

1. Copy the diagram below and label each line with its equation. One has been filled in for you already.

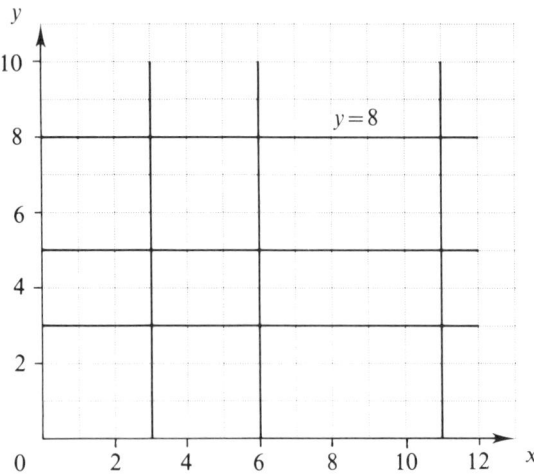

2. On a diagram like the one in question **1** draw and label the following lines:
   (a) $x = 5$ (b) $y = 6$ (c) $y = 1$
   (d) $x = 0$ (e) $y = 4\frac{1}{2}$ (f) $y = x$

3. Copy the diagram below.

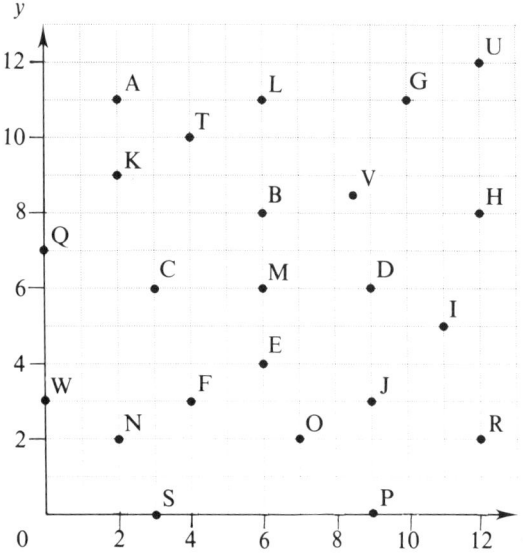

   (a) List the points on the line $x = 6$.
   (b) List the points on the line $y = 6$.
   (c) List the points on the line $x = 12$.
   (d) List the points on the line $y = 0$.
   (e) List the points on the line $y = x$.

   (f) Write down the equation of the line on which the following points lie:
   (i) W, F, J   (ii) T, F
   (iii) A, L, G   (iv) A, K, N
   (v) S, P   (vi) N, M, V, U.

   (g) How many points lie above the line $y = 9$?

4. On squared paper draw the lines $x = 2$, $x = 8$, $y = 3$ and $y = 6$. What is the area of the rectangle formed by the four lines? (Give the answer as a number of squares.)

5. On squared paper draw the lines $y = 3$, $x = 8$ and $y = x$. What is the area of the triangle formed by the three lines?

6. (a) On squared paper plot and join the points (2, 5), (6, 2), (10, 8) as shown below.

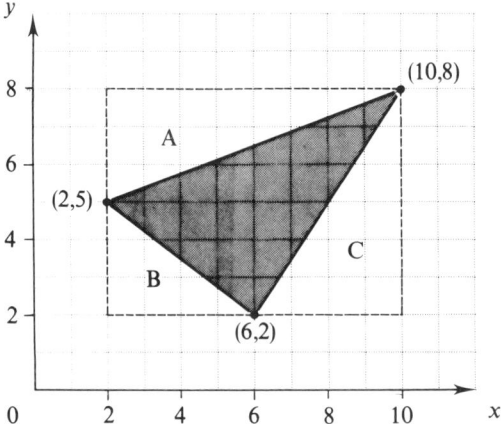

   (b) Find the area of the triangles A, B, C.
   (c) Find the area of the shaded triangle.

In questions **7** to **12** draw a set of axes for x and y from 0 to 10. Plot and join the points in order and find the area of the shape formed. Use the same method as in question **6**.

7. (2, 4), (6, 9), (8, 3), (2, 4).
8. (2, 2), (3, 8), (9, 2), (2, 2).
9. (1, 5), (5, 8), (8, 2), (1, 5).
10. (1, 6), (8, 8), (5, 2), (1, 6).
11. (2, 7), (10, 9), (8, 2), (3, 3), (2, 7).
12. (1, 2), (2, 9), (9, 7), (7, 3), (1, 2).

8 The metric system

In the metric system all the units of measurement are related to one another by powers of 10. This makes converting between units very easy using decimal notation.

Length

10 mm = 1 cm
100 cm = 1 m
1000 m = 1 km

Weight

1000 g = 1 kg

Volume

1000 ml = 1 l

Exercise 8.1

Do these calculations for revision of decimal notation.

1. 3·4 × 10
2. 2·53 × 10
3. 6·24 × 100
4. 7·3 × 100
5. 7·823 × 1000
6. 6·48 × 1000
7. 5·62 × 100
8. 7·5 × 10
9. 8·4 × 1000
10. 9·65 × 100
11. 78 ÷ 10
12. 5·7 ÷ 10
13. 123 ÷ 100
14. 25·9 ÷ 100
15. 5286 ÷ 1000
16. 93·8 ÷ 10
17. 425 ÷ 1000
18. 4·7 ÷ 100
19. 259 ÷ 10
20. 7·6 ÷ 1000
21. 54 × 10
22. 370 ÷ 10
23. 6·2 ÷ 100
24. 4·3 × 100
25. 0·6 × 10
26. 0·008 × 1000
27. 541 ÷ 1000
28. 0·5 × 100
29. 0·2 ÷ 10
30. 6·2 × 1000
31. 8·4 × 10
32. 76·7 ÷ 100
33. 0·007 × 100
34. 6 ÷ 1000
35. 5047 ÷ 100
36. 0·03 × 1000
37. 11 ÷ 1000
38. 0·99 ÷ 10
39. 0·9 × 100
40. 5·5 × 10
41. 156 ÷ 10
42. 37 × 100
43. 794 ÷ 100
44. 450 ÷ 10
45. 0·67 × 1000
46. 548 ÷ 100
47. 80 × 10
48. 42·6 × 1000
49. 0·0005 × 100
50. 7227 ÷ 1000
51. 578 ÷ 10
52. 0·2 × 1000
53. 7·63 × 1000
54. 4·4 ÷ 100
55. 627 ÷ 100
56. 0·52 × 10
57. 61·3 × 1000
58. 2·5 ÷ 100
59. 640 × 10
60. 37·5 ÷ 100

Length

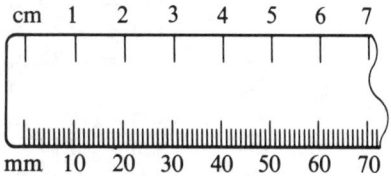

Centimetres and metres

Since there are 100 cm in every metre, the following rules apply.

To change from metres to centimetres we multiply by 100 (since there are more cm than m).

To change from centimetres to metres we divide by 100 (since there are less m than cm).

Examples

Convert the following lengths to cm.

(a) 6·42 m
6·42 m = (6·42 × 100) cm
= 642 cm

(b) 5·8 m
5·8 m = (5·8 × 100) cm
= 580 cm.

Examples

Convert the following lengths to m.

(a) 164 cm
164 cm = (164 ÷ 100) m
= 1·64 m

(b) 3120 cm
3120 cm = (3120 ÷ 100) m
= 31·2 m

Exercise 8.2

In questions **1** to **50**, copy and complete.

1. 2.47 m = cm
2. 135 cm = m
3. 3.51 m = cm
4. cm = 2.88 m
5. m = 728 cm
6. cm = 1.56 m
7. 4.94 m = cm
8. cm = 9.12 m
9. m = 326 cm
10. 507 cm = m
11. 2.05 m = cm
12. cm = 1.21 m
13. 4.07 m = cm
14. 936 cm = m
15. m = 309 cm
16. cm = 4.22 m
17. 7.06 m = cm
18. cm = 1.04 m
19. m = 55 cm
20. 282 cm = m
21. m = 47 cm
22. cm = 0.55 m
23. 0.87 m = cm
24. cm = 7.13 m
25. m = 24 cm
26. 517 cm = m
27. m = 5 cm
28. 2483 cm = m
29. 0.09 m = cm
30. cm = 19.26 m
31. 0.02 m = cm
32. 5355 cm = m
33. m = 6 cm
34. cm = 45.86 m
35. 24.18 m = cm
36. 197 cm = m
37. m = 3726 cm
38. 344 cm = m
39. 41.42 m = cm
40. cm = 2.19 m
41. m = 6037 cm
42. cm = 16.38 m
43. 21.59 m = cm
44. 97 cm = m
45. 30.28 m = cm
46. cm = 0.08 m
47. m = 432 cm
48. cm = 0.64 m
49. m = 76 cm
50. 2471 cm = m

Kilometres and millimetres

We use millimetres for measuring small distances and kilometres for measuring large distances.

1000 m = 1 km
To change kilometres to metres we multiply by 1000 (since there are more m than km).

To change metres to kilometres we divide by 1000 (since there are less km than m).

Exercise 8.3

In questions **1** to **40**, copy and complete.

1. 5.214 km = m
2. m = 6.139 km
3. 6.372 km = m
4. 4126 m = km
5. km = 4918 m
6. m = 3.147 km
7. km = 2163 m
8. 7318 m = km
9. 4.842 km = m
10. 5245 m = km
11. km = 3027 m
12. m = 1.3 km
13. 4.018 km = m
14. 2130 m = km
15. km = 378 m
16. m = 0.219 km
17. km = 400 m
18. m = 0.318 km
19. 0.727 km = m
20. 1246 m = km
21. km = 497 m
22. m = 3.198 km
23. 0.8 km = m
24. m = 0.09 km
25. km = 56 m
26. m = 0.552 km
27. km = 1310 m
28. 21 460 m = km
29. 0.005 km = m
30. m = 13.26 km
31. km = 19 222 m
32. 61 623 m = km
33. 42.6 km = m
34. m = 2.186 km
35. 0.0008 km = m
36. m = 0.359 km
37. km = 426 m
38. 500 m = km
39. 2.644 km = m
40. m = 20.43 km

10 mm = 1 cm

To change centimetres to millimetres we multiply by 10 (since there are more mm than cm).

To change millimetres to centimetres we divide by 10 (since there are less cm than mm).

Exercise 8.4

In questions **1** to **40**, copy and complete.

1. 3.7 cm = mm
2. mm = 5.7 cm
3. 4.9 cm = mm
4. mm = 63 cm
5. cm = 61 mm
6. mm = 8.8 cm
7. 2.6 cm = mm
8. mm = 9.2 cm
9. cm = 48 mm
10. 7 mm = cm
11. 1.5 cm = mm
12. mm = 0.5 cm
13. cm = 9 mm
14. 11 mm = cm
15. cm = 98 mm
16. 127 mm = cm
17. 31.8 cm = mm
18. mm = 22.3 cm
19. 72.4 cm = mm
20. mm = 41.6 cm
21. cm = 688 mm
22. 19 mm = cm
23. 90 cm = mm
24. mm = 7.9 cm
25. cm = 443 mm
26. 371 mm = cm
27. cm = 827 mm
28. mm = 52 cm
29. 62.5 cm = mm
30. 647 mm = cm
31. 40.4 cm = mm
32. 498 mm = cm
33. cm = 85 mm
34. mm = 20.3 cm
35. 1.35 cm = mm
36. 2.5 mm = cm
37. cm = 22.5 mm
38. mm = 13.75 cm
39. 29.05 cm = mm
40. 87.5 mm = cm

Exercise 8.5

1. On a certain day, an athlete in training runs 7.5 km in the morning and 6.7 km in the afternoon. Find how far he runs during the day altogether.
2. On a model railway, two straight pieces of track are joined together. If the two pieces measure 16.5 cm and 24.5 cm respectively, find their combined length.

3. The distance between two railway stations is 3·45 km. A signal lies between the stations at a distance of 1·94 km from one of the stations. How far is the signal from the other station?
4. At the beginning of the year a young tree is 2·67 m tall. During the year it grows another 44 cm. How tall is the tree at the end of the year?
5. A candle is 12·7 cm long. After burning for a while it is 8·9 cm long. What length has been burnt?
6. On a journey of 9·7 km, how far is there left to go after travelling 5·624 km?
7. A £1 note is 13·3 cm long, a £5 note is 14·6 cm long and a £10 note is 15·1 cm long. If one note of each kind is taken and the three are laid end to end, what is their combined length?
8. A piece of wood 4·33 m long needs to be shortened to 3·5 m. How much must be cut off?
9. A journey is done in two stages. The first stage is 12·5 km and the second stage is 27·8 km. Find the total length of the journey.
10. Three pencils laid end to end have a combined length of 48 cm. If two of the pencils are 17·3 cm and 19·9 cm long respectively, how long is the third pencil?
11. A pound note is 13·3 cm long. Find the combined length of six pound notes laid end to end.
12. The distance round a running track is 420 m. If a woman runs 6 laps, how far does she run altogether?
13. A piece of wire 15·6 cm long is to be divided into 4 equal parts. How long will each part be?
14. A metal rail 3·15 m long is cut into 7 identical sections. Calculate the length of each section.
15. An athlete runs 6·5 km every day. How far does he run in a week?
16. A piece of thread 24 cm long is to be cut into 5 equal parts. How long will each part be?
17. A tree grows 39 cm every year. How much does it grow in 8 years?
18. A matchbox is 5·4 cm long. Find the combined length of 8 matchboxes laid end to end.
19. A plank of wood 8·28 cm long is to be cut into 9 equal pieces. How long will each piece be?
20. A sponsored walk of 28 km is divided into 5 equal stages. Find the length of each stage.

Mixed problems

Exercise 8.6

Copy and complete each question.

1. 1·72 m =   cm
2. 4·213 km =   m
3. 4·8 cm =   mm
4. 244 cm =   m
5. 5000 m =   km
6. 12 mm =   cm
7. 2·1 km =   m
8. 3·87 m =   cm
9. 9·3 cm =   mm
10. 7214 m =   km
11. 56 mm =   cm
12. 6·169 km =   m
13. 122 cm =   m
14. 7·1 cm =   mm
15. 0·27 m =   cm
16. 2046 m =   km
17. 30 mm =   cm
18. 52 cm =   m
19. 0·09 m =   cm
20. 0·355 km =   m
21. 0·7 cm =   mm
22. 22 mm =   cm
23. 13 cm =   m
24. 217 m =   km
25. 0·5 cm =   mm
26. 0·614 km =   m
27. 3·29 m =   cm
28. 34 mm =   cm
29. 80 m =   km
30. 166 cm =   m
31. 2·95 m =   cm
32. 1·342 km =   m
33. 0·2 cm =   mm
34. 603 cm =   m
35. 42 300 m =   km
36. 62 mm =   cm
37. 4·15 m =   cm
38. 0·125 km =   m
39. 4·4 cm =   mm
40. 127 cm =   m
41. 20 400 m =   km
42. 1 mm =   cm
43. 53·242 km =   m
44. 8·2 cm =   mm
45. 2·45 m =   cm
46. 37 mm =   cm
47. 817 m =   km
48. 3472 cm =   m
49. 2·144 km =   m
50. 4·2 cm =   mm

Exercise 8.7

(This exercise is harder than the previous one.) Copy and complete each question.

1. 0·195 m =   cm
2. 0·1062 km =   m
3. 0·75 cm =   mm
4. 322·5 cm =   m
5. 2345·5 m =   km
6. 14·2 mm =   cm
7. 19·625 km =   m
8. 1·06 cm =   mm
9. 2·385 m =   cm
10. 1·253 m =   cm
11. 0·989 km =   m
12. 3·25 cm =   mm
13. 162·4 cm =   m
14. 1248 m =   km
15. 41·5 mm =   cm
16. 71·4 m =   km
17. 1269·4 cm =   m
18. 35·8 mm =   cm
19. 0·1725 km =   m
20. 7·94 cm =   mm
21. 3 m =   mm
22. 2 km =   cm
23. 1 km =   mm
24. 7 m =   mm
25. 5 km =   cm
26. 6 km =   mm
27. 2400 mm =   m
28. 700 000 cm =   km
29. 5 000 000 mm =   km
30. 5·6 m =   mm
31. 1·3 km =   cm
32. 2·7 km =   mm
33. 3 900 000 mm =   km
34. 240 000 cm =   km
35. 2240 mm =   m
36. 1·75 m =   mm
37. 4·22 km =   mm
38. 7·6 km =   cm
39. 425 000 cm =   km
40. 6 350 000 mm =   km
41. 8300 mm =   m
42. 2·124 m =   mm
43. 5·879 km =   mm
44. 3·512 km =   cm
45. 2500 cm =   km
46. 2 050 000 mm =   km

Perimeters

Example

Find the perimeter of the following triangle, giving your answer in metres.

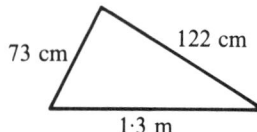

The perimeter is the distance round the triangle. Since we want the answer in metres, we want the 3 sides in metres. The 3 sides measure 1·3 m, 1·22 m and 0·73 m.

```
  1·3
  1·22
+ 0·73
------
  3·25
```

The perimeter of the triangle is 3·25 m.

Exercise 8.8

In questions **1** to **5**, find the perimeter of each quadrilateral, giving your answer in *centimetres*.

1.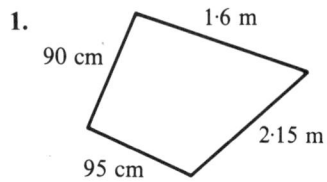

2.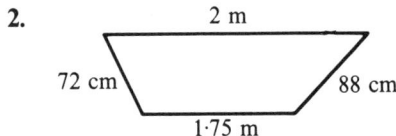

3.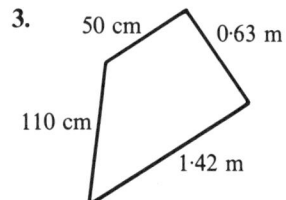

4.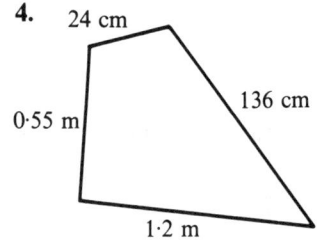

5.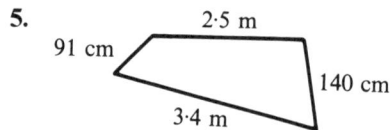

In questions **6** to **10**, find the perimeter of each quadrilateral, giving your answer in *metres*.

6.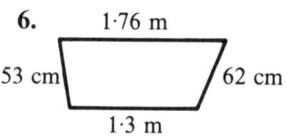

7.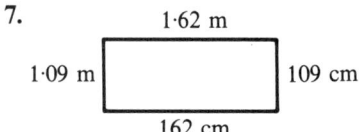

8.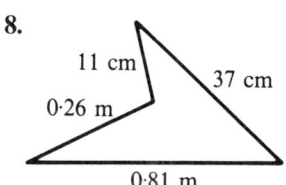

9.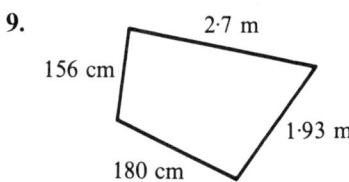

10.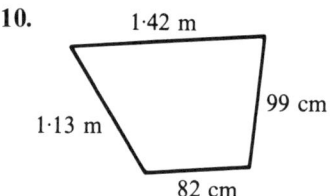

In questions **11** to **15**, find the perimeter of each triangle, giving your answer in *metres*.

11.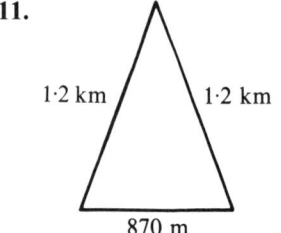

12.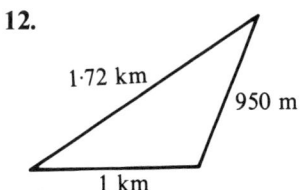

13.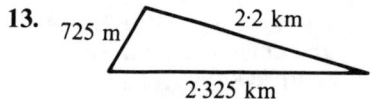

14.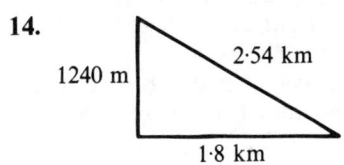

15.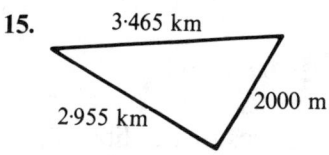

In questions **16** to **20**, find the perimeter of each triangle, giving your answer in *kilometres*.

16.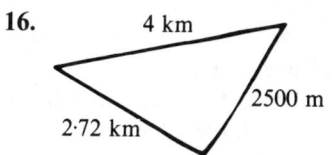

17.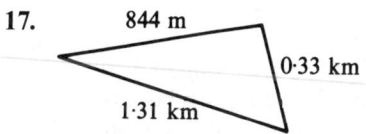

18.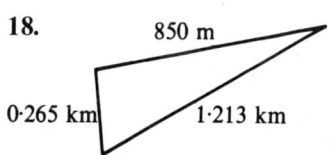

19.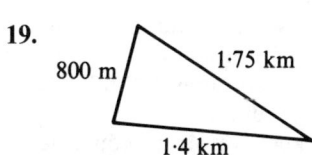

20.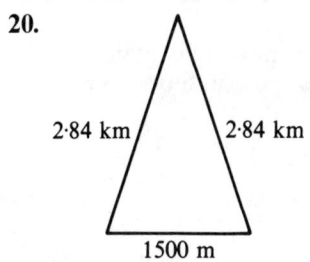

Areas

Example

Find the area of the rectangle below, giving your answer in mm².

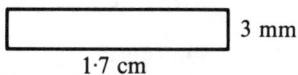

The area of a rectangle is 'length × breadth'. Since we want the answer in mm², we want all distances in mm.

    The length of the rectangle is 17 mm
    The breadth is 3 mm.
    So the area is 17 × 3
        = 51 mm²

Exercise 8.9

Below are the dimensions of some rectangles.
    In questions **1** to **10** calculate the area of the rectangles giving your answer in mm².

	length	breadth
1.	2·6 cm	6 mm
2.	3·7 cm	4 mm
3.	4·8 cm	5 mm
4.	53 mm	0·7 cm
5.	62 mm	0·9 cm
6.	2·7 cm	5 mm
7.	32 mm	0·8 cm
8.	4·4 cm	9 mm
9.	18 mm	0·6 cm
10.	0·6 cm	2 mm

In questions **11** to **20** calculate the area of the rectangles giving your answer in cm².

	length	breadth
11.	2·8 cm	4 mm
12.	4·1 cm	7 mm
13.	3·3 cm	6 mm
14.	35 mm	0·5 cm
15.	57 mm	0·4 cm
16.	7·2 cm	9 mm
17.	65 mm	0·7 cm
18.	2·6 cm	8 mm
19.	0·4 cm	2 mm
20.	24 mm	0·5 cm

Weight

In everyday life we measure weights in grams (g) and kilograms (kg).

Just as there are 1000 m in every km, so there are 1000 g in every kg.

Exercise 8.10

Copy and complete each of the following.

1. 3 kg =   g
2.   g = 5 kg
3.   kg = 7200 g
4.   g = 4·6 kg
5. 8·5 kg =   g
6. 1300 g =   kg
7. 5·3 kg =   g
8. 3540 g =   kg
9.   kg = 2460 g
10.   g = 7·214 kg
11. 3·14 kg =   g
12.   g = 3·607 kg
13.   kg = 7150 g
14. 2105 g =   kg
15.   kg = 10400 g
16.   g = 11·72 kg
17. 4·219 kg =   g
18. 12862 g =   kg
19.   kg = 410 g
20. 725 g =   kg
21. 0·3 kg =   g
22.   g = 0·42 kg
23. 0·058 kg =   g
24. 28 g =   kg
25.   kg = 8 g
26.   g = 5·63 kg
27.   kg = 572 g
28. 4900 g =   kg
29. 12·86 kg =   g
30.   g = 0·07 kg

31. Find the total weight of the three fish below.

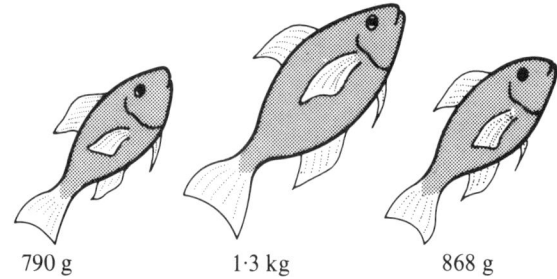

790 g   1·3 kg   868 g

32. There are 7·5 kg of sand in a container. If 725 g of sand are removed, find how much sand remains in the container, giving your answer in kilograms.
33. A sculptor carves a small figure from a piece of stone weighing 3 kg. If the finished work of art weighs 1·34 kg, find the weight of stone that was removed, giving your answer in grams.
34. A large jar of mincemeat weighs 822 g. Find the combined weight of three such jars, giving your answer in kilograms.
35. Three lumps of dough weigh 240 g, 1·72 kg and 0·9 kg. Find their combined weight in grams.
36. A tin of baked beans weighs 450 g. Find the combined weight of 4 such tins, giving your answer in kilograms.
37. There are 4·8 kg of cement in a bag. If 2750 g of cement are removed, find how much cement remains in the bag, giving your answer in grams.
38. Two pineapples weigh 0·45 kg and 0·725 kg respectively. Find the difference between their weights, giving your answer in grams.
39. A bag of flour weighs 1500 g and a bag of sugar weighs exactly 1 kg. Find the combined weight of 3 bags of flour and 2 bags of sugar, giving your answer in kilograms.
40. A quantity of sand weighs 950 g. Find how much sand must be added to this in order to make the weight up to 2·2 kg, giving your answer in kilograms.

Volume of a liquid

Volumes of liquids are measured in litres (l) and millilitres (ml).

There are 1000 ml in every litre (just as there are 1000 mm in every metre).

Exercise 8.11

In this exercise, if the answer comes out to be 1000 ml or more, then it should be written in litres (e.g. if your answer is 2450 ml, then rewrite it as 2·450 l).

1. If one bottle of milk contains 568 ml, how much is there in 2 bottles?
2. If one container of fly-killer contains 213 ml, how much is there in 7 containers?
3. If one container of washing-up liquid contains 540 ml, how much is there in 5 containers?
4. If one bottle of vanilla flavouring essence contains 28 ml, how much is there in 6 bottles?
5. If one can of beer contains 440 ml, how much is there in 7 cans?
6. If one bottle of anti-freeze contains 1·200 l, how much is there in 4 bottles?
7. If one bottle of liqueur contains 350 ml, how much is there in 8 bottles?
8. If one bottle of tonic water contains 250 ml, how much is there in 6 bottles?
9. If one bottle of whisky contains 750 ml, how much is there in 9 bottles?
10. If one bottle of blackcurrant drink contains 500 ml, how much is there in 4 bottles?
11. If one tin of paint contains 2·500 l, how much is there in 5 tins?
12. If one bottle of cough mixture contains 325 ml, how much is there in 6 bottles?

9 Algebra

Simple equations

Examples

(a) Solve the equation $x + 5 = 7$

When we are told to 'solve an equation' we have to find the number that the letter stands for.

$x + 5 = 7$
So $x = 2$

(b) Solve the equation $y - 2 = 24$

$y - 2 = 24$
So $y = 26$

Exercise 9.1

Solve the following equations.

1. $y + 2 = 5$
2. $a + 5 = 7$
3. $x - 2 = 17$
4. $y - 6 = 10$
5. $x + 6 = 11$
6. $d - 4 = 1$
7. $t + 1 = 7$
8. $c - 7 = 3$
9. $u - 6 = 12$
10. $x + 4 = 12$
11. $y + 2 = 9$
12. $n - 10 = 4$
13. $m + 3 = 4$
14. $x + 5 = 15$
15. $a - 4 = 0$
16. $b - 1 = 12$
17. $a + 10 = 19$
18. $x + 4 = 24$
19. $y - 11 = 7$
20. $c + 3 = 10$
21. $x - 3 = 6$
22. $d + 7 = 9$
23. $y + 3 = 14$
24. $t - 10 = 1$
25. $u - 12 = 16$
26. $d - 4 = 20$
27. $b + 9 = 17$
28. $a + 1 = 8$
29. $x - 1 = 23$
30. $u + 2 = 11$
31. $c + 17 = 22$
32. $d - 2 = 15$
33. $e + 21 = 28$
34. $n - 6 = 2$
35. $x - 13 = 5$
36. $y + 6 = 46$
37. $m + 8 = 29$
38. $x - 17 = 3$
39. $y - 20 = 2$
40. $t + 3 = 17$
41. $10 - x = 1$
42. $5 - y = 2$
43. $y - 5 = 2$
44. $7 - a = 4$
45. $a - 7 = 4$
46. $9 - b = 9$
47. $x + 13 = 54$
48. $t - 15 = 17$
49. $13 - x = 3$
50. $y + 17 = 28$
51. $x - 18 = 12$
52. $16 - t = 9$
53. $c + 23 = 31$
54. $y - 22 = 33$
55. $22 - y = 19$
56. $t + 63 = 76$
57. $17 - x = 10$
58. $d + 44 = 62$
59. $32 - t = 27$
60. $x - 42 = 2$

Values of expressions

$x + 7$ is called an expression.
Its value will depend on the value of x, as is seen below in the examples.

Examples

(a) Find the value of the expression $x + 7$ when $x = 11$.

$x + 7$
$= 11 + 7$
$= 18$.

(b) Find the value of the expression $x + 7$ when $x = 2$.

$x + 7$
$= 2 + 7$
$= 9$

Note. These questions are better done working *down* the page as in the examples above, especially when the questions become more difficult.

Exercise 9.2

1. Find the value of each of these expressions when $x = 7$
   (a) $x + 6$ (b) $x - 4$ (c) $x - 2$
   (d) $x + 1$ (e) $20 - x$ (f) $10 + x$

2. Find the value of each of these expressions when $x = 9$
   (a) $x + 6$ (b) $x - 4$ (c) $x - 7$
   (d) $x + 2$ (e) $3 + x$ (f) $11 - x$

3. Find the value of each of these expressions when $x = 13$
   (a) $x + 6$ (b) $x - 4$ (c) $x - 2$
   (d) $x + 12$ (e) $17 - x$ (f) $5 + x$

4. Find the value of each of these expressions when $x = 10$
   (a) $x + 6$ (b) $x - 4$ (c) $x + 10$
   (d) $x - 1$ (e) $7 + x$ (f) $15 - x$

5. Find the value of each of these expressions when $y = 5$
   (a) $y + 7$ (b) $y - 1$ (c) $4 + y$
   (d) $15 - y$ (e) $y + 17$ (f) $y - 3$

6. Find the value of each of these expressions when $y = 8$
   (a) $y + 7$ (b) $y - 1$ (c) $y - 8$
   (d) $y + 11$ (e) $4 + y$ (f) $9 - y$

7. Find the value of each of these expressions when $y = 11$
   (a) $y + 7$ (b) $y - 1$ (c) $y + 19$
   (d) $y - 11$ (e) $9 + y$ (f) $21 - y$

8. Find the value of each of these expressions when $a = 12$
   (a) $a - 7$ (b) $a + 3$ (c) $a - 11$
   (d) $a + 12$ (e) $8 + a$ (f) $17 - a$

9. Find the value of each of these expressions when $c = 3$
   (a) $c - 3$ (b) $c + 10$ (c) $6 + c$
   (d) $c - 1$ (e) $c + 21$ (f) $4 - c$

10. Find the value of each of these expressions when $d = 6$
    (a) $d + 5$ (b) $7 - d$ (c) $d - 5$
    (d) $d - 1$ (e) $16 + d$ (f) $d + 35$

11. Find the value of each of these expressions when $x = 17$
    (a) $x + 4$ (b) $19 - x$ (c) $x - 12$
    (d) $x + 15$ (e) $x - 4$ (f) $22 + x$

12. Find the value of each of these expressions when $y = 15$
    (a) $y + 18$ (b) $y - 7$ (c) $y - 15$
    (d) $25 - y$ (e) $14 + y$ (f) $y + 32$

13. Find the value of each of these expressions when $a = 20$
    (a) $a + 7$ (b) $31 - a$ (c) $11 + a$
    (d) $a - 11$ (e) $a - 7$ (f) $a + 42$

14. Find the value of each of these expressions when $n = 19$
    (a) $n + 3$ (b) $n - 3$ (c) $n - 9$
    (d) $n + 17$ (e) $23 + n$ (f) $23 - n$

15. Find the value of each of these expressions when $b = 27$
    (a) $b + 4$ (v) $b - 18$ (c) $b - 9$
    (d) $b + 13$ (e) $16 + b$ (f) $36 - b$

$5 \times y$ can be written more simply as $5y$
$a \times b$ can be written more simply as ab
(or ba)
$7 \times c \times y$ can be written more simply as $7cy$
(or $7yc$)
Similarly, $2a$ means $2 \times a$
ty means $t \times y$
$8cbx$ means $8 \times c \times b \times x$.

You can only use this shorthand method when doing multiplication.
There is no short way of writing $7 + a$ or $5 - x$.

Examples

(a) Rewrite the following without using the '×' sign.

   (i) $8 \times y = 8y$
   (ii) $10 \times x = 10x$
   (iii) $c \times a = ca$ (or ac)
   (iv) $4 \times a \times c \times d = 4acd$

(b) Rewrite the following in full, using the '×' sign.

   (i) $3x = 3 \times x$
   (ii) $2y = 2 \times y$
   (iii) $ad = a \times d$
   (iv) $2axy = 2 \times a \times x \times y$.

(c) Rewrite the following without using the '×' sign.

   (i) $2 \times a \times 4 \times c = 8ac$
   (ii) $3 \times a \times y \times d = 3ayd$
   (iii) $6 \times a \times 2 \times x = 12ax$

Notice that when there are two *numbers*, we can actually multiply these together.

Exercise 9.3

In questions **1** to **40**, rewrite *without* using the '×' sign.

1. $a \times b$ 2. $5 \times c$ 3. $y \times z$
4. $8 \times t$ 5. $5 \times u$ 6. $3 \times y$
7. $t \times x$ 8. $11 \times d$ 9. $12 \times y$
10. $a \times c$ 11. $c \times x$ 12. $10 \times t$
13. $5 \times b$ 14. $11 \times a$ 15. $a \times n$
16. $b \times e$ 17. $6 \times t$ 18. $5 \times a$
19. $m \times x$ 20. $a \times x$ 21. $a \times d$
22. $9 \times y$ 23. $11 \times c$ 24. $5 \times y$
25. $13 \times d$ 26. $d \times x$ 27. $3 \times b$
28. $m \times u$ 29. $x \times y$ 30. $9 \times n$
31. $4 \times a \times y$ 32. $2 \times c \times x$ 33. $3 \times a \times d$
34. $5 \times b \times y$ 35. $2 \times t \times y$ 36. $7 \times c \times u$
37. $4 \times c \times d$ 38. $a \times x \times d$ 39. $c \times n \times y$
40. $4 \times n \times a$

In questions **41** to **60**, rewrite in full, using the '×' sign.

41. $6x$ 42. $2a$ 43. $3d$ 44. ce
45. mx 46. $5n$ 47. ct 48. mt
49. ya 50. $10a$ 51. $12y$ 52. yd
53. $2z$ 54. $6x$ 55. xat 56. $5cw$
57. $7dy$ 58. $5cn$ 59. amx 60. $3cdt$

In questions **61** to **80**, rewrite *without* using the '×' sign.

61. $2 \times x \times 3 \times y$ 62. $3 \times a \times 4 \times d$
63. $4 \times a \times c \times b$ 64. $5 \times e \times h \times t$
65. $5 \times 2 \times x \times a$ 66. $3 \times m \times 3 \times n$

67. $3 \times t \times a \times d$
69. $2 \times a \times 2 \times c$
71. $7 \times b \times c \times n$
73. $4 \times c \times 4 \times y$
75. $4 \times y \times x \times z$
77. $2 \times b \times 7 \times a$
79. $6 \times 4 \times c \times d$
68. $10 \times x \times 2 \times y$
70. $6 \times t \times 3 \times z$
72. $4 \times u \times 2 \times t$
74. $5 \times c \times 3 \times e$
76. $2 \times t \times d \times h$
78. $a \times x \times y \times b$
80. $5 \times x \times 4 \times z$

Example

Solve the equation $2x + 3 = 15$

$$2x + 3 = 15$$
So $2x = 12$
So $x = 6$.

Exercise 9.5

Solve the following equations.

1. $4a = 28$
2. $t - 7 = 3$
3. $5x = 40$
4. $9y = 45$
5. $8 - c = 0$
6. $d + 11 = 20$
7. $2m = 18$
8. $11t = 88$
9. $x + 13 = 21$
10. $x - 11 = 0$
11. $10y = 30$
12. $7u = 7$
13. $x - 5 = 11$
14. $2 + m = 39$
15. $12y = 36$
16. $8c = 64$
17. $3 - u = 1$
18. $t - 8 = 7$
19. $12d = 60$
20. $8x = 32$
21. $10 + y = 41$
22. $7x = 70$
23. $w + 9 = 22$
24. $9n = 63$
25. $4t = 44$
26. $10 - x = 10$
27. $t + 6 = 19$
28. $a - 11 = 17$
29. $6x = 0$
30. $13y = 0$
31. $2a + 1 = 11$
32. $3c + 2 = 14$
33. $4d - 3 = 17$
34. $6t + 1 = 13$
35. $2u + 5 = 11$
36. $4n - 3 = 5$
37. $5y - 1 = 19$
38. $3a + 2 = 17$
39. $4x + 3 = 27$
40. $5y + 2 = 27$
41. $6d - 1 = 17$
42. $2y - 3 = 7$
43. $3t + 2 = 20$
44. $2x - 4 = 16$
45. $7x + 1 = 15$
46. $6y - 2 = 28$
47. $8x + 1 = 9$
48. $10a + 5 = 5$
49. $9c - 3 = 24$
50. $5d + 2 = 37$

Solving harder equations

Examples

(a) Solve the equation $2x = 8$

$$2x = 8$$
So $x = 4$

(b) Solve the equation $x + 5 = 8$

$$x + 5 = 8$$
So $x = 3$

Exercise 9.4

Solve the following equations.
(Remember that $3a$ means $3 \times a$)

1. $a + 7 = 9$
2. $c - 3 = 5$
3. $3c = 12$
4. $7d = 14$
5. $d - 2 = 7$
6. $4e = 20$
7. $2y = 10$
8. $e + 3 = 11$
9. $h + 8 = 9$
10. $3t = 9$
11. $2u = 6$
12. $6w = 18$
13. $m + 11 = 15$
14. $t - 1 = 11$
15. $4m = 8$
16. $5h = 15$
17. $9 - c = 2$
18. $2 + u = 7$
19. $y - 3 = 1$
20. $2k = 8$
21. $1 + a = 13$
22. $c - 9 = 2$
23. $5n = 25$
24. $7t = 21$
25. $6a = 12$
26. $3 + d = 9$
27. $5c = 50$
28. $5 - e = 4$
29. $h + 2 = 20$
30. $11 - k = 8$
31. $n - 4 = 10$
32. $3e = 21$
33. $2x = 12$
34. $3 + x = 21$
35. $4k = 4$
36. $x + 4 = 17$
37. $8n = 0$
38. $13 - y = 10$
39. $7t = 49$
40. $9x = 36$
41. $a + 5 = 12$
42. $7 + x = 13$
43. $8y = 40$
44. $7x = 56$
45. $m - 2 = 16$
46. $6c = 54$
47. $8 + t = 16$
48. $3d = 18$
49. $12 - x = 9$
50. $9 + y = 17$

Values of harder expressions

Example

Find the value of each of the following expressions when $a = 2, c = 5$.

(a) $\quad a + c$
$\quad = 2 + 5$
$\quad = 7$

(b) $\quad a + 11 - c$
$\quad = 2 + 11 - 5$
$\quad = 8$

(c) $\quad 4c$
$\quad = 20$

(d) $\quad 3a + c$
$\quad = 6 + 5$
$\quad = 11$

Algebra

Exercise 9.6

Part A.

Find the value of each of the following expressions when $a = 5$, $b = 4$, $c = 2$.

1. $a + 3$
2. $b + 2$
3. $6c$
4. $3b$
5. $c - 1$
6. $a + 8$
7. $5a$
8. $a + b$
9. $4b$
10. $a - c$
11. $b + c$
12. $7c$
13. $a + b + c$
14. $11a$
15. $c + 9$
16. $a - b$
17. $8c$
18. $a + b - c$
19. $9a$
20. $b + 37$
21. $2a - 3$
22. $3c + 2$
23. $4a + b$
24. $3b - a$
25. ab
26. ac
27. bc
28. $2bc$
29. abc
30. $ac + 5$

Part B.
Repeat part A, this time with $a = 7$, $b = 5$, $c = 3$.

Part C.
Repeat part A, this time with $a = 10$, $b = 6$, $c = 5$.

Part D.
Repeat part A, this time with $a = 8$, $b = 3$, $c = 1$.

Part E.
Repeat part A, this time with $a = 11$, $b = 9$, $c = 4$.

Examples

If $a = 7$, $b = 2$, $c = 5$ find the value of

(a) $\quad 3a + 7b$
$\quad\quad = 21 + 14$
$\quad\quad = 35$

(b) $\quad 7c - 10b$
$\quad\quad = 35 - 20$
$\quad\quad = 15$

(c) $\quad 2a + 3c - 4$
$\quad\quad = 14 + 15 - 4$
$\quad\quad = 25.$

Exercise 9.7

Given that $a = 2$, $b = 3$, $c = 6$, $d = 10$, find the value of each of the given expressions.

1. $2a + 3b$
2. $3a + 4c$
3. $5c - 2b$
4. $5a + 3d$
5. $4c - 2d$
6. $3a + 2c$
7. $4d - 7a$
8. $2a + 3d$
9. $2c - 4a$
10. $6b + 2d$
11. $7b + 4c$
12. $2d - 3a$
13. $6c - 2b$
14. $7d - 8c$
15. $4a + 5c$
16. $5d + 5b$
17. $6c - 9b$
18. $3d - 12a$
19. $10c - 3b$
20. $2a + 11b$
21. $7a + 3c$
22. $3d - 10a$
23. $4c + 7d$
24. $3d - 5c$
25. $10c - 5a$
26. $7a + 9d$
27. $8c - 7a$
28. $6a + 4c$
29. $10c - 2a$
30. $11c - 3b$
31. $3a + 7b - 2$
32. $6d + 3a - 50$
33. $7a - 3b + 11$
34. $6b + 2c + 10$
35. $4c + 2a - 28$
36. $7a + 3c - 9$
37. $4d + 5 - 3c$
38. $20 + a + 7b$
39. $3 + 2d - c$
40. $4a + 10c - 1$
41. $6a + 10b + 2c$
42. $3a + 2d + 5c$
43. $5d + 4a - 8b$
44. $3c + 2b - 11a$
45. $12a - b + 3c$
46. $4b + 4c - 7a$
47. $2d - 4a + 5b$
48. $3a + 4c + 12b$
49. $4c - 7a + 8b$
50. $2d + 4c + 13a$

Powers and indices

7^2 means 7×7, or 7 multiplied by itself.
5^2 means 5×5, or 5 multiplied by itself.
$2 \cdot 3^2$ means $2 \cdot 3 \times 2 \cdot 3$
a^2 means $a \times a$

7^3 means $7 \times 7 \times 7$
5^4 means $5 \times 5 \times 5 \times 5$
2^7 means $2 \times 2 \times 2 \times 2 \times 2 \times 2 \times 2$

Notice that 7^2 does *not* mean 7×2!
$\quad\quad\quad\quad\quad 5^4$ does *not* mean 5×4!

a^2 is pronounced 'a squared'.
a^3 is pronounced 'a cubed'.
a^4 is pronounced 'a to the power of 4'.

Examples

Find the value of each of the following.

(a) $\quad 3^2 = 3 \times 3$
$\quad\quad\quad = 9$

(b) $\quad 6^2 = 6 \times 6$
$\quad\quad\quad = 36$

(c) $\quad 2^3 = 2 \times 2 \times 2$
$\quad\quad\quad = 8$

(d) $\quad 1^2 = 1 \times 1$
$\quad\quad\quad = 1$

(e) $\quad 2^4 = 2 \times 2 \times 2 \times 2$
$\quad\quad\quad = 16$

Exercise 9.8

Work out the following.

1. 4^2
2. 10^2
3. 7^2
4. 2^2
5. 5^2
6. 8^2
7. 1^2
8. 9^2
9. 2^3
10. 1^3
11. 0^2
12. 12^2
13. 3^3
14. 4^3
15. 1^4
16. 2^4
17. 10^3
18. 1^7
19. 11^2
20. 5^3

Algebra

Examples

Solve the following equations

(a) $x^2 = 16$
So $x = 4$.

(b) $d^2 + 3 = 28$
So $d^2 = 25$
So $d = 5$.

Find the value of the following expressions when $x = 5$.

(a) $\quad x^2 - 2$
$= 25 - 2$
$= 23$

(b) $\quad x^2 + 3x + 4$
$= 25 + 15 + 4$
$= 44$.

Exercise 9.9

In questions 1 to 20, solve the given equation.

1. $x^2 = 9$
2. $y^2 = 25$
3. $a^2 = 4$
4. $d^2 = 1$
5. $x^2 = 100$
6. $b^2 = 16$
7. $y^2 = 81$
8. $a^2 = 36$
9. $c^2 = 49$
10. $x^2 = 64$
11. $a^2 = 144$
12. $t^2 = 0$
13. $y^2 - 1 = 3$
14. $a^2 + 1 = 50$
15. $y^2 - 3 = 97$
16. $u^2 + 4 = 40$
17. $x^2 + 3 = 52$
18. $40 - x^2 = 31$
19. $a^3 = 8$
20. $x^3 = 1000$

In questions 21 to 40, find the value of the given expression, given that $x = 3$, $y = 4$, $a = 1$.
(Remember that a^2 means $a \times a$, but $2a$ means $2 \times a$.)

21. $x^2 + 1$
22. $y^2 + 1$
23. $a^2 + 5$
24. $x^2 + 10$
25. $y^2 - 4$
26. $x^2 - 7$
27. $a^2 + 22$
28. $x^2 + y^2$
29. $y^2 - x^2$
30. $a^2 + x^2$
31. $7 + x^2$
32. $20 - y^2$
33. $y^2 - y$
34. $y^2 + x$
35. $y^2 - 2y$
36. $4x + x^2$
37. $x^3 - 5$
38. $x^3 + 3x$
39. $xa - 1 + y$
40. $x^2 + y^2 + a^2$

Examples

Find the value of each of the following.

(a) $0 \cdot 3^2 = 0 \cdot 3 \times 0 \cdot 3$
$= 0 \cdot 09$

(b) $(\frac{1}{2})^2 = \frac{1}{2} \times \frac{1}{2}$
$= \frac{1}{4}$

(c) $(\frac{2}{3})^2 = \frac{2}{3} \times \frac{2}{3}$
$= \frac{4}{9}$

(d) $0 \cdot 2^3 = 0 \cdot 2 \times 0 \cdot 2 \times 0 \cdot 2$
$= 0 \cdot 008$

Notice that $0 \cdot 3^2$ is *not* equal to $0 \cdot 9$!

Exercise 9.10

Work out the following

1. $0 \cdot 4^2$
2. $0 \cdot 2^2$
3. $0 \cdot 1^2$
4. $0 \cdot 5^2$
5. $0 \cdot 6^2$
6. $0 \cdot 9^2$
7. $0 \cdot 8^2$
8. $0 \cdot 7^2$
9. $(\frac{1}{3})^2$
10. $(\frac{1}{4})^2$
11. $(\frac{3}{4})^2$
12. $(\frac{2}{5})^2$
13. $(\frac{3}{10})^2$
14. $(\frac{3}{8})^2$
15. $(\frac{1}{9})^2$
16. $(\frac{5}{6})^2$
17. $0 \cdot 2^3$
18. $0 \cdot 1^4$
19. $(\frac{1}{2})^3$
20. $(\frac{1}{10})^3$
21. $0 \cdot 03^2$
22. $0 \cdot 04^2$
23. $(\frac{7}{10})^2$
24. $(\frac{1}{100})^2$
25. $(\frac{3}{10})^3$
26. $(\frac{2}{7})^2$
27. $0 \cdot 12^2$
28. $(\frac{1}{2})^5$
29. $0 \cdot 004^2$
30. $0 \cdot 02^3$

In questions 31 to 50, solve the given equation.

31. $t^2 = 0$
32. $a^2 = 1$
33. $x^2 = 49$
34. $y^2 = 121$
35. $x^2 + 1 = 10$
36. $a^2 + 1 = 37$
37. $x^2 + 2 = 27$
38. $b^2 - 5 = 11$
39. $x^2 + 8 = 8$
40. $y^2 - 10 = 15$
41. $c^2 + 1 = 2$
42. $10 - a^2 = 6$
43. $20 - t^2 = 11$
44. $150 - h^2 = 50$
45. $b^3 = 27$
46. $x^5 = 32$
47. $a^2 = 900$
48. $d^2 = 4900$
49. $t^2 = 1600$
50. $x^2 = 10\,000$

In questions 51 to 70, find the value of the expression, given that $a = 5$, $b = 3$, $c = 4$.
(Remember that a^2 means $a \times a$, but $2a$ means $2 \times a$.)

51. $a^2 + 3$
52. $b^2 - 7$
53. $22 - c^2$
54. $a^2 + c^2$
55. $3a + 2$
56. $7c - 3$
57. $a^2 + 2b$
58. $c^2 + 2c$
59. $c^2 - 3a$
60. $4a + b^2$
61. $ac + 3$
62. $a^2 - bc$
63. $7c + b^2$
64. $ab + c^2$
65. $5c + a^2 + 3$
66. $c^2 + a^2 + 2b$
67. $6a + bc - 2$
68. $6a - 4b + c^2$
69. $a^2 + b^2 + c^2$
70. $2a + b^2 - 2c$

10 Area

Triangles

The easiest way to find the area of a triangle is to multiply its base by its height and then divide the result by 2.

We can write this more clearly by using algebra as follows.

If A stands for the area of the triangle, b stands for its base and h stands for its height, then

$$A = \frac{bh}{2}$$

(where bh means $b \times h$, as is usual in algebra)

Example

Find the area of the triangle below, giving your answer as a number of squares.

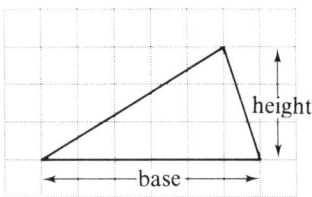

The base of this triangle is 6
The height is 3

So the area is $\dfrac{6 \times 3}{2}$

$= \dfrac{18}{2}$

$= 9$ squares.

Exercise 10.1

In this exercise, copy down each triangle onto squared paper and then find its area, giving your answer as a number of squares.

1.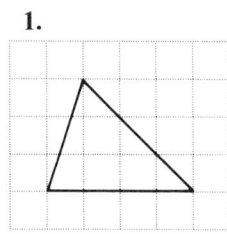

2.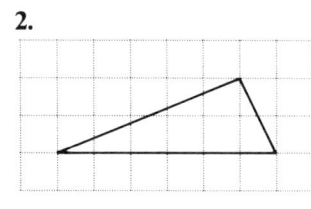

3.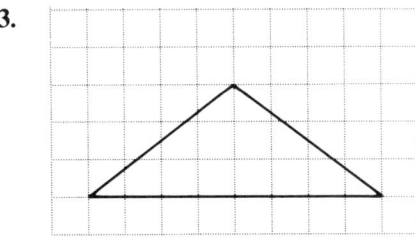

4.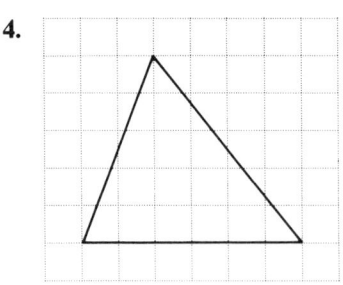

5.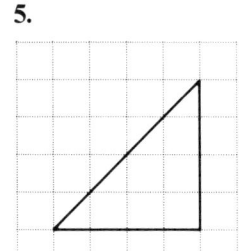

6.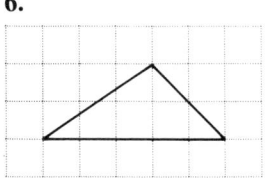

Area   67

7.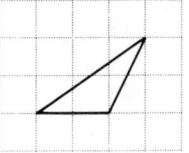

8.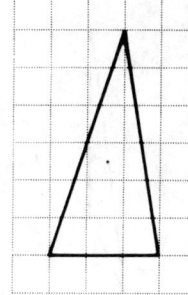

9.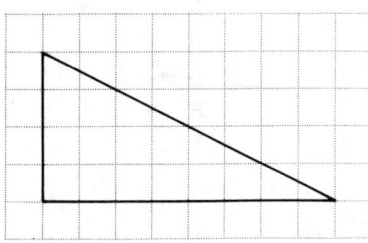

10.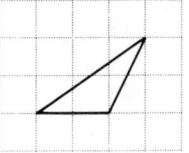

11.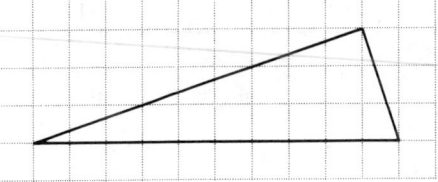

12.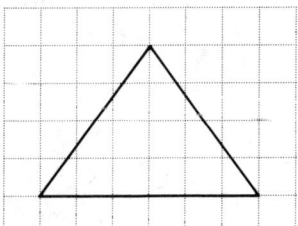

13.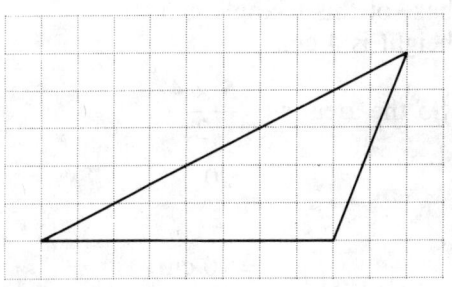

14.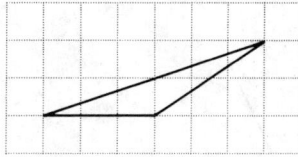

15.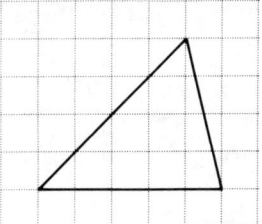

16.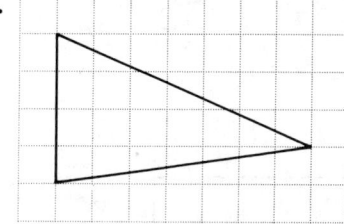

17.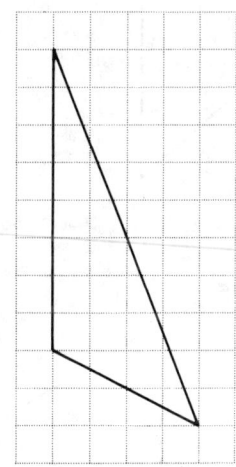

18.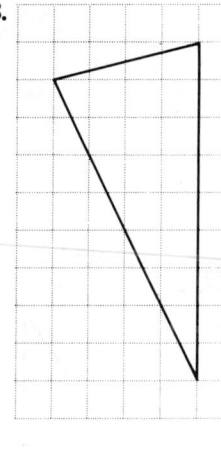

19.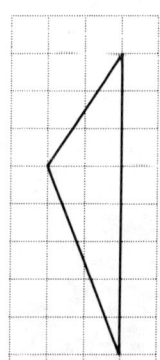

20.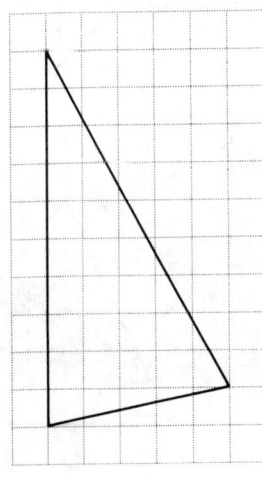

68 Area

21.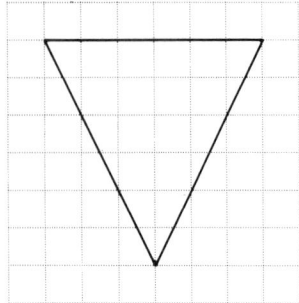

22.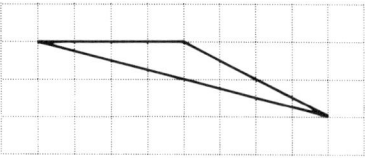

23.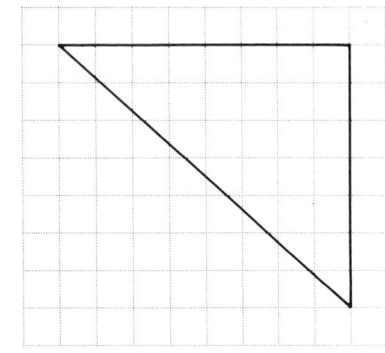

24. 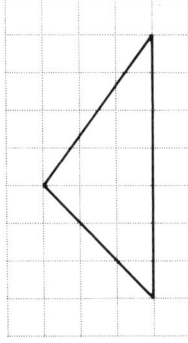 **25.**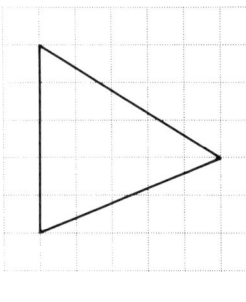

26.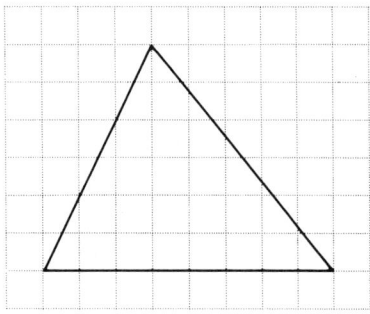

27.  **28.**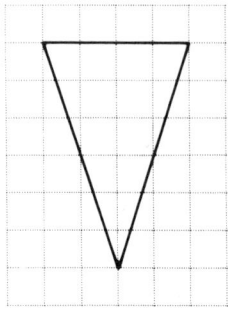

29.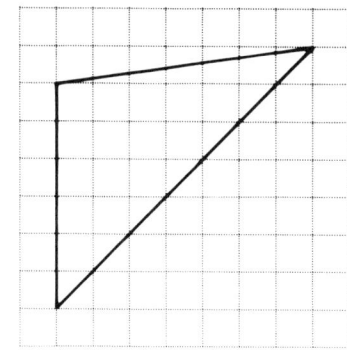

30.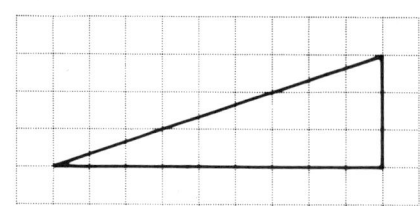

Example

Calculate the area of the triangle below.

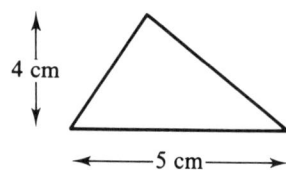

The base of this triangle is 5 cm.
The height is 4 cm.

$$\text{So the area is } \frac{5 \times 4}{2}$$
$$= \frac{20}{2}$$
$$= 10 \text{ cm}^2$$

Exercise 10.2

In each question use a pencil and ruler to make a neat labelled sketch of the triangle shown, and then calculate its area, giving your answer in the proper units.
 Do *not* draw the triangles to scale.

13. **14.**

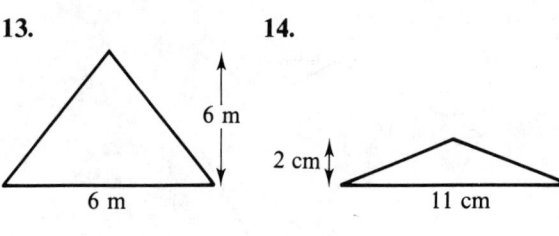

1. **2.** **15.**

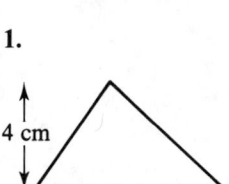 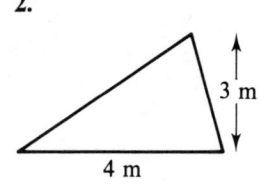 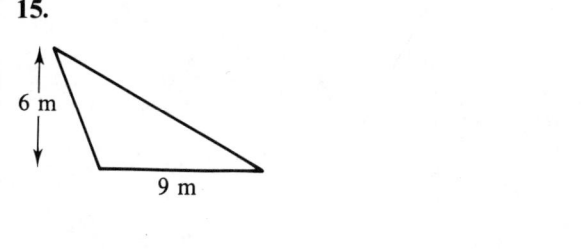

3. **4.**

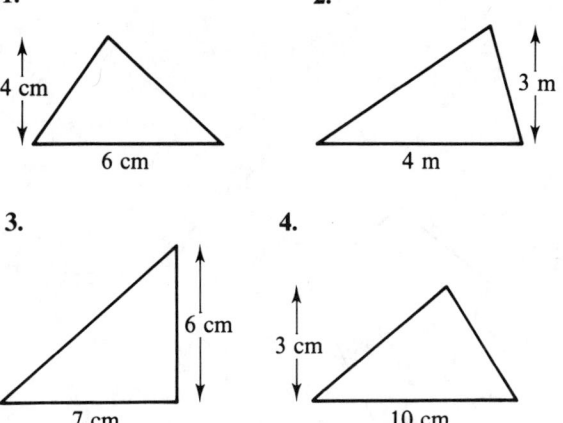

Kites

Exercise 10.3

In questions **1** to **15**, make a neat copy of the kite onto squared paper and then find its area by dividing it into two triangles.

5. **6.**

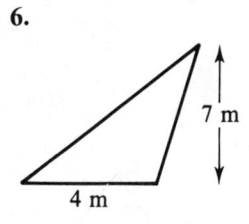 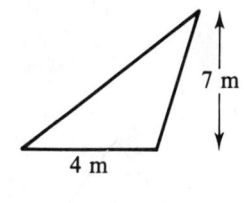

1. **2.**

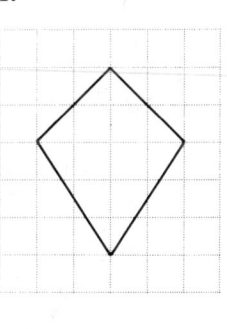 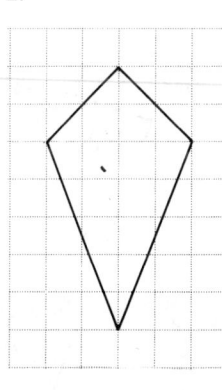

7. **8.**

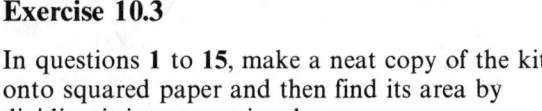 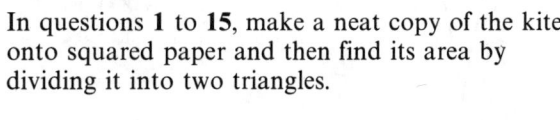

9. **10.**

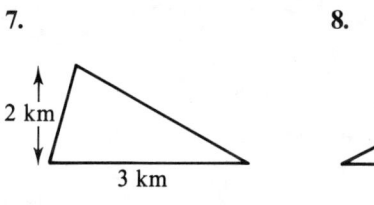 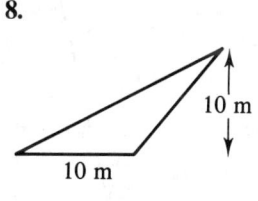

3.

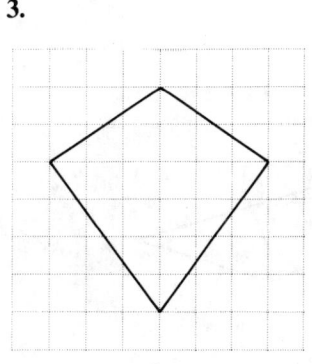

11. **12.**

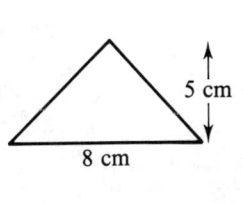 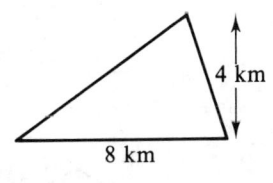
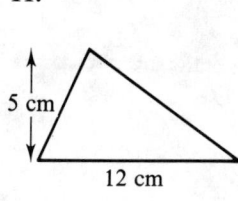
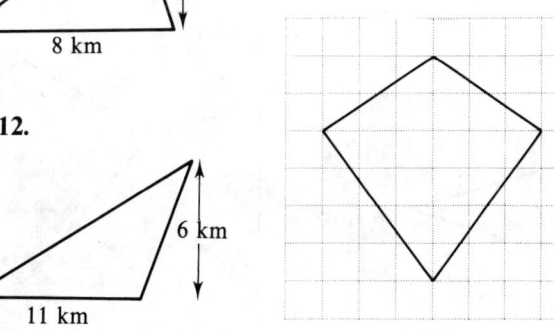

70 Area

4.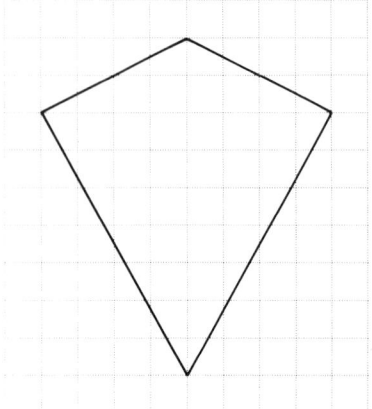

5.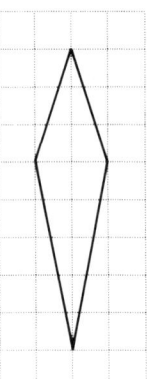

6.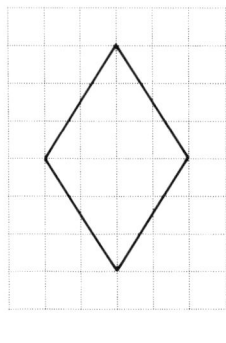

7.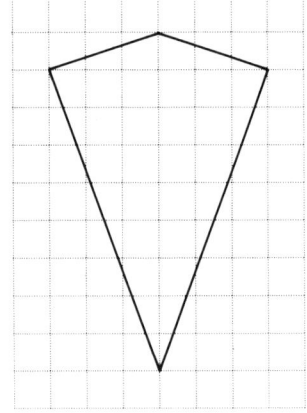

8.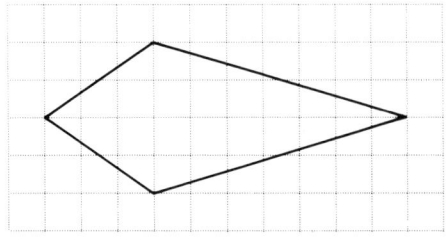

9.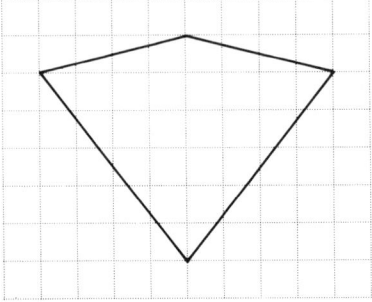

10.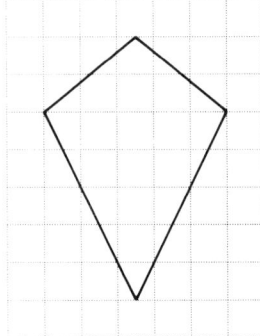

11.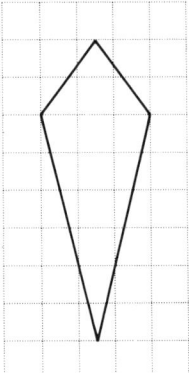

12.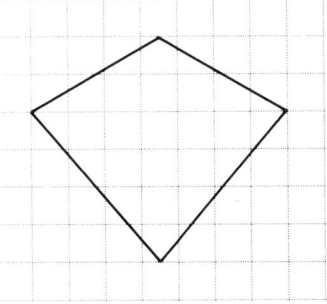

Area 71

13.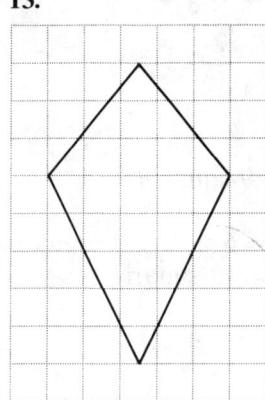

14.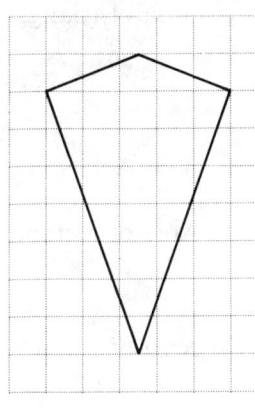

20.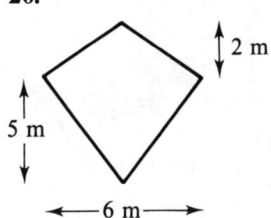

21.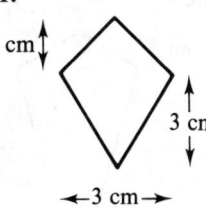

15.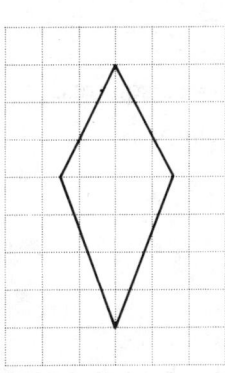

22.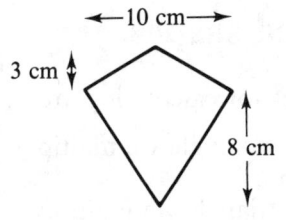

23.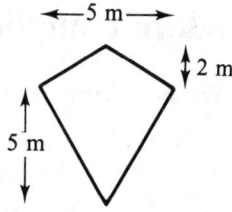

24.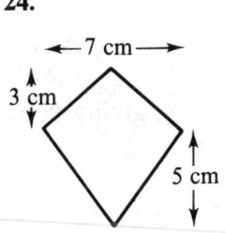

25.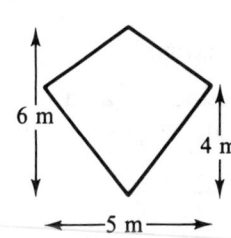

In questions **16** to **30** calculate the area of the kite, giving your answer in the proper units. Make sure you draw a neat sketch of the kite first.

16.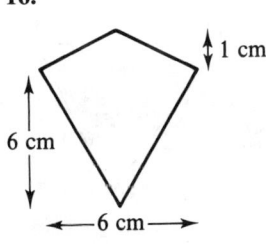

17.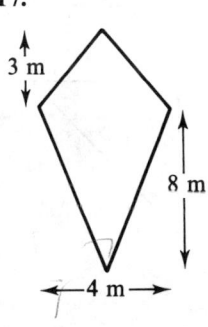

26.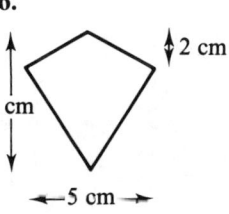

27.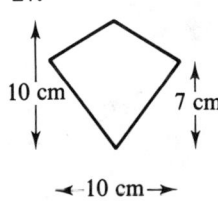

28.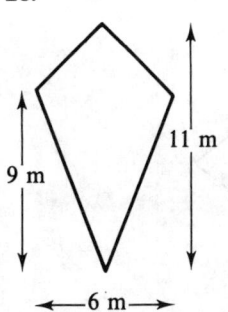

29.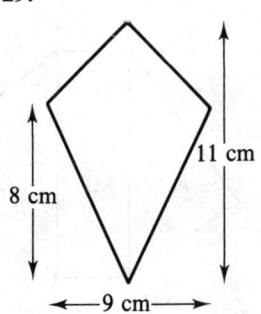

18.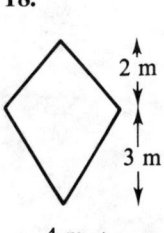

19.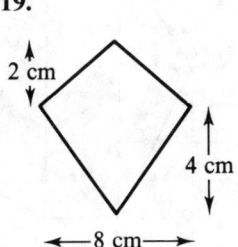

72 Area

30.

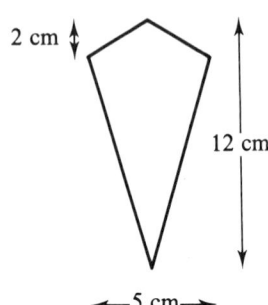

More complicated shapes

We now know two rules for calculating areas.

To find the area of a rectangle we multiply its length by its breadth.

To find the area of a triangle we multiply its base by its height and then divide the result by 2.

Example

Find the area of the shape below, giving your answer as a number of squares.

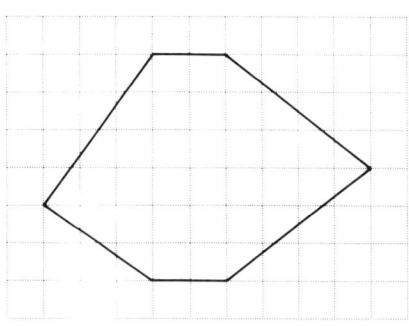

We divide up the shape as shown.

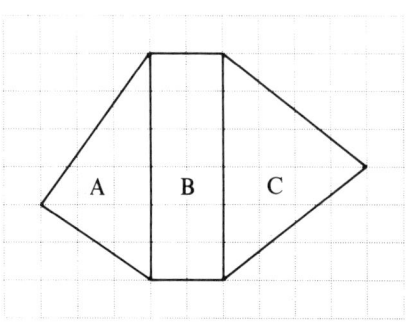

Area of triangle A = $\dfrac{6 \times 3}{2}$

$= \dfrac{18}{2}$

$= 9$ squares.

Area of rectangle B = 6×2
$= 12$ squares.

Area of triangle C = $\dfrac{6 \times 4}{2}$

$= \dfrac{24}{2}$

$= 12$ squares.

So the total area of the shape is

$9 + 12 + 12$
$= 33$ squares.

Exercise 10.4

In questions **1** to **7** copy the shape onto squared paper and find its area, giving your answer as a number of squares.

1. 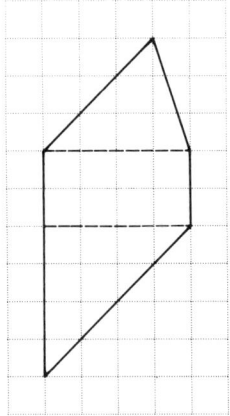 2.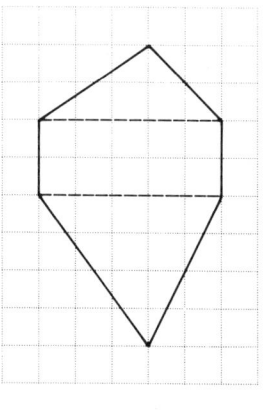

3.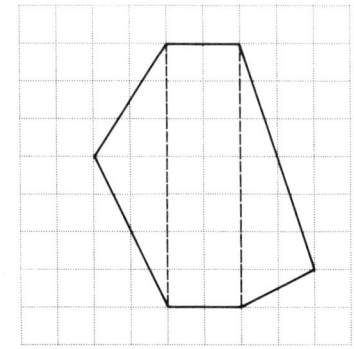

Area 73

4.
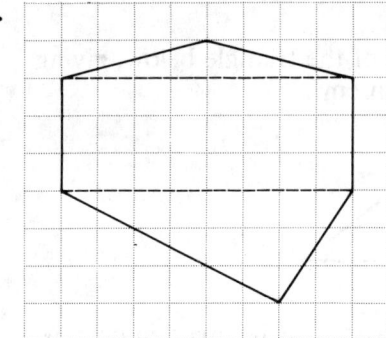

5.
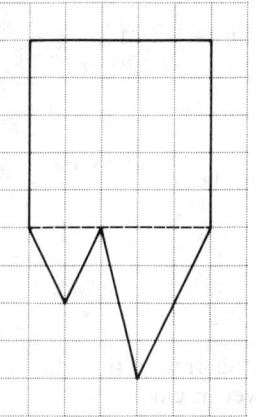

6.
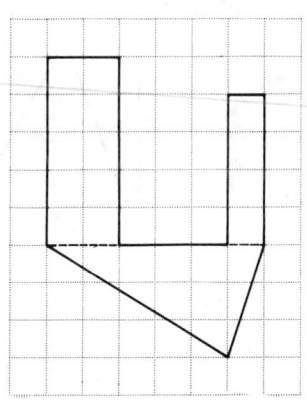

7.
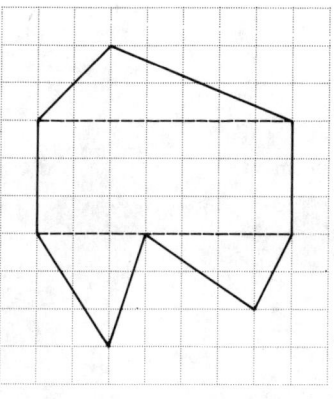

In questions **8** to **18** calculate the area of the given shape, giving your answer in the proper units.

8.   9.
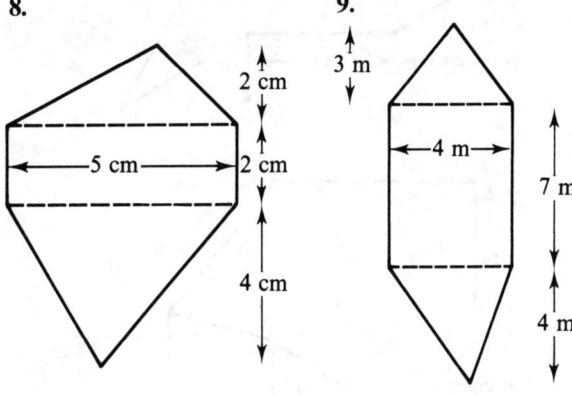

10.
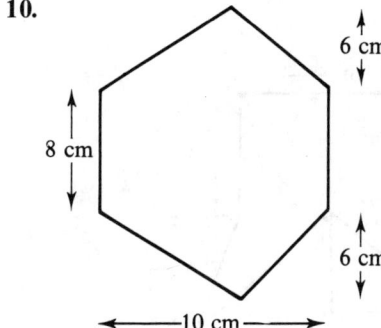

11.
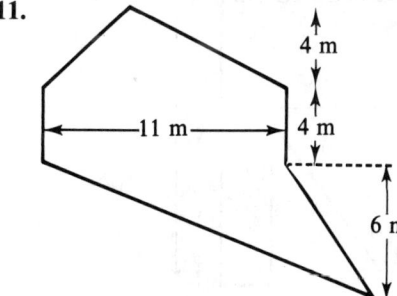

12.
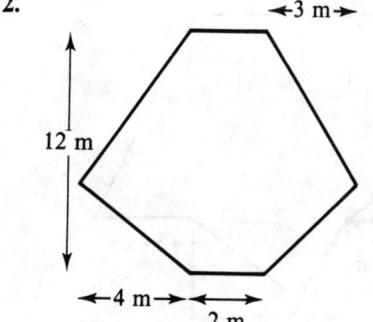

74 Area

13.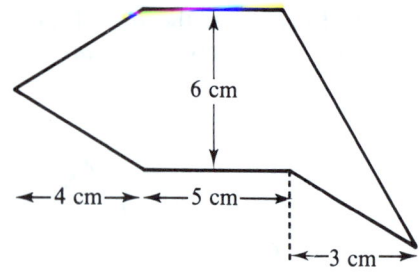

14.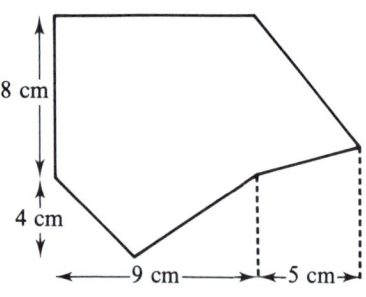

15.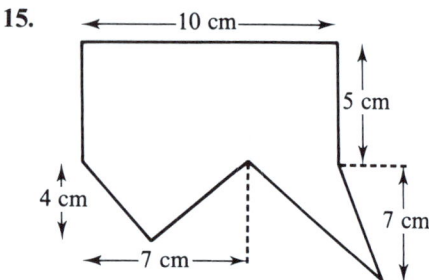

16.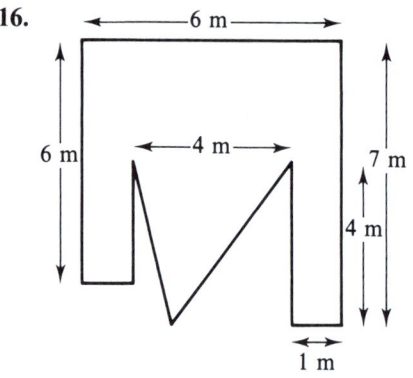

17.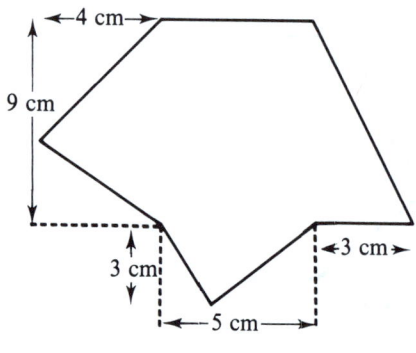

Example

Find the area of the triangle below, giving your answer in cm².

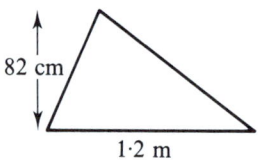

Since the answer must be given in cm², we must make sure all lengths are in cm.

The base of this triangle is 1·2 m
= 120 cm.

The height of the triangle is 82 cm.

So the area of the triangle is $\dfrac{120 \times 82}{2}$

= 4920 cm².

Exercise 10.5

In questions **1** to **5** find the area of the triangle shown, giving your answer in cm².

1.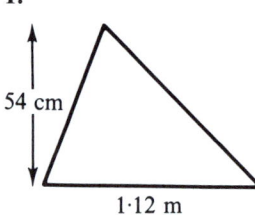

2.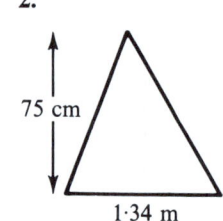

3.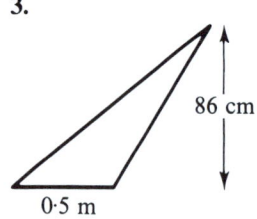

4.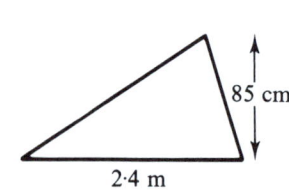

5.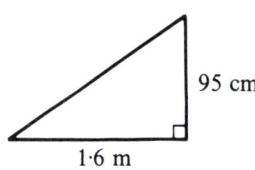

In questions **6–15** find the areas of the triangles in the table. Give your answer in cm².

	base	height
6.	0·75 m	42 cm
7.	65 cm	1·24 m
8.	90 cm	2·14 m
9.	70 cm	2 m
10.	140 cm	2·5 m
11.	1·22 m	65 cm
12.	0·25 m	66 cm
13.	110 cm	1·1 m
14.	0·1 m	12 cm
15.	95 cm	1·38 m

In questions **16 to 20** find the area of the triangle shown, giving your answer in m².

16. **17.**

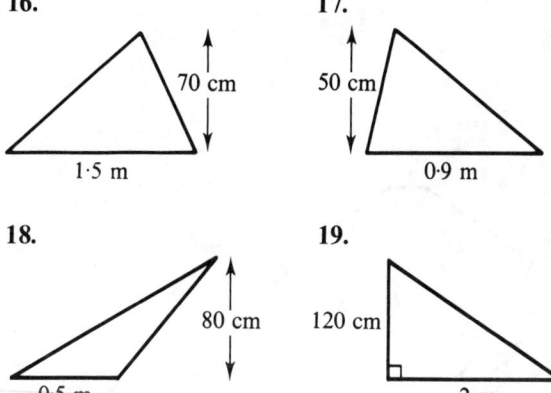

18. **19.**

20.

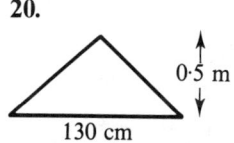

In questions **21 to 30** find the areas of the triangles in the table. Give your answer in m².

	base	height
21.	350 cm	3 m
22.	4 m	320 cm
23.	1·2 m	75 cm
24.	1·8 m	135 cm
25.	85 cm	2·2 m
26.	1·2 m	120 cm
27.	1·1 m	90 cm
28.	250 cm	2·4 m
29.	35 cm	0·3 m
30.	460 cm	5 m

11 Symmetry

Line symmetry

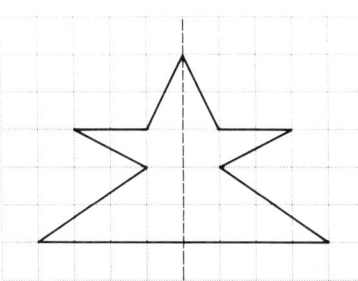

If we fold the shape above along the broken line, the left half fits exactly over the right half.

We say that such a shape has *line symmetry*, or that it is *symmetrical*. The broken line is called an *axis of symmetry*

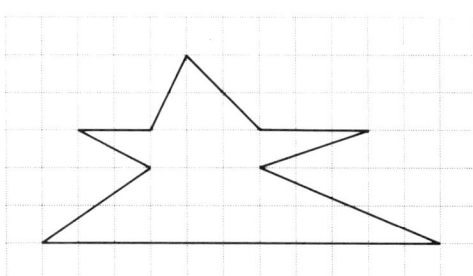

This shape is not symmetrical. It has no axis of symmetry.

Exercise 11.1

In this exercise, each shape shown has exactly one axis of symmetry. Copy each shape onto squared paper and mark in its axis of symmetry with a broken line, using colour if possible.

1.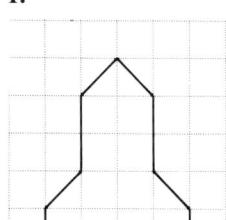

2.

3.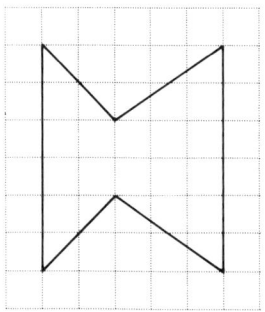

4.

5.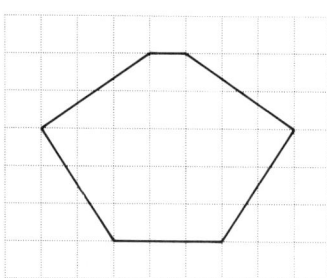

6.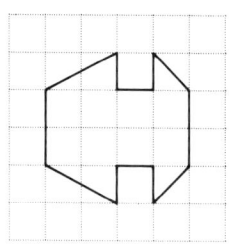

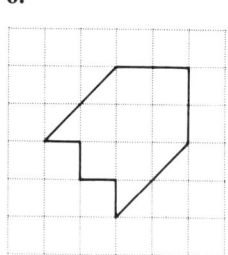

7.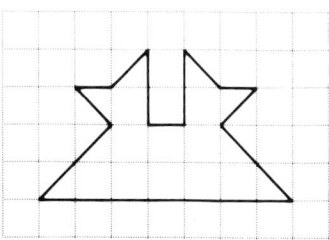

Symmetry 77

8.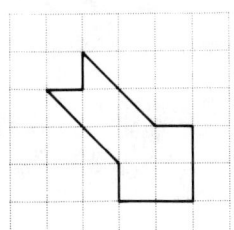

9.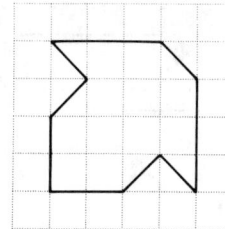

10.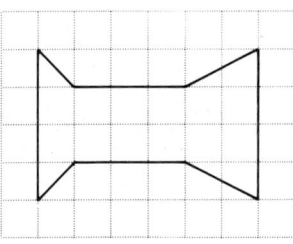

11.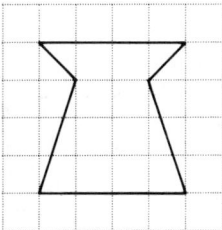

12.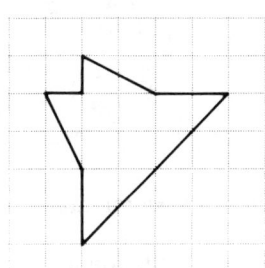

13.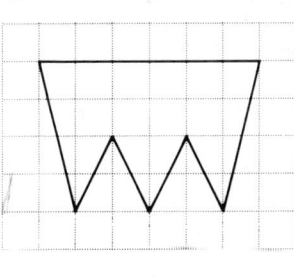

14.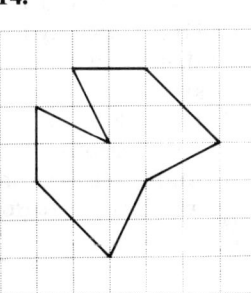

15.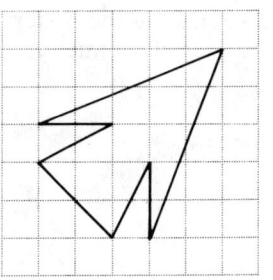

Exercise 11.2

Use colours to make a large, interesting pattern which has exactly one axis of symmetry. Make sure the axis of symmetry is clearly marked.

Some shapes have more than one axis of symmetry.

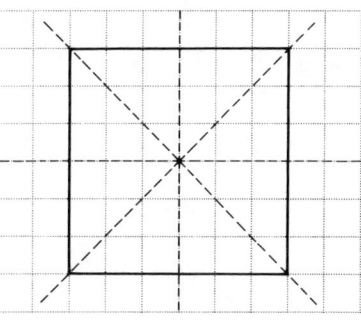

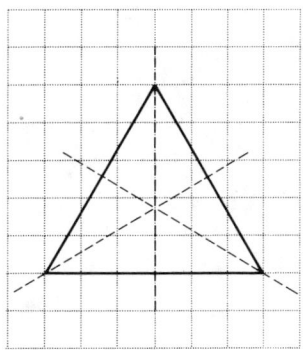

The square on the left has 4 axes of symmetry. The equilateral triangle on the right has 3 axes of symmetry.

Exercise 11.3

In questions **1** to **12** copy the shape onto squared paper and then draw in all the axes of symmetry with broken lines.

(In two of the questions there are no lines of symmetry! In these cases, just copy down the shape and leave it as it is.)

1.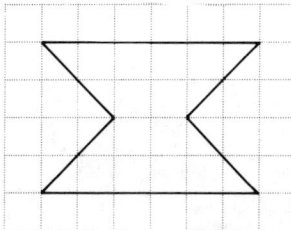

2.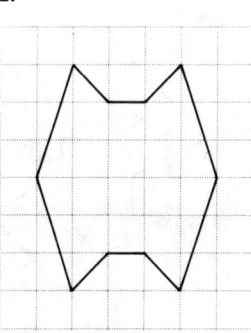

78 Symmetry

3.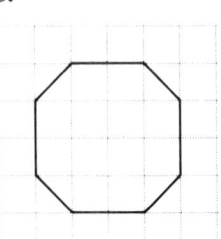

4.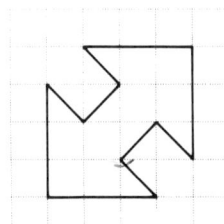

5.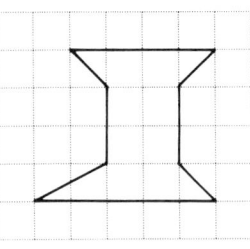

6.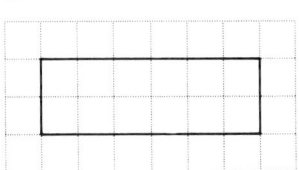

7.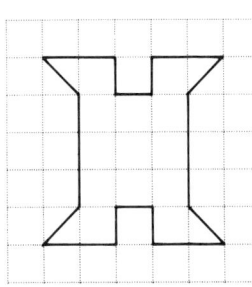

8.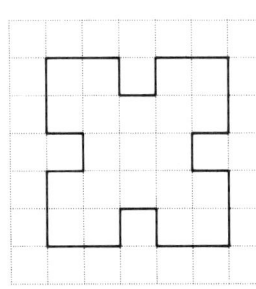

9.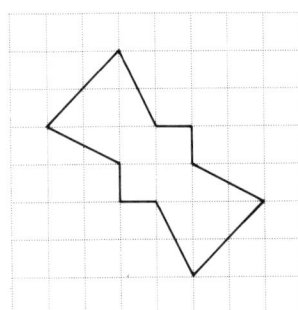

10.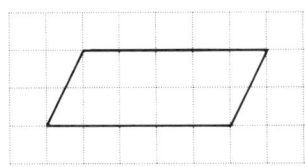

11.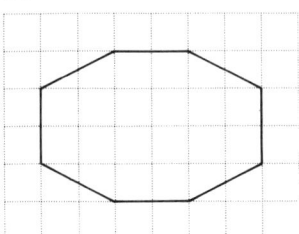

12.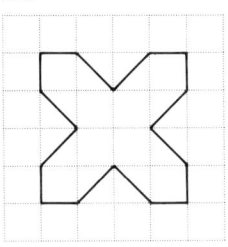

13. Construct (or trace) a regular hexagon and draw in its axes of symmetry.
14. Construct (or trace) a regular pentagon and draw in its axes of symmetry.
15. Draw a circle. Say why it would be unfair to ask you to draw in all the axes of symmetry.
16. Draw carefully round a 50p coin. On the shape that you get, draw in all the axes of symmetry.
17. Is any human face perfectly symmetrical? Give your reasons.
18. Make a list of common everyday objects which could reasonably be said to be symmetrical.

Exercise 11.4

1. Make a colourful, interesting pattern which has exactly two axes of symmetry.
2. Repeat question **1**, this time making the pattern so that it has exactly three axes of symmetry. (This is quite difficult.)

Symmetry

Exercise 11.5

This exercise consists of shapes having exactly one axis of symmetry. In each question *only part of the shape* is given, along with its axis of symmetry. In each case copy what is given onto squared paper and then carefully complete the shape.

1.

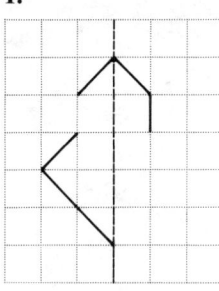

2.

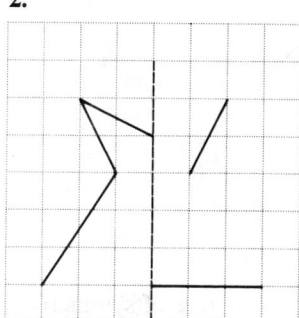

3.

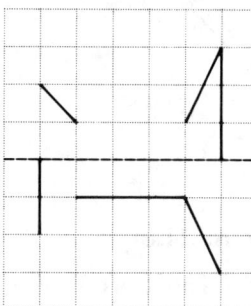

4.

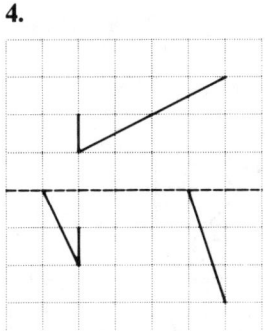

5.

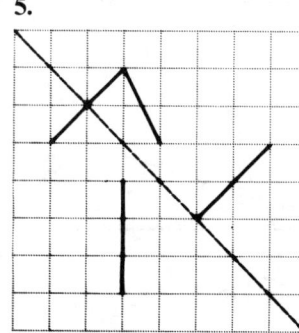

6.

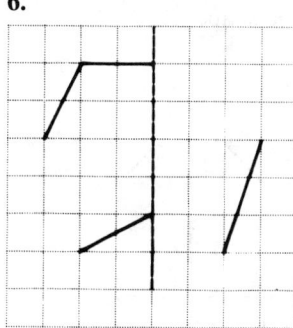

7.

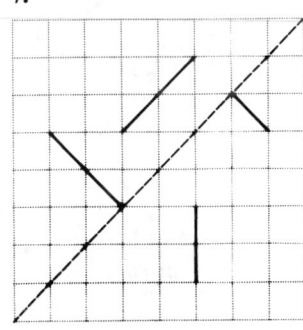

8.

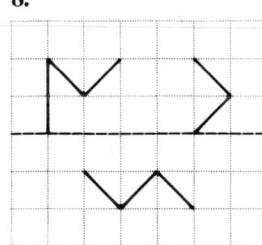

9.

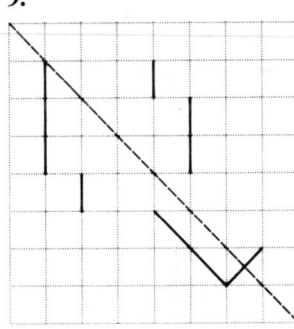

10.

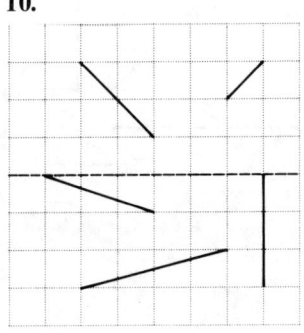

11.

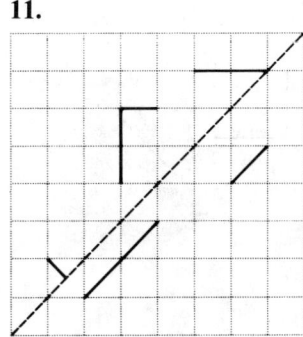

12.

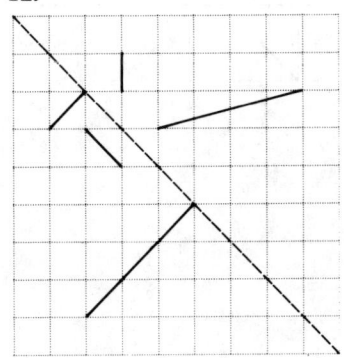

80 Symmetry

13.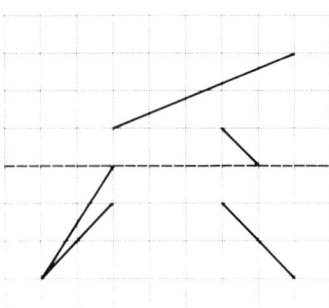

14.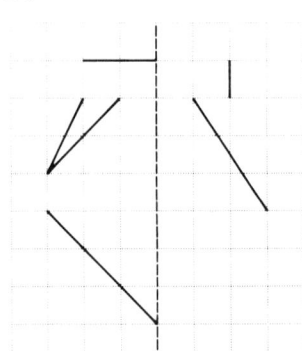

15.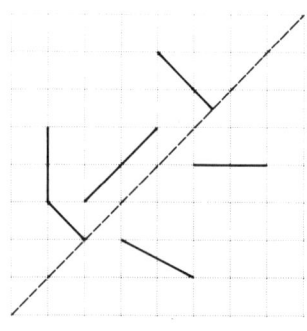

Exercise 11.6

This exercise consists of shapes having exactly two axes of symmetry. In each question *only part of the shape* is given, along with its two axes of symmetry. In each case copy what is given onto squared paper and then carefully complete the shape.

1.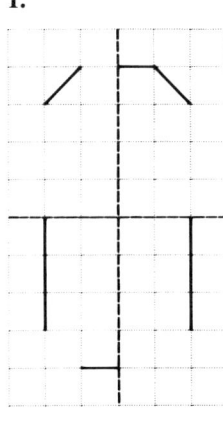

2.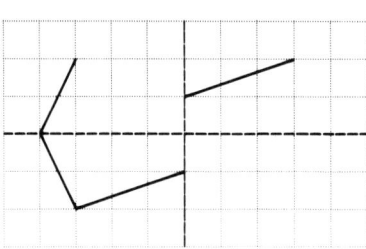

3.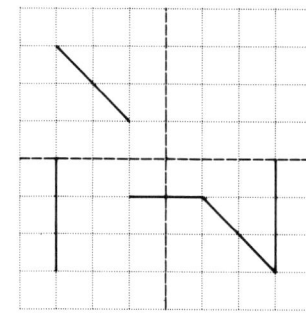

4.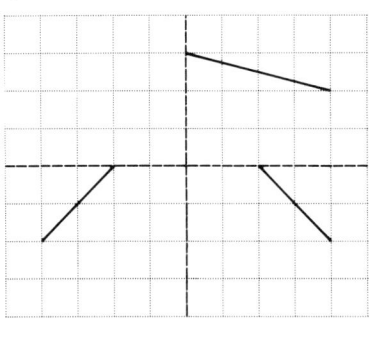

5.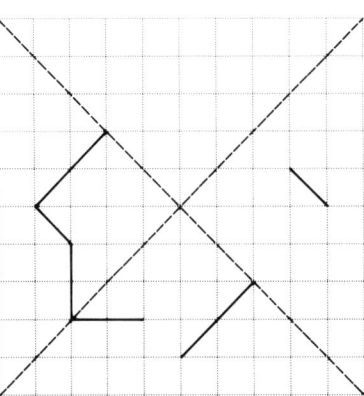

6.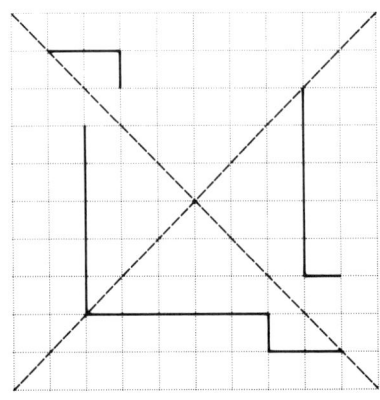

Symmetry 81

7.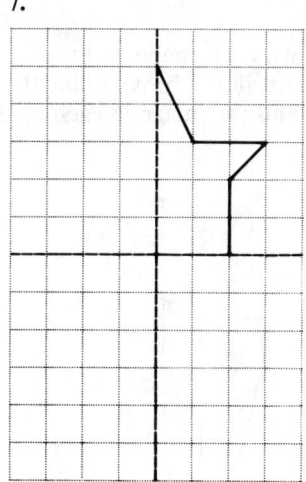

8.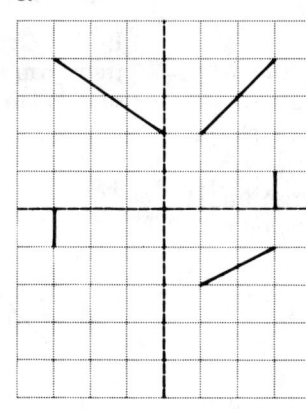

9.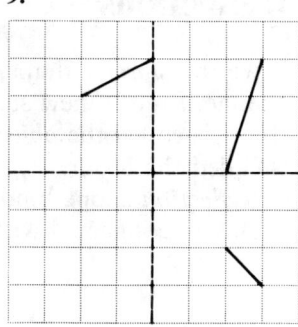

10.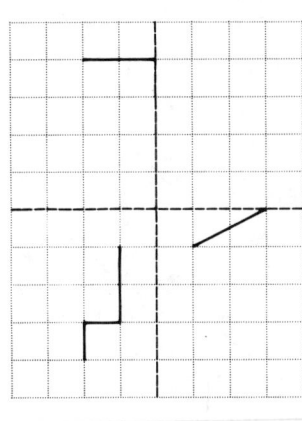

11.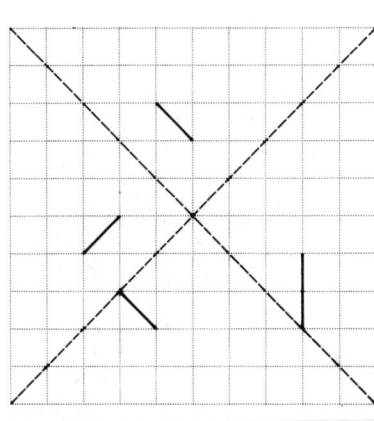

12.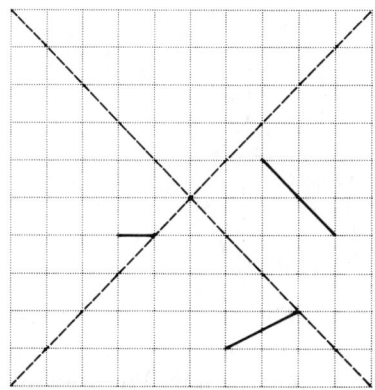

13.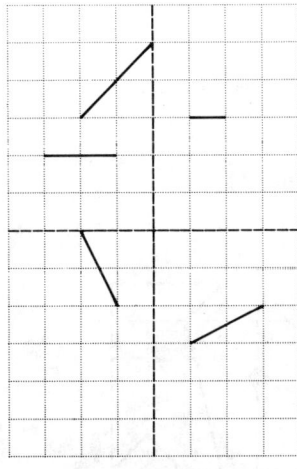

14.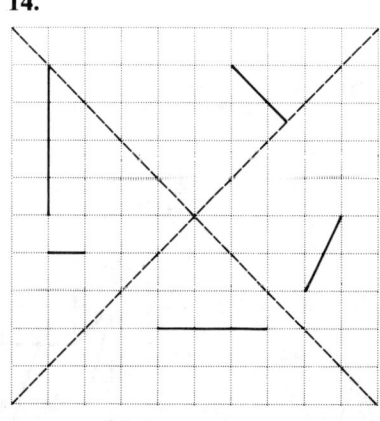

15.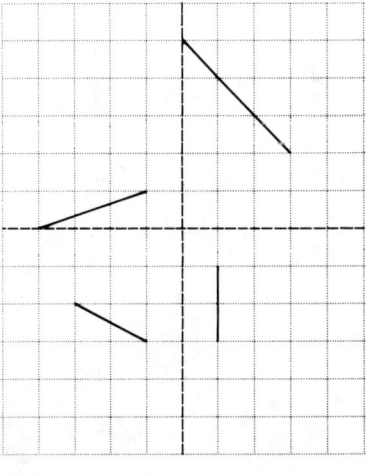

Reflections

If we *transform* a shape, this means that we change it into a new shape. The original shape is called the *object*, and the new shape is called the *image*.

Reflection is one kind of transformation. It is closely connected with the idea of line symmetry.

Example

Transform the object shown below by reflecting it in the broken line. Label the image.

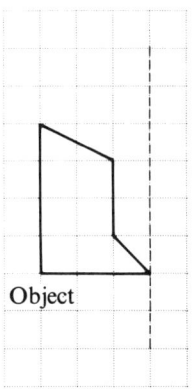

The broken line acts as a line of symmetry. It is sometimes called the mirror line. We draw in the image as shown below.

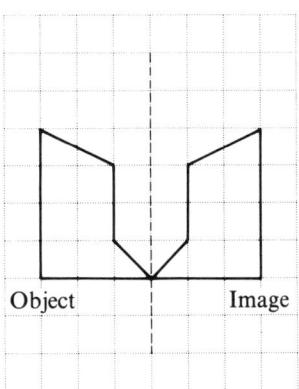

Exercise 11.7

In this exercise copy down each shape and then transform it by reflecting it in the broken line. Be sure to label the object and the image in each case.

1.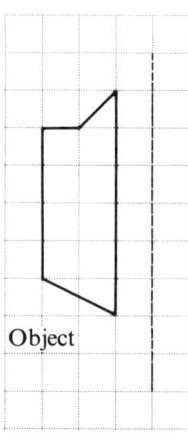

2.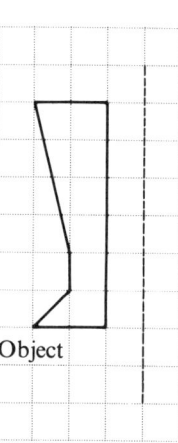

3.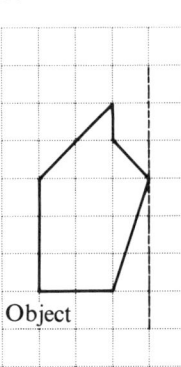

4.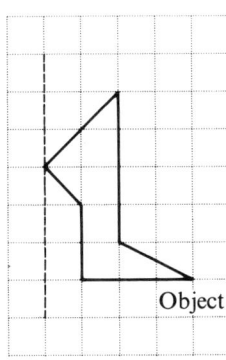

5.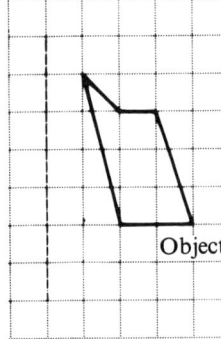

6.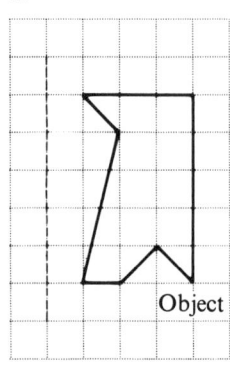

Symmetry 83

7.
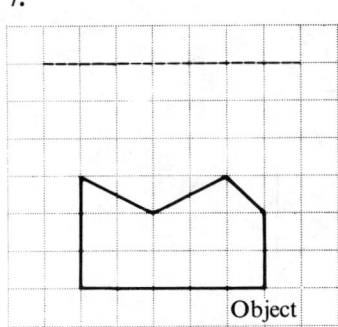

13.
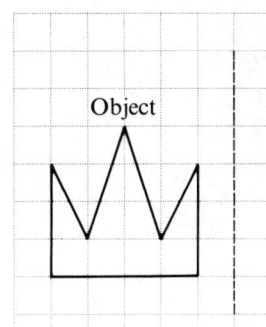

14.
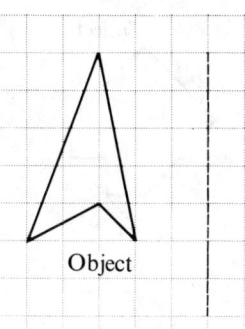

8.
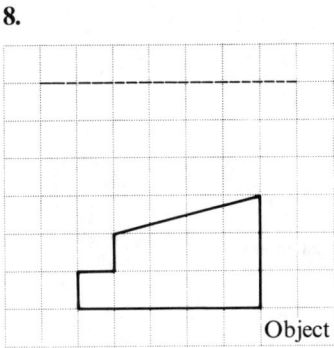

15.
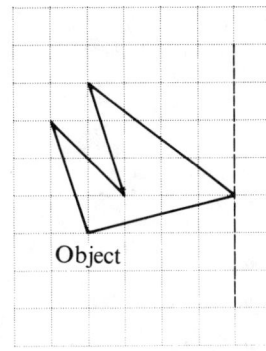

9.
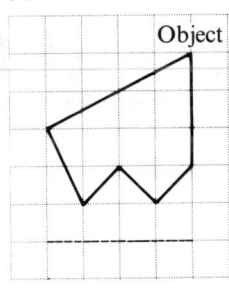

10.
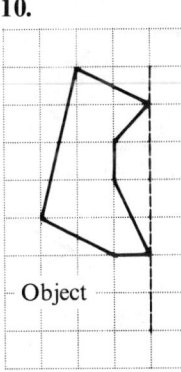

Exercise 11.8

In this exercise copy down each shape and then transform it by reflecting it in the broken line. Be sure to label the object and the image in each case.

1.
2.
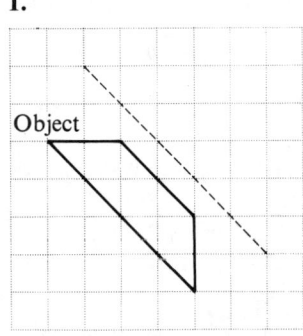
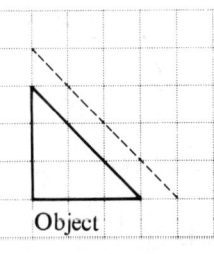

11.
12.
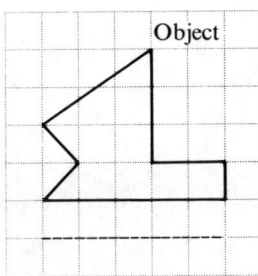
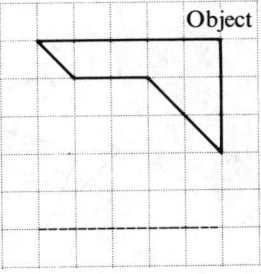

3.
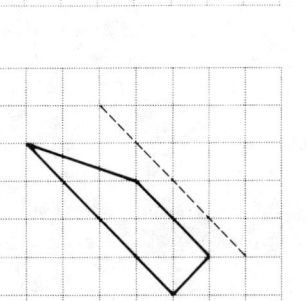

84 Symmetry

4.
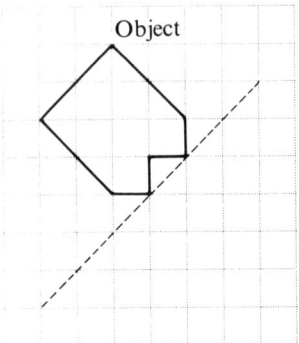

5.
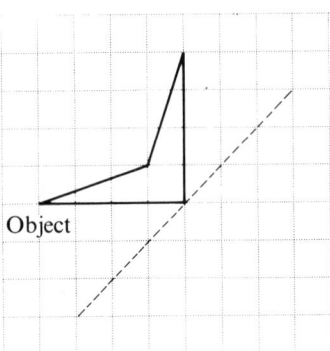

6.
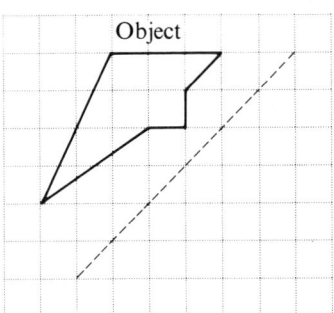

7.
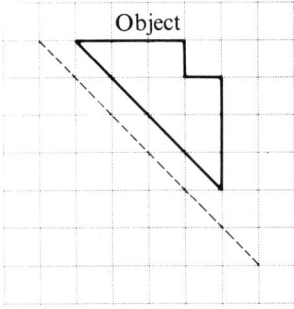

8.
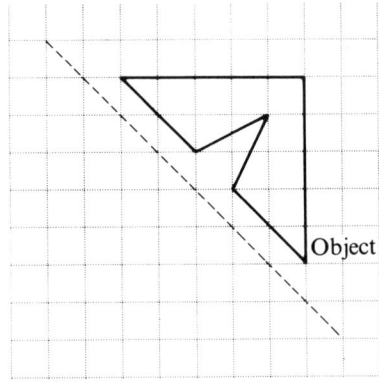

9.
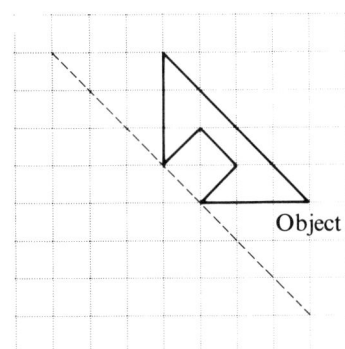

10.
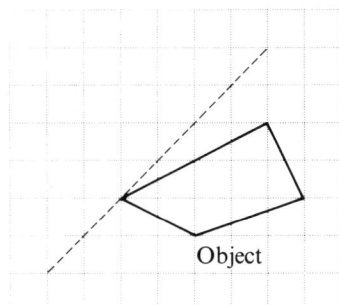

11.
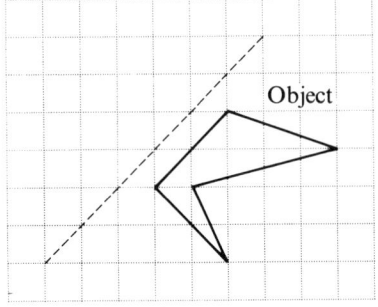

12.

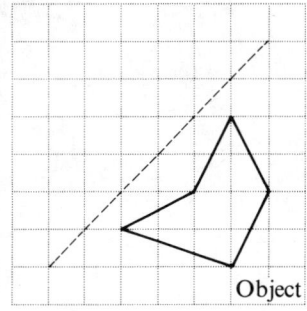

Object

Example

Reflect the words below in the broken line.

We draw the images of each word as follows.

| TOP | qOT |
| STUN | NUTS |

(mirror reflections shown)

Exercise 11.9

In each question, carefully copy the word given and the broken line, and then do the reflection. Try to get all the letters the same height and evenly spread out.

1. NEW
2. TIP
3. MAN
4. SET
5. TWO
6. COD
7. SIX
8. TRY

Example

(a) On a set of axes, draw and label the object formed by joining these points in order: (2, 1), (9, 2), (9, 3), (6, 3), (5, 4), (4, 3), (2, 3), (2, 1).

(b) Draw and label the straight line $y = 4$.

(c) Transform the object by reflecting it in the line $y = 4$. Label the image.

The line $y = 4$ is the line that passes through the points (0, 4), (1, 4), (2, 4), (3, 4), etc. When we have done the question we are left with the following diagram.

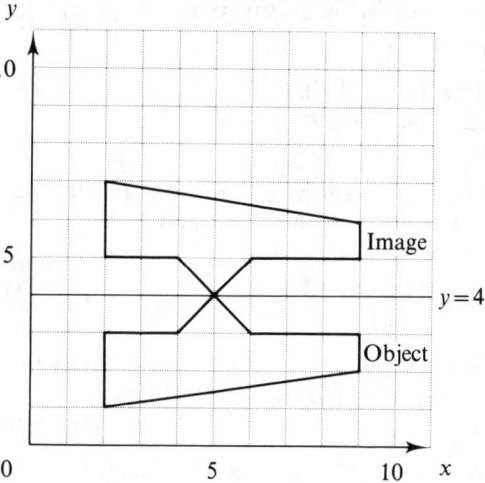

Exercise 11.10

In questions **1** to **10** draw a set of axes with x and y both going from 0 to 10. In each case draw and label the object given and then draw and label the line given. Transform the object by reflecting it in the line, and then label the image.

1. Object (7, 2), (8, 3), (9, 2), (9, 7), (10, 8), (6, 8), (7, 7), (7, 2)
   Line $x = 6$
   (i.e. the line that passes through (6,0), (6, 1), (6, 2), (6, 3), etc.)

2. Object (0, 5), (3, 5), (2, 6), (2, 9), (1, 10), (1, 6), (0, 5)
   Line $x = 3$
   (i.e. the line that passes through (3, 0), (3, 1), (3, 2), (3, 3), etc.)

3. Object (3, 1), (2, 4), (3, 3), (4, 4), (5, 3), (6, 4), (7, 3), (8, 4), (7, 1), (3, 1)
   Line $y = 5$
   (i.e. the line that passes through (0, 5), (1, 5), (2, 5), (3, 5), etc.)

4. Object (5, 2), (8, 4), (4, 8), (5, 5), (6, 4), (5, 2)
   Line $x = 4$

5. Object (2, 6), (3, 5), (2, 4), (8, 4), (4, 5), (8, 6), (2, 6)
   Line $y = 7$

6. Object (2, 7), (4, 4), (4, 5), (5, 5), (5, 4), (7, 6), (10, 6), (10, 7), (2, 7)
   Line $y = 4$

7. Object   (4, 2), (1, 2), (2, 3), (1, 3), (2, 4), (0, 4), (2, 9), (4, 2)
   Line $x = 5$

8. Object   (2, 0), (3, 3), (4, 1), (5, 4), (6, 2), (7, 5), (9, 1), (2, 0)
   Line $y = 5$

9. Object   (8, 2), (8, 6), (9, 7), (8, 8), (8, 9), (10, 9), (10, 5), (9, 4), (10, 3), (10, 2), (8, 2)
   Line $x = 7$

10. Object   (2, 9), (4, 7), (9, 7), (10, 9), (8, 9), (8, 8), (4, 8), (2, 9)
    Line $y = 6$

In questions **11** to **16** the procedure is exactly the same except that this time the x and y axes will both need to go from 0 to 15.

11. Object   (7, 1), (8, 3), (11, 1), (12, 8), (4, 7), (7, 1)
    Line $y = 8$

12. Object   (10, 5), (12, 4), (15, 7), (12, 10), (10, 9), (12, 9), (10, 7), (12, 5), (10, 5)
    Line $x = 9$

13. Object   (2, 3), (1, 10), (2, 9), (3, 12), (4, 10), (5, 13), (6, 5), (2, 3)
    Line $x = 7$

14. Object   (5, 15), (4, 12), (6, 10), (5, 12), (10, 12), (9, 10), (11, 12), (10, 15), (8, 14), (7, 14), (5, 15)
    Line $y = 9$

15. Object   (8, 1), (11, 2), (14, 5), (13, 6), (14, 7), (14, 8), (13, 8), (13, 9), (12, 9), (11, 8), (10, 9), (7, 6), (6, 3), (8, 1)
    Line $y = x$
    (i.e. the line that passes through (0, 0), (1, 1), (2, 2), (3, 3), etc.)

16. Object   (9, 9), (9, 10), (8, 11), (9, 12), (9, 13), (8, 13), (7, 14), (6, 13), (5, 13), (5, 12), (4, 11), (5, 10), (5, 9), (6, 9), (7, 10), (8, 9), (9, 9)
    Line $y = x$.

Revision exercises 3

Quick tests

Test 1
1. What is x, if $x + 7 = 20$?
2. What is y, if $y - 5 = 9$?
3. Change 250 cm into metres.
4. Change 500 m into km.
5. Change 1·2 m into cm.
6. Change 600 g into kg.
7. Change $\frac{1}{2}$ m into cm.
8. Change $\frac{3}{4}$ kg into g.
9. What is z, if $3z = 24$?
10. What is b, if $b - 6 = 11$?
11. Work out 3^2.
12. Work out 2^3.
13. Work out 10^3.
14. $6 - 2\cdot4$.
15. $11 - 1\cdot2$.
16. $18 - 1\cdot6$.
17. $53 - 19$.
18. 16×9.
19. $0\cdot2 \times 0\cdot3$.
20. $0\cdot2^2$.

Test 2
1. Which is greater: 0·2 or 0·15?
2. Which is greater: 5·3 or 5·21?
3. £5 − 60p.
4. £2 − 15p.
5. £20 − £8·40.
6. $\frac{1}{3} \times \frac{1}{4}$.
7. $\frac{2}{3} \times \frac{1}{5}$.
8. $\frac{1}{2}$ of 51.
9. $\frac{1}{2}$ of 5·2.
10. What is next in the sequence 2, 4, 8 . . .
11. What is next in the sequence 1, 6, 11, 16 . . .
12. $20 + 30 + 40$.
13. 20×30.
14. $0\cdot6 \times 100$.
15. $0\cdot4 \div 10$.
16. $3\cdot1 \times 1000$.
17. Change 0·6 litres into ml.
18. Change 50 ml into litres.
19. Change 50 cm into m.
20. Change 50 cm into km.

Cross-numbers

Revision exercise 3.1

Make three copies of the cross-number and then fill in the numbers using the clues given.

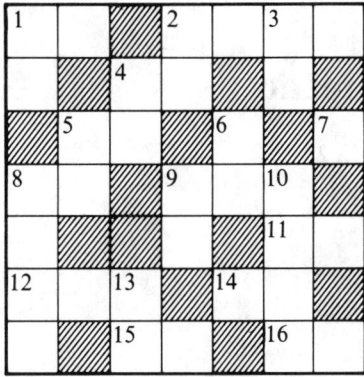

1.

Across
1. 13×7
2. $0\cdot214 \times 10\,000$
4. $5 + 4 \times 3$
5. $2 \times 2 \times 2 \times 2 \times 2 \times 2$
7. $90 - 9 \times 9$
8. $\frac{1}{20}$ of 1400
9. $2226 \div 7$
11. $216 \div (18 \div 3)$
12. $800 - 363$
14. $93 - 6 \times 2$
15. $0\cdot23 \times 100$
16. $8 \times 8 - 1$

Down
1. $101 - 7$
2. $2\cdot7 \div 0\cdot1$
3. $63 - 3 \times 6$
4. $(2 \times 9) - (8 \div 2)$
6. 9^2
8. $0\cdot372 \times 20\,000$
9. $418 \div 11$
10. $216 + 81 \times 100$
13. $2 \times 2 \times 2 \times 3 \times 3$

2.

Across
1. $2\cdot4 \times 40$
2. $11 \times 11 \times 13$
4. $913 - 857$
5. $2 + 9 \times 9$
7. $0\cdot4 \div 0\cdot05$
8. $27 \times 5 - 69$
9. $4158 \div 7$
11. $2^6 + 6$
12. $5\cdot22 \div 0\cdot03$
14. $201 - 112$
15. 7 million $\div 100\,000$
16. $1\cdot023 \div 0\cdot011$

Down
1. $558 \div 6$
2. $6\cdot4 \div 0\cdot4$
3. $0\cdot071 \times 1000$
4. $11\cdot61 + 4\cdot2 + 37\cdot19$
6. $(7 - 3\cdot1) \times 10$
8. 78×81
9. $0\cdot08 \times 700$
10. $40 \times 30 \times 4 - 1$
13. $\frac{1}{5}$ of 235

3.

Across
1. 2·6 × 10
2. 6·314 × 1000
4. 600 − 563
5. 0·25 × 100
7. 3 ÷ 0·5
8. 0·08 × 1000
9. 3·15 ÷ 0·01
11. 1·1 × 70
12. 499 + 103
14. 1 ÷ 0·1
15. 0·01 × 5700
16. 1000 − 936

Down
1. 0·2 × 100
2. 6·7 ÷ 0·1
3. 1800 ÷ 100
4. 21 ÷ 0·6
6. 420 × 0·05
8. 0·8463 × 10 000
9. 0·032 × 1000
10. 5·706 ÷ 0·001
13. 5^2

Mixed arithmetic

Revision exercise 3.2

1. 34·7 + 2·02
2. 37·2 − 5·1
3. 68·39 + 2·17
4. 16·3 − 2·9
5. 5·724 − 0·68
6. 3·264 + 102·08
7. 12·7 − 1·34
8. 62·36 + 0·943
9. 4·12 + 13·664 + 310·025
10. 73·2 − 4·17
11. 8 − 2·38
12. 37·6 + 1·48 + 20·027
13. 3·62 − 0·213 + 11·4
14. 113·2 + 2·025 + 67·81
15. 87·52 + 1·009 + 673·281
16. 67·3 + 2·07 − 15·79
17. A man buys a chair for £13·55 and then a table for £43·25. How much has he spent altogether?
18. A woman buys a cardigan for £8·49. How much change should she get from a £10 note?
19. In a hardware shop, a man purchases four articles costing £3·40, £5·27, £7·13 and £11 respectively. Find the total cost.
20. Mrs Green buys two articles costing £1·72 and £2·14. How much change should she get from £5?
21. Mr White wants to pay for a load of coal costing £11·20. He only has £8·34 with him. How much more money does he need?
22. Mr Ford buys three plants costing £3·47, £9·15 and £4·22 respectively. How much change should be get if he pays for them with a £20 note?
23. Michael buys four records costing £3·99, £4·99, £4·99 and £7·99 respectively. How much does he pay altogether?

24. Mrs Perkins buys her friend a house warming gift. What is the total cost of the two items?

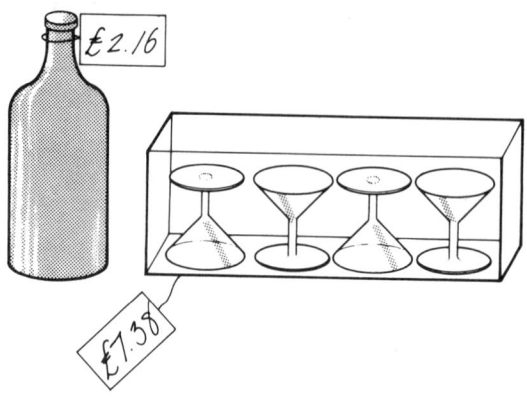

25. 2·3 × 6
26. 4·5 × 7
27. 6·23 × 8
28. 21·64 × 3
29. 5·52 ÷ 2
30. 3·24 ÷ 3
31. 0·37 × 6
32. 1·274 ÷ 7
33. 2·24 × 9
34. 30·9 × 3
35. 11·28 ÷ 4
36. 17·5 ÷ 5
37. 21·6 × 5
38. 15·43 × 4
39. 331·8 ÷ 6
40. 22·08 × 6

Revision exercise 3.3

1. 3·724 + 10·38
2. 12·7 + 2·482 + 27
3. 16·6 + 205·84
4. 8·76 − 4·37
5. 7·2 − 1·7
6. 92·3 + 12·7 + 0·55
7. 11·2 − 0·38
8. 23·1 − 4·42
9. 20·62 + 2·551 + 34
10. 12 − 9·3
11. Find the total cost of three shirts where two of them cost £8·99 each and the other one costs £10·49.
12. Find the total cost of the four items shown.

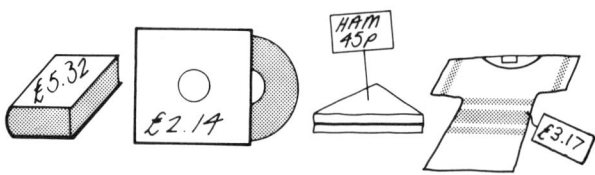

13. Paul has saved £13·24 and Susan has saved £9·83. Find how much more money Paul has than Susan.
14. On a car journey, Mrs Jackson drives 75·2 miles, then Mr Jackson drives 46·7 miles, and then Mrs Jackson drives another 24·6 miles. How long was their journey?
15. Bill is saving up for a pair of binoculars which cost £94·50. So far he has saved £39·45. How much more does he need to save?
16. Three books cost £4·50, £6·50 and £3·75 respectively. If the customer pays for them with two £10 notes, how much change should be given?
17. 3·28 × 2
18. 1·07 × 4
19. 2·94 ÷ 2
20. 13·5 ÷ 5
21. 0·37 × 3
22. 2·7 ÷ 5

23. 24.2×6 **24.** $4.3 \div 2$
25. 1.68×5 **26.** 12.19×4
27. A man puts 5 gallons of petrol in his car. If the petrol costs £1·73 per gallon, calculate how much he pays altogether.
28. How much would you have to pay for four pairs of socks if each pair cost £1·34?
29. A woman buys seven gallons of petrol and it costs her £12·32 altogether. Find the price of the petrol per gallon.
30. A maths teacher buys six calculators, each one costing £7·14. Find the total cost.
31. £28·05 is to be divided equally between you and four other people. How much will you receive?
32. A man is going to give five people £3·24 each, but he then decides to divide the same sum of money between six people instead. If you are one of those six people, calculate how much you will receive.

Equations

Revision exercise 3.4

Solve the equations

1. $m + 3 = 7$ **2.** $p + 7 = 12$
3. $x - 5 = 10$ **4.** $y - 6 = 20$
5. $a - 3 = 1$ **6.** $5 + c = 9$
7. $6 + d = 12$ **8.** $e - 12 = 20$
9. $m - 17 = 1$ **10.** $p + 100 = 200$
11. $12 = x + 7$ **12.** $15 = 9 + y$
13. $21 = 9 + z$ **14.** $17 = 12 + c$
15. $3 = d - 9$ **16.** $19 = s - 15$
17. $32 = x - 31$ **18.** $19 = 7 + f$
19. $1\frac{1}{2} = x + 1$ **20.** $3\frac{1}{4} = e + 2$
21. $5 - a = 3$ **22.** $7 - c = 3$
23. $9 - m = 3$ **24.** $15 - z = 7$
25. $t - 7 = 10$ **26.** $u - 11 = 15$
27. $5 = 13 - g$ **28.** $9 = 18 - h$
29. $31 = 40 - t$ **30.** $50 = 63 - a$

In questions **31** to **60** find the value of the expressions when $a = 3$, $b = 1$, $c = 4$.

31. $a + 5$ **32.** $b + 6$ **33.** $c - 2$
34. $a + 11$ **35.** $c + 10$ **36.** $a + b$
37. $c + b$ **38.** $c - b$ **39.** $2a$
40. $3b$ **41.** $5c$ **42.** $10 - a$
43. $7 - c$ **44.** $12 - b$ **45.** $a + c - b$
46. $c + b - a$ **47.** $37 - c$ **48.** $6a$
49. $3b + 1$ **50.** $7c - 1$ **51.** $3 + 2a$
52. $4 + 2b$ **53.** ab **54.** ac
55. cb **56.** $2a + 3b$ **57.** $3c + 4b$
58. $5a - c$ **59.** $2ab$ **60.** $3bc$

Revision exercise 3.5

Solve the equations

1. $3x = 12$ **2.** $4a = 20$
3. $3c = 27$ **4.** $6y = 30$
5. $2a + 1 = 5$ **6.** $3b + 2 = 8$
7. $3z + 3 = 9$ **8.** $4m - 1 = 7$
9. $10p = 500$ **10.** $n - 7 = 20$
11. $s - 12 = 2$ **12.** $5 - p = 3$
13. $18 = 3a$ **14.** $25 = 5c$
15. $42 = 6r$ **16.** $50 = 2n$
17. $60 = 3t$ **18.** $15 = 21 - x$
19. $y + 7 = 20$ **20.** $3x - 5 = 4$
21. $y^2 = 36$ **22.** $x^2 = 9$
23. $c^2 = 1$ **24.** $m^2 = 100$
25. $y^2 + 2 = 18$ **26.** $t^2 - 1 = 24$
27. $u^2 - 3 = 61$ **28.** $e^2 + 10 = 91$
29. $v^2 = 400$ **30.** $y^2 - 2 = 142$

Work out the following

31. 3^2 **32.** 2^3 **33.** 4^2 **34.** 2^4
35. 5^2 **36.** 3^3 **37.** 1^5 **38.** 0^3
39. 2^5 **40.** $(\frac{1}{2})^2$ **41.** $(0.1)^2$ **42.** $(0.2)^3$
43. 10^3 **44.** 7^2 **45.** 10^4 **46.** $(0.01)^2$
47. $(\frac{1}{3})^2$ **48.** $(\frac{1}{3})^3$ **49.** 7^1 **50.** $(\frac{2}{5})^2$

In questions **51** to **80** find the value of the expressions when $x = 3$, $y = 2$, $z = 1$.

51. xy **52.** $3y + 4z$
53. $x^2 + 2$ **54.** $y^2 + 4$
55. $4z + 3x$ **56.** $3xy$
57. $x^2 + y^2$ **58.** $2xz + 3y$
59. $x^2 + 2x$ **60.** $y^2 - 2$
61. $x^2 - x$ **62.** $y^2 - z$
63. $4xz + 5$ **64.** $6 + xy$
65. xyz **66.** $3zyx$
67. $x^2 + 2x + 1$ **68.** $y^2 + 3y + 1$
69. $z^2 + 4z$ **70.** $x^3 + 1$
71. $y^3 + y$ **72.** $y^3 + y^2 + y$
73. $x + x^2 + x^3$ **74.** $10 - x^2$
75. $16 - xyz$ **76.** $100 - z^2$
77. $x^3 + y^3$ **78.** z^y
79. y^x **80.** x^y

Angles

Revision exercise 3.6

1.

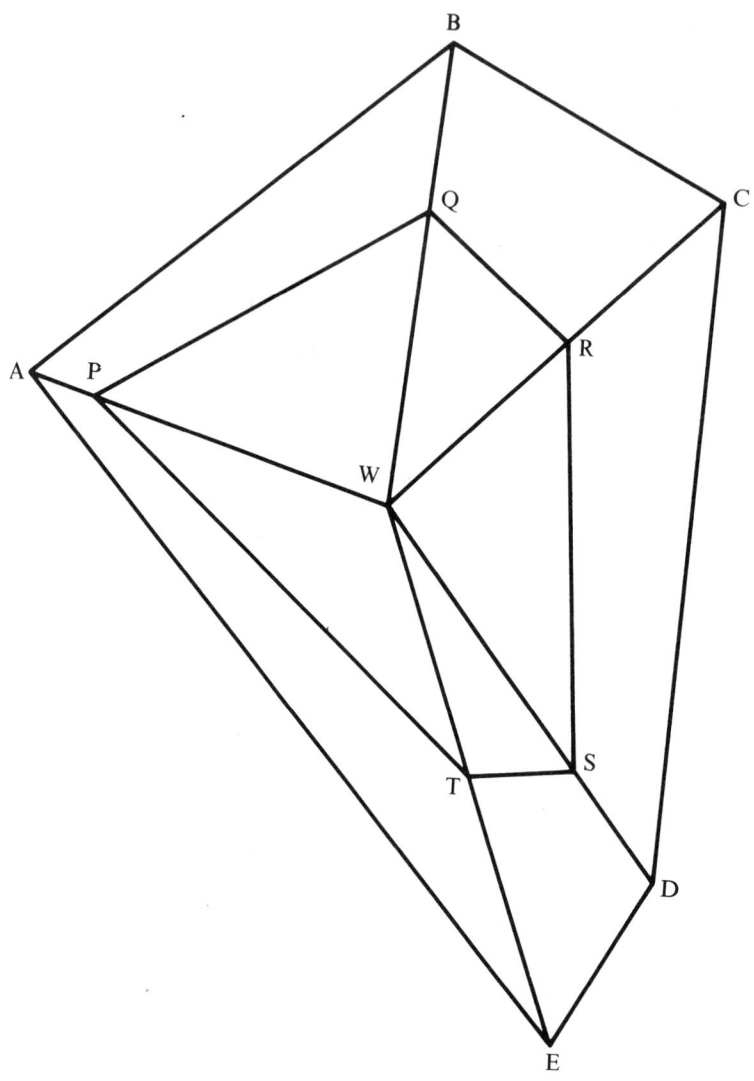

Use a protractor to measure the following angles.

(a) AŴB   (b) SŴB   (c) AŴE
(d) RŜW   (e) EDŴ   (f) QR̂S
(g) QP̂T   (h) EDĈ   (i) BŴC
(j) AÊD   (k) TŴD   (l) CŴE
(m) DŴQ   (n) BÂW   (o) CŴD